THE SOMERSET & DORSET

Aftermath of the Beeching axe

The final full month of through workings finds BR 9F 2-10-0 No. 92245 entering Evercreech Junction station with an up express on 4th August 1962, and passes BR Standard Class 4 No. 75009.

BR 4MT 4-6-0 No. 75071 departs from Evercreech Junction station with a down working in June 1962.

THE SOMERSET & DORSET

Aftermath of the Beeching axe

Tim Deacon

OPC

Oxford Publishing Co.

RCTS and SLS 'Farewell Specials' pass at Blandford on 6th March 1966.   *Michael Gates*

Dedication

To the Memory of my late Father – John.

First published in 1995.

A catalogue record for this book is available from the British Library.

ISBN 0 86093 527 2

Oxford Publishing Co. is an imprint of Haynes Publishing, Sparkford, near Yeovil, Somerset, BA22 7JJ.

Printed and bound in Great Britain by BPC Hazell Books Ltd
Typeset in Times Roman Medium by Character Graphics (Taunton) Ltd.

Publisher's note: Some of the illustrations have been reproduced from poor quality originals, but have been included because of their unique historical value.

Contents

		page
Preface and Acknowledgements		6
Introduction		7

Chapter

1	A Brief History of the Somerset & Dorset Joint Railway	11
2	The Beginning of the End	16
3	Services Remaining after March 1966	25
4	Timetable of Track Lifting and Rationalisation	51
5	Demolition and Redevelopment of S&DJR Land	100

Appendix

1	Stations and Halts	140
2	Closures and Major Changes since 1925	142
3	S&DJR Main Line and Branch Line Bridges	151
4	S&DJR Viaducts	185

Bibliography	189
Index	191

Preface

"**B**orn too Late", a rock and roll classic that describes perfectly my position as far as the railways of Britain were concerned. Having been born in early March 1957, I was unaware at the time of how lucky I was to see the last few years of steam on BR. Also, living in North Kent and travelling regularly to Dorset I was fortunate to travel on one of the last steam main lines in the country. Even so memories are few, the most vivid are those of Waterloo and Swanage. Waterloo station on a busy August Saturday, with my late Father taking me along to see our locomotive, but being only four or five years old I found the experience, to say the least, daunting. The locomotive appeared huge and the noise and smell was overwhelming for one so small. We met again at journey's end as my parents always thanked the crew for our safe arrival. Perhaps this ritual had something to do with the fact that my Father was an engineer by profession.

At Swanage my Aunt's home backed on to the railway and I can recall many a night as I settled down to sleep hearing the last train for Wareham passing by. If the window was open I could smell that unique steam locomotive smoke as the train passed into the distance. Just as pleasant was to awake to the sound of shunting in the station yard. All this came, to what I considered, a very abrupt end after steam's demise and the rundown of the branch which closed in 1972. Still worse was the undignified speed with which the track was lifted during the summer of that year. The line did catch out one of the 'vandals'; a large articulated lorry was driven in beside Swanage station on the ballast to collect the redundant chairs and bolts. Heavy rain that night left the lorry totally bogged down in the ballast. It took three days to retrieve the lorry, and some 20 years to re-open the Swanage branch.

As I stated in the introduction, my interest in the subject of this book was sparked-off by Mac Hawkins' book. My curiosity just kept me asking questions on how things could change so dramatically in only 20 years. In the beginning I had no intention of writing a book – it just seemed to happen. People I contacted had information, photographs and names of other possible contributors; events just snowballed to the point where a book seemed the logical conclusion. One could well say how much hard work and time went into the project, but it never seemed like work, as all my informants gave so freely of their time, knowledge and encouragement, that the research became a pleasure. It seemed I had a huge jigsaw puzzle of events that just had to fit together to form the complete picture. Several pieces are still missing but one day I will answer the few remaining questions. Having said all that, at times I found it a very sad job. I can, in some small way, understand the anger of the railway's employees at the line's unnecessary rundown and closure by a vindictive Western Region. I take this opportunity to thank everyone who has helped me with this project.

Acknowledgements

It would have been impossible to write this book without the considerable contribution made by Chris Handley and Peter James, both with their personal recollections and photographs. Bob Bunyar and Mike Ware have gone out of their way to help me with photographs, information and to locate useful names and addresses. Rev. Alan Newman, Michael Gates, Colin Maggs, Tony Witt, Mark Shore, Kevin Regan, Andy Read and the Somerset & Dorset Railway Trust have either loaned or sold me irreplaceable photographs, slides and negatives. Unless stated otherwise photographs are from the author's collection.

I must also thank the following people and organisations for their help in supplying the remaining information needed to complete this book. Working in alphabetical order: Mike Arlett, Robin Atthill, Mike Bailey, Mr D. Bell, Miss S. Berry, John Baxter, Jim Boudreau, John Brice, Mr J. Brownlow, Miss A. Clark, Colin Divall, Mike Dodd, John Eaton, Jonathon Edwards, Derek Fear, Paul Fear, Mr R. Fraser, Mr Froggatt, Mr M. Garland, David Grimwood, Duncan Harper, Paul Hayes, Richard Hayes, Mr Hillman, Mr Hutchinson, Robin Linsley, Will Locke, Brian Macdermott, Ken Marchant, David Milton, Tony Owen, Mike Palmer, Nick Piggot, Maurice Shaw, John Smith, Richard Stevens, Col. Edward Trotman and Bernard Ware.

Also, Bath City Council, BR Western Region, BR Southern Region, BR South Western Property Board, Dorset County Council, Dorset Record Office, East Dorset District Council, Mendip District Council, Shepton Town Council, Somerset County Council and Somerset Records Office.

Introduction

On the 7th March 1966 I was nine years and four days old, and the Somerset & Dorset Joint Railway had had sentence passed on it. Now, like a condemned man on death row it awaited execution.

It took nine months for the executioner to be appointed – perhaps a reprieve? The South Western Regional Economic Planning Council suggested a review of this closure, being one of the first main lines in Britain to be closed, and suggested a limited service on perhaps a single track could be introduced. Comments on hardship for the local population and the poor quality replacement bus services were made, but British Railways would have none of it, the line would close regardless. By 3rd January 1967 the executioner had struck, simultaneously, at Bath (Green Park) station and Highbridge.

I never travelled on, photographed or even saw the Somerset & Dorset before its closure. The nearest I came to it was at Broadstone Junction station, on a diverted Waterloo to Swanage Summer Saturday express in the early 1960s. But as soon as I was old enough to purchase railway books I became aware of this independent railway company, which had managed to maintain its individual identity even though run jointly by two much larger companies. It was never referred to as just part of the LMS or SR, always as the Somerset & Dorset.

The Somerset & Dorset stood for something different, something special. With a fierce loyalty from employees and local management alike, this loyalty and love for the Somerset & Dorset Railway united employees and local people in a common cause when the proposal for closure was first announced. Unfortunately the same could not be said of the senior BR management of the Western Region, stubbornly set on closure regardless of sense or reason. They got their own way on 7th March 1966.

The line from Bath Green Park to Bournemouth West must be just about the most photographed and documented line in Britain. For any line to travel through 63 miles of pure countryside must be unique. Industrial development in this part of the country was minimal, mostly coal, stone, light engineering and agriculture.

The development of the line is very well covered in a multitude of books and magazine articles. However, events *after* closure are sparsely covered. Freight traffic continued to use four sections of the S&DJR, some as late as 1973, and enthusiasts' specials ran on the Blandford and Radstock sections. Closure of the S&DJR was also to bring the demise of the Mangotsfield to Bath and Poole to Wimborne lines, and the fate of these two lines is also covered here. The general rundown of the S&DJR started in 1960. This, along with the final track lifting and demolition, are covered in greater detail than ever before. This work, which started in early October 1966, was not completed until the last track was lifted in late 1976. Mother nature has taken hold of a great deal of the abandoned trackbed and man has changed most of the remainder beyond recognition in only a few short years.

Mac Hawkins' book *The Somerset and Dorset Railway, Then & Now* exemplified this change perfectly, with his excellent then and now comparison of 1960s photographs to 1980s equivalents. I intend to fill the gap between 'then' and 'now', by showing how and when these dramatic changes came about. Every effort has been made to be as accurate as possible with events and dates of trains and closures, but it has proved difficult on occasions. For example, Moorewood signalbox has three different closure dates depending on who you are dealing with! The same problem occurred with the removal of sidings at various locations when the date quoted by BR for their removal was not in fact the date on which the work was undertaken. Weeks or even months elapsed until the man power was available to undertake the work. In most cases I have quoted the official date, so it is likely that some dates could be disputed.

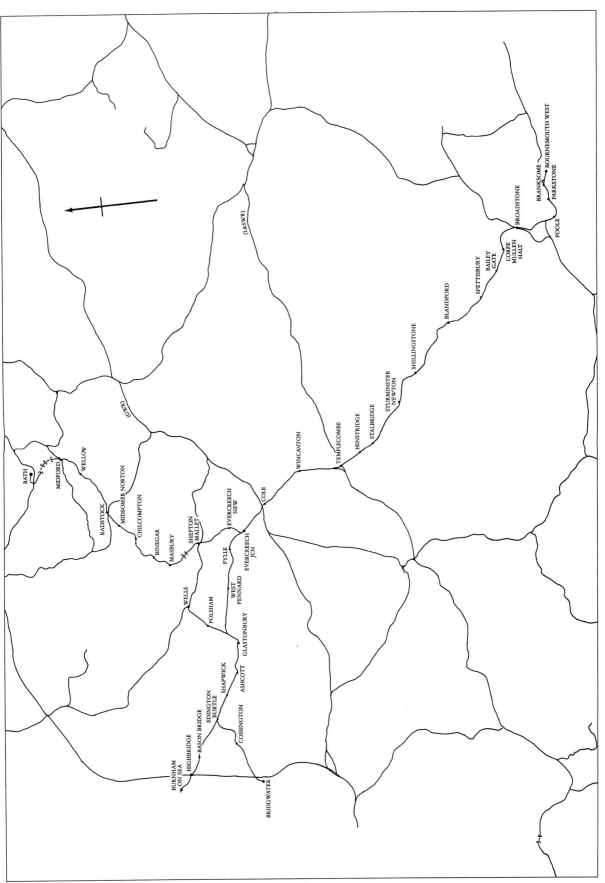

Courtesy Derek Phillips

1962
The Final Year of Express Workings

BR 9F 2-10-0 No. 92233 at Blandford Forum station on 7th July 1962 with a down train.

A Templecombe to Highbridge train at Shapwick station in the charge of GWR Class 2251 0-6-0 No. 2247.

GWR 0-6-0 pannier tank No. 3758 with former Southern Railway coaching stock on a down train at Blandford Forum station on 7th July 1962.

LMS 2-8-0 No. 48706 and BR 2-6-4T No. 80043 at Templecombe Upper with the down working of the SLS railtour on 6th March 1966.
John Scrace

1

A Brief History of the Somerset & Dorset Joint Railway

The first section of line to be opened was from Highbridge Wharf to Glastonbury on 28th August 1854, constructed by the Somerset Central Railway. By 30th July 1855 the Somerset Central Railway had approval for two short extensions; from Highbridge to Burnham-on-Sea, and a branch to Wells from Glastonbury. The Highbridge extension to Burnham was the first to open on 3rd May 1858 followed on 15th March 1859 by the new branch to Wells. All this work was carried out by the Somerset Central Railway, its partner to be, the Dorset Central Railway, had started life as the South Midland Union Railway, which had conceived the building of a line from Mangotsfield on the Midland Railway to Poole on the London & South Western Railway via Radstock and Blandford in 1852. The plan was to be dropped in favour of a line from Wimborne on the Southampton to Dorchester LSWR main line for 10½ miles to Blandford. Royal Assent was given on 29th July 1856, the same day as the Somerset Central's Act for an extension from Glastonbury to Bruton, a distance of 13 miles.

An Act of Parliament for a 24-mile extension from Blandford to Templecombe passed into law on 10th August 1857 and the line was opened on 31st August 1863. By this time the line from Wimborne to Blandford had been in use for nearly three years having been opened on 1st November 1860. The year 1862 was not only to see the opening of the Glastonbury to Bruton extension on 3rd February but also the coming together of the Somerset Central and the Dorset Central Railways on 1st

September 1862. The union of these two railway companies had also required a Bill to be approved by Parliament during the session of 1862. Royal Assent for the amalgamation of the Somerset Central and Dorset Central into the Somerset & Dorset Railway was granted on 7th August 1862.

By 31st August 1863 the now Somerset & Dorset Railway covered a total distance of 61½ miles from Burnham to Wimborne. Also on this date the final section from Blandford to Templecombe was opened allowing through traffic to run. An Act authorised on 21st August 1871 allowed for an extension from Evercreech to Bath via Shepton Mallet and Radstock. This would connect with the Midland Railway from Mangotsfield to Bath which had opened on 4th August 1869. This project would cover 26 miles of very difficult terrain, consisting of steep gradients and sharp curves which would necessitate large, often deep, earthworks with enormous viaducts. The first public train to use the new line (to be called the Bath extension) departed from Bath Queen Square station at 7.25 am on 4th August 1874. The Somerset & Dorset Railway was still plagued by financial problems and soon turned to the Midland Railway and London & South Western Railway to form a joint committee to run the line. The leasing agreement was signed on 1st November 1875 and the necessary Act of Parliament was passed on 13th July 1876. So the Somerset & Dorset Joint Railway was born.

The very last section of the S&DJR to receive Parliamentary approval was the seven-mile Edington to Bridgwater branch line on 18th August 1882. The branch was in fact an independent company worked by the S&DJR. Eight years elapsed before services commenced on 21st July 1890.

With the S&DJR being constructed throughout as a single track line, powers had to be obtained from Parliament between 1885 and 1902 to double the line in stages, including the necessary work on viaducts and bridges. One example was Tucking Mill viaduct in 1891. The line was doubled in the order shown below and the double track timetable started on these dates:

Radstock to Binegar	1885*
Evercreech New to Evercreech Junction	28/8/1886
Evercreech Junction to Templecombe	16/1/1887
Shepton Mallet to Evercreech New	5/2/1888
Midford to Wellow	28/8/1892
Binegar to Shepton Mallet	20/11/1892
Wellow to Radstock	1/7/1894
Blandford to Bailey Gate	29/4/1901
Bailey Gate to Corfe Mullen	16/2/1902

* An accident occurred with a locomotive on this section of new track in 1885, implying that the track was at least in situ by 1885, though a report would indicate that trains were using the new double track by this time.

Even as early as March 1870 a small section of the S&DR was closed, this being the connection between the Dorset Central and the LSWR main line at Templecombe. The connection to the west replaced one to the east, up to an enlarged

Templecombe Upper station. The old connection then became a long siding which survived until July 1967 when the Lower yard was lifted. On 16th January 1897 the original Templecombe (DCR) station was closed, along with the No. 1 Templecombe Junction signalbox. At the same time the building-less Templecombe Lower Halt was opened and construction work started on Templecombe motive power depot on the original Templecombe (DCR) station site.

The first important section of the S&DJR to close was the original line from Wimborne Junction to Corfe Mullen Junction. This occurred after the Corfe Mullen Junction to Broadstone Junction station cut-off had been constructed in 1884/5 and had required an Act of Parliament, which was granted to the LSWR on 20th August 1883. The new cut off was opened to freight traffic on 14th December 1885 and passenger traffic started on 1st November 1886. The old line to Wimborne continued to be used by some trains up to 17th June 1933. After termination of use as a through line, a short section from Corfe Mullen Junction to Carters Clay Pit sidings remained until September 1969, used for the last ten years to store wagons.

The next major closure was of the branch lines to Bridgwater and Wells. These occurred on 29th October 1955 and 1st October 1954 respectively, followed on 20th May 1963 by the Highbridge to Burnham-on-Sea branch.

The rarely photographed Nettlebridge Viaduct with LMS 8F 2-8-0 No. 48706 on the down leg of the Great Western Society rail tour on 5th March 1966.

John Scrace

The Lull Before the Storm, 1963 and 1964

A GWR Class 2251 0-6-0 in the ex GWR Highbridge yard shunting milk tankers from Bason Bridge Creamery for their journey to London in 1963.

Bath (Green Park) S&DJR depot on 2nd June 1963.

Glastonbury & Street station on 21st August 1963. Ivatt 2MT No. 41296 waits to depart east whilst GWR Class 2251 No. 3206 is seen approaching with an Evercreech Junction to Highbridge train.

Ivatt 2MT 2-6-2T No. 41243 is seen at Stalbridge station in the spring of 1964 on a down train.

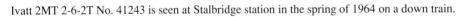

BR 4MT 2-6-0 No. 76057 departs from Radstock on a down train on 5th August 1964. Note the closed Clandown Colliery branch is on the left.

BR 5MT 4-6-0 No. 73049 passes Henstridge station on an up train on 5th September 1964.

2

The Beginning of the End

From 1st November 1875 a leasing agreement was made between the Midland Railway and the London & South Western Railway to safeguard the future of the S&DR. With the grouping of railways in 1923 the arrangement continued with the London, Midland & Scottish Railway and Southern Railway, and the tradition continued into British Railways' time. Unfortunately, the S&DJR was the baby that nobody wanted, and by 2nd February 1948 the line was under Southern Region commercial control from Southampton, while responsibility for the operation of the line was with the London Midland Region at Bath which allocated motive power from its large Bristol Bath Road depot.

January 1950 brought regional boundary changes which had the line split at Bruton, with everything to the north under Western Region control, including the three branch lines, and to the south under Southern Region control, though still operated throughout by Southern Region to whom the LMR loaned most of the required motive power. In 1953 all LMR stock was transferred outright to Southern Region control, including all group 71 code motive power depots excluding Bath Green Park.

This all changed again on 1st February 1958. The boundary was redrawn, this time between Templecombe and Henstridge, at Templecombe Junction Distant signal from Henstridge. Templecombe Upper station remained in the Southern Region, whilst Templecombe depot along with Bath, Radstock and Highbridge were all transferred to the Western Region. In early 1962 another adjustment transferred the line between Temple-

combe and a point just north of Shillingstone to the Western Region. The Western Region now had control of about 80% of the S&DJR and its fate was sealed. One last change of boundaries occurred on 1st January 1963 when the Salisbury to Exeter line was transferred to the Western Region, along with more of the S&DJR to the south of Shillingstone.

Closure of the line became a talking point as soon as the Western Region took over the responsibility for running the majority of the route. Changes came as sure as night follows day. Diversion of traffic away from the line began in 1960 as the Western Region showed its authority, starting with the beer traffic from Burton being re-routed via Taunton. This traditional S&DJR freight train had run since 1874, the 11 am from Bath always having been known as the 'Burton'. Through freights dropped away one by one until even the fertilizer traffic from Avonmouth to Blandford was re-routed on a 135 mile new route compared to 65 miles over the S&DJR – that was progress! Local freight started to diminish as road haulage made inroads. So followed the obvious withdrawal of freight facilities at most stations, along with the removal of their sidings, run-round facilities and signalboxes from 1963. All freight traffic was withdrawn from the Wincanton–Blandford section on 14th June 1965 followed by the Radstock–Wincanton section on 3rd January 1966 (except coal from Norton Hill Colliery). The remaining freight traffic was terminated on 7th March 1966 with the exception of the four sections that remained open.

A real turn for the worse came in 1962 when it was announced that all express passenger traffic was to be diverted away from the S&D at the end of the 1962 season. Most of this traffic would be re-routed via Oxford and overnight express working would be withdrawn. A downfall in passenger numbers had occurred over the previous few summers as more people purchased their own transport and all trains were re-routed at the end of the 1962 season, some never to run again. Even the Somerset & Dorset's best known express, the 'Pines', was diverted away and would in future run via Oxford and Basingstoke until finally being withdrawn altogether at the end of the 1967 season. (In 1992 this train, much re-routed, made a welcome return to the railway timetable.) These express passenger diversions were really the final nail in the coffin for the S&DJR.

The 1962 Transport Act was to be behind the closure of many lines in the West Country, leading as it did to the BR report – The Reshaping of British Railways – in March 1963. This report proposed the closure of all branch lines in Dorset, except the Wareham to Swanage branch, along with the S&DJR and the Southampton to Poole line (the Old Road).

There was however an immediate outcry. A meeting was held in October 1963 by the relevant Transport User Consultative Committee who led a flood of objections to the closure of the S&DJR. As a result of this the Ministry of Transport consent for the closure of the S&DJR did not emerge until September 1965, after the Conservative Government had been defeated in a general election. During the two-year delay the Western Region continued its rundown of the S&DJR.

On 7th September 1964 all the remaining night freight traffic, including the 2.40 am mail train were withdrawn. Thereafter the S&D closed at night for the first time since the early 1870s, and this also had the effect that the night shift in all signalboxes ceased and many signalmen were relocated away from the S&DJR. At around this time the passenger timetable was changed, with the result that many trains just missed connections at Bath, Highbridge and Bournemouth for locations further afield. It was now much more difficult to arrange Bank Holiday excursions from locations on the S&D and local people had to resort to road coaches.

A line of this difficulty to operate would always be a prime target for closure regardless of the hatred that the Great Western Railway, then Western Region, had for it. One wonders how much a very busy summer Saturday must have cost to operate, with every through working having a pilot as well as a train locomotive; a large number of pilot locomotives awaiting their next turn of duty; light engines running back to various locations; the costs of extra crews and problems arranging for extra locomotives and crews to be in the right place at the right time. The time taken for an express to travel from Bath (Green Park) to Bournemouth West in relation to the distance covered was poor, particularly as expresses had to run into Bath (Green Park) station, change locomotives and then proceed back the way they had come in. A similar delay was inflicted on passengers at Templecombe Junction as trains were shunted up to Templecombe Upper station for connections with the Waterloo–Exeter line. A pilot locomotive was required in at least one direction of this trip. Due to the nature of the S&DJR, with severe gradients and tight curves, overall speed was low and the time taken to travel the line was greater than lines of a similar length elsewhere. Could diesels have made a more efficient and faster job of this journey? Unfortunately, we will never know, as with the exception of a few diesel multiple units on specials the S&D never saw diesel workings on a regular basis.

Taking into account the problems confronting the railway staff at all levels, it is a miracle the heavy summer Saturday traffic ran as smoothly as it did. This line, which must have been not only a nightmare to construct but also to operate, with rarely a mile of level straight track – excluding the branch lines – each obstacle adding fuel to the arguments for closure.

Many may say that the events of 1875, when the S&DR leased the line to the Midland Railway and the London & South Western Railway, going behind the back of the Great Western, had much to do with the final outcome. Certainly the Western Region won control of the line by stealth until a majority of the line was theirs, yet there is early evidence that the Western Region saw the S&D only as an operating inconvenience. Their subsequent behaviour was beyond belief when it came to stating a case for closure, which would, no doubt, have happened regardless of Beeching and his axe.

Western Region conducted a passenger traffic census during the school holiday period, when some local trains which normally conveyed a large number of children were running relatively empty. This summertime census was criticised by local railway staff, so another, just before Christmas was carried out. Now not only were school children on holiday but so also were local students using colleges in

Class 2MT 2-6-2T No. 41243 is just north of Corfe Mullen crossing on 24th April 1965 with the 12.23 Templecombe–Bournemouth West service.

Class 2MT No. 41307 is seen approaching Pylle station on 29th May 1965. There would appear to be twice as much mail as passengers on the branch by this time.

The rare sight in 1965 of a Bulleid Pacific on the S&DJR. Rebuilt 'West Country' No. 34046 *Braunton* is seen on the 4.20 Bath to Bournemouth service at Moorewood on 25th April. This was probably the last use of a Bulleid Pacific on a timetabled train.

Michael Gates

Class 4MT 2-6-4T No. 80059 on a down local at Midford station in the summer of 1965.

Ken Marchant

A Class 4MT 2-6-4T is seen on a down afternoon local from Bath to Templecombe at Winsor Hill Tunnel in 1965.

Ken Marchant

Bath. Such little tricks all enhanced the case for closure. Even railway staff were encouraged not to use the trains. For example, the signalmen at Midford had their salaries delivered each Friday from Bath by taxi from 1964 until closure.

With no attempt ever being made to try diesel multiple units or, indeed diesels of any kind it is a hypothetical question now to ask if the S&D could ever have been made viable, but one suspects that if proper marketing techniques had been applied from the early 1960s the line might just have been able to survive. It would have been important to introduce large scale modernisation of the complete line. Not just diesel traction but signalling, unmanned stations and possibly the singling of large parts of the line but still using the complete width of the trackbed to reduce the severity of the curves to increase train speeds and reduce journey times. At the end of the day would the costs have been met by increased traffic receipts?

When one looks back at the case that Western Region put forward at that time it really was very shallow, but there was no enlightened force around to put up a really good defence. The poor railwaymen tried hard, as did a number of local people, but it was all too little too late as Western Region had made up their minds that the S&D would close regardless.

Interestingly, final consent for the sale of the S&D's assets, made up of land, buildings and track, was not fully granted until July 1967. Though by this time track lifting and demolition was well under way and at least one station had been sold to become a private dwelling and several plots of land had found new owners.

Proposals for remaining sections of the line
British Railway's first attempt to close the S&D was in 1963, with a condition to maintain several remaining sections for freight traffic. In fact 90% or 370,000 tons of the previous three years – 1960 to 1962 – was average. The remaining sections would be: Broadstone Junction to Blandford for coal and general merchandise, also to serve the Blandford army camp, plus milk traffic to the creamery at Bailey Gate. The second section was from Highbridge to Glastonbury, again for general merchandise at Glastonbury and the traffic generated by C. & J. Clark's shoes at Street, plus Bason Bridge station for the exclusive use of the United Dairies Creamery which would produce no less than 1,238 3,000-gallon rail tankers of milk mostly for London, in 1969. Third, and largest, would be at Radstock

serving the local collieries with a link to the GWR line for the journey to Bristol, the lines at Radstock would extend north to the Lower Writhlington Colliery sidings, and south as far as Moorewood sidings between Chilcompton and Binegar for stone to be worked out of Emborough Quarries. Further coal traffic would come from the Norton Hill Colliery at Midsomer Norton plus possible new traffic from the New Rock Colliery at Chilcompton, which never had rail facilities, instead using road haulage to the New Rock sidings at Chilcompton station. Further traffic was generated at Radstock in the form of the Wagon Repair Company and general merchandise. Radstock would act as the hub of all local freight. The last and shortest section to remain in use would be from Bath Junction a few chains up to the Co-op bakery at Twerton, with coal.

Between the original 1963 plan and final closure in March 1966, the rundown of the line continued and was matched by the rundown of freight traffic, so on closure the Southern Region section to Blandford remained open as agreed, while those to be run by Western Region were drastically changed. The section to Glastonbury & Street would not now remain open, but just a short stretch to Bason Bridge for the United Dairies Creamery. Plans to serve Radstock were altered since nothing to the south would remain open as Norton Hill Colliery had closed in February 1966. The New Rock Colliery had closed, plus the Emborough Quarry was using road haulage. The line from Bath Junction to the Co-op siding at Twerton would remain open.

As the Somerset & Dorset closed so did the Mangotsfield to Bath line, at least as far as passenger services were concerned. Freight was running as usual, supplying the Bath gas works up to conversion to natural gas, and Midland Bridge goods depot remained open for general freight. This traffic was gradually reduced until May 1971 when the gas works was closed and all remaining freight traffic to Bath was terminated with the track being lifted between May and September 1972. The situation at the southern extremity of the S&D was very similar with the Southampton to Poole line being closed in March 1966 to passenger traffic. Freight traffic would continue to run as far as Ringwood, with the line being singled from 24th July 1966. Track lifting of the redundant line was carried out over the next couple of years commencing at Broadstone Junction. Freight traffic was soon cut back to West Moors and by late 1970 only two sources of traffic remained to and from Wimborne and the Doulton's sidings. All traffic finally ceased on the Poole yard to Wimborne line on 2nd May 1977 and the track had all been lifted by July 1978.

The remaining freight services were not to prove as long-term as had at first been hoped. Competition from road haulage continued to eat away at the line's share of business. This was compounded by recession in the early 1970s, which in itself led to a sharp rise in the value of scrap metal; not a good omen for the remains of the S&DJR. The first and not unexpected casualty was the Bath Junction to Twerton section which succumbed in November 1967. Just over a year later came the demise of what had seemed a very secure and busy service to Blandford due to the opening of a freight concentra-

tion depot at Bournemouth. Also, in mid-1968 a rail linked fertiliser store was opened at Gillingham with the result that rail originated freight would in future have to travel from Bournemouth to Blandford by lorry. Road traffic would be the downfall of a section that appeared to have a long and bright future, due to the strong desire of its customer to remain true to a rail based distribution service. Unfortunately the builders of the M5 motorway had a different idea and in October 1972 the last milk train ran from Bason Bridge to Highbridge. Exactly one year later the last operational section of the old S&DJR closed, that being from Radstock to Writhlington and with it ended the last rail traffic on the unique Somerset & Dorset Joint Railway.

The last freight train from Writhlington to Bath departs on 4th March 1966 behind LMS 8F 2-8-0 No. 48760.

Michael Gates

The Final Timetabled Trains – 5th March 1966

Class 4MT 2-6-4T No. 80043 on the 07.00 Templecombe to Bath service, sweeps over Charlton Road Viaduct in the early light.

John Scrace

Class 8F 2-8-0 No. 48760 on the 08.15 Bath to Templecombe service is seen departing south from Binegar station.

John Scrace

The 3-coach 14.00 Templecombe to Bath service climbs away from Radstock behind BR Class 4MT No. 80138 and Ivatt 2MT No. 41307.

John Scrace

The Farewell Rail Tours – 6th March 1966

The SLS railtour is seen climbing vigorously south from Radstock behind LMS 8F No. 48706 and BR 4MT No. 80043.

John Scrace

The same pair are well into their stride as they haul the 10-coach special over the summit at Masbury.

John Scrace

Having worked through to Templecombe Upper station the rail tour continued its journey, here seen passing a deserted Templecombe Depot.

John Scrace

The LCGB rail tour is seen passing over bridge No. 41 as it enters Radstock from the south, behind Bulleid Pacifics Nos 34006 *Bude* and 34057 *Biggin Hill*.

John Scrace

On the branch line the RCTS rail tour passes Elbow Corner Crossing as it heads for Templecombe behind LMR 2MT Nos 41283 and 41249.

John Scrace

At Templecombe the two Class 2MTs were replaced by 'Merchant Navy' No. 35028 *Clan Line* here seen heading towards Henstridge.

John Scrace

3

Services Remaining after March 1966

**Bath Junction to Twerton Bakery Siding
1966–1967**

The shortest section at only 68 chains from Bath Junction to Twerton Co-op bakery siding, using the former single track main line from Bath Junction up towards Devonshire Tunnel, the Co-op siding being on the down side of the line. Traffic for the bakery was only minimal with movements of coal in, and empty wagons out, being performed as required by a diesel shunter from Bath Midland Bridge yard. Mostly the motive power was Class 08 but on occasions any spare locomotive was used whilst awaiting a return trip from Bath, even a Class 52. At the siding itself the points were always kept selected for the main line, only being altered when shunting was in progress. Predictably it was only a short time before the Western Region decided to terminate this very light traffic, and with that all traffic down the S&D from Bath Junction ceased and the line was closed completely on 3rd November 1967.

Motive power used on this section: Classes 08, 14, 22, 35, 44, 45, 47 and 52.

**Radstock to Lower Writhlington Colliery
1966–1975**

Radstock North to Writhlington was to become the most active remaining section of the S&DJR after March 1966. Between the original announcement of closure in 1963 and the actual closure in March 1966 two of the three main sources of mineral traffic on this section of the line had ceased production, although this was clearly not apparent when the original arrangements were drawn up. Firstly the

New Rock Colliery ceased operation at Moorewood before the end of 1965 immediately before the second revised date of line closure in January 1966. At that time Norton Hill Colliery was working and in fact it was the most modern in North Somerset, but during 1965 it began to lose money at such a rate that the NCB had to close it. The closure took place in February 1966 but work there was completed just before the S&D closed in March. This was very convenient for BR as it meant they could abandon the Radstock to Moorewood section of the line. Nevertheless the section up to Writhlington would still be required and the wagon repair works was still open. BR, in proposing to connect the S&D with the GWR at this point, now decided to stable a Class 08 diesel at Radstock permanently. This was to be used to shunt not only the S&D line but also the GWR West goods yard and Kilmersdon Colliery sidings. Radstock depot was transferred from Bath MPD control to Bristol MPD on 7th March 1966.

To keep the line open a certain amount of constructional work had to be carried out just west of the two level crossings. At this point the two former rivals ran side by side, albeit at different levels. A junction between the two lines had been proposed when the S&DR line was originally constructed in 1872/74 but never executed, so when the civil engineering department moved into the area towards the end of 1965 to construct the short connecting spur they were doing no more than had been allowed for in the original S&DR Bath Extension Act! Construction of the new connection was completed in time for the proposed January 1966 closure

Two views of the slewed connection between the S&DJR and the B&NS lines at Radstock in 1966.   *Both Ken Marchant*

deadline. The connection with the S&D itself was left so that a set of points could be laid into the down main line on the weekend of closure. As things turned out this did not happen for a few more weeks.

Regular passenger services ceased on the evening of Saturday 5th March 1966 leaving Sunday free for several enthusiasts' specials. Two were scheduled to pass Radstock in both directions during the day. However the new connection had to be ready to clear coal from Writhlington Colliery on the Monday morning. Therefore on the Sunday the civil engineering department were given the down main-line. As a result all down specials crossed to the up line at Radstock, then returned to the down line at Midsomer Norton. As Norton Hill Colliery was now closed no point was required in the down line, and instead it was merely slewed to connect with the new spur.

The new arrangements came into effect first thing on the Monday morning from which time only the down main line remained in use between Radstock and Writhlington, the diesel shunter arriving from Bristol using the GWR line and the new spur. The diesel would return to Bristol at monthly intervals for servicing and refuelling.

Employed at Radstock in 1966 and 1967 were two engine drivers and about four or five shunters. Originally they opted to use the S&DJR station's offices as a staff mess room but later a shed in the yard near to the locomotive depot was used. At this time two shifts were required each day. On 22nd December 1966 the morning shift routine was like this:

Driver on morning shift, oil and grease locomotive, fill sand hopper and check fuel. Proceed from the shed through the station to the connecting spur and thence to the North Somerset (GWR) line. Proceed along the GWR line to Midsomer Norton & Welton station yard to shunt Blatchford's siding (they were a large engineering firm). Return along North Somerset line to Radstock West and thence on to Kilmersdon exchange sidings. Remove full coal wagons and replace with empties. Return via connecting spur to S&DJR line and proceed to Wagon Repairs Ltd. Remove repaired wagons to North yard and replace with those awaiting repair. Proceed up the line to Writhlington Colliery, traverse colliery branch, remove all full wagons from colliery screens and replace with empties. Make up a train of full coal wagons in the sidings, place brake van at the rear, and haul the complete train back

to Radstock North. Complete the makeup of the train in the North yard by adding any other wagons from the goods yard including repaired wagons. Leave train on the down main line, remove shunter from main line in preparation for the arrival of a locomotive from Bristol between 13.30 and 14.30. This departed about an hour later.

At this point the afternoon shift took over to complete any further shunting duties. Incoming trains brought the empty wagons for the colliery and the wagons for repair. These had to be shunted and, if necessary, empties taken back up to Writhlington Colliery sidings.

The above diagram was changed according to requirements and at that time it was more than adequate to keep the engine crews busy all day. At one time early in 1967 the S&DJR yard was so full that extensive use of the up main line was made for the storage of wagons both at Radstock and just beyond the crossover at Writhlington.

Once demolition trains began to use Radstock the area became even busier and the up main line was regularly used at Radstock to store both full and empty trains of wagons, then moved either off the line to Bristol or down to the scene of demolition. Coal and goods trains from Radstock North were scheduled to leave for Bristol at 14.30 each weekday.

Fears that the Radstock to Writhlington section would close in the late 1960s proved to be unfounded following a review by the NCB in January 1967 of their remaining North Somerset collieries. They stated that two of the remaining three collieries would continue to work until the early 1970s, these being Writhlington and Kilmersdon.

There was, however, a smaller shock to the area with the announcement at the end of the 1967 summer that Wagon Repairs Ltd, were going to close their works at Radstock at the end of the year. By the middle of November they were completing their last half dozen or so repairs. This now left the future of the line entirely dependent on the fortunes of the Lower Writhlington Colliery at just about the same time that the future of this coalfield was again under discussion. Almost certainly Writhlington and Kilmersdon would go – or so it was thought locally. Strangely they escaped the immediate cuts and were given instead a limited life extension!

The next major event to affect the line occurred in July 1968 when the county suffered some of the worst flooding for many years in a freak summer storm. Serious damage to the North Somerset line at Pensford put it out of service and it was never repaired. In consequence all trains would now have to work out of Radstock via Frome to Bristol, a much longer and more inconvenient route and one which, between Mells Road and Radstock, would have to be reinstated. The North Somerset line was closed completely from a point a few chains to the west of the 1966 spur and subsequently lifted, but enough track was retained to form a headshunt on this spur to allow continued access to the S&D. It was now impracticable to bring main line diesel locomotives over to the S&D so all traffic was transferred by shunter across to Radstock West where completed trains were made up for despatch via Frome. The first passenger train since the closure of the S&DJR was on 6th April 1968 run by the Railway Correspondence & Travel Society (RCTS) in the form of a 4-car dmu 'The Thames–Avon Railtour' which travelled up the line as far as Writhlington Colliery and back. A second special, planned for 29th June 1968 had to be postponed because of industrial trouble but then had to be cancelled for good because of the storm damage to the North Somerset line in July 1968 at Pensford.

In 1969 another unexpected move occurred when Wagon Repairs partially re-opened their works at the end of the summer to deal with heavy repairs, mainly to privately owned vehicles, such as petrol tankers and coal wagons for the electricity authority. Alas, this re-opening was to be decidedly short-lived and within two years had closed for good.

Removal of the track between Bristol and Radstock (North Somerset Line) took place during 1969. It was reported on 14th November 1969 that the Norton-Radstock UDC were agitating for the complete removal of the two level crossings over the main road in the centre of the town. They wanted the two railways linked by re-instating a former private siding connection between the two lines through the closed Ludlows Colliery. By doing this it would release a lot of land in the centre of the town to allow for the redevelopment of the road system. Neither BR nor the highway authority were willing to stand the cost of the work and a stalemate was reached and the crossings remained.

In the depths of a Mendips' winter, 8th December 1967, Class 08 No. D3182 is shunting the Writhlington Colliery sidings. Note that Writhlington signalbox has been removed and the lines north to Bath have already been lifted.

Peter James

Later the same day No. D3182 is seen at Radstock with its load of coal from Writhlington Colliery.   *Peter James*

On 6th April 1968 the RCTS arranged a rail tour to visit various locations in and around Avon called 'The Thames–Avon Railtour'. The four car dmu is seen returning from Writhlington Colliery.

Michael Gates

By 1970 much of the existing track not used between Radstock North and Writhlington Colliery was recovered, this including most of the former up main line except the part which ran from the level crossing gates through the up platform and yard as far as Tyning. Various sidings in and around the yard were lifted at this time as well. On 14th November 1970 the Wirral Railway Circle and Great Western Society (Bristol Group) organised the 'Somerset Rambler II'. The 3-car dmu running from Bristol to Radstock via Frome before taking a round trip to Writhlington Colliery. The rail tour also included an unscheduled stop at Radstock North station to visit the headquarters of the Somerset & Dorset Railway Circle. From Radstock the special returned via Frome along the B&NS line and up to Highbridge to run out to Bason Bridge Creamery. The final part of the tour was to visit Bath Midland Bridge goods yard.

Looking thoroughly run-down and dilapidated, the remainder of the line existed in a sort of half-life with each month bringing the inevitable abandonment closer. In April 1972 the Locomotive Club of Great Britain ran another special from Radstock to Writhlington Colliery, formed of a 3-car dmu. This again stopped at Radstock North station to view the S&DRC collection but by this time the end seemed near. Then quite suddenly during the early part of 1973 coal output from Writhlington was increased although sadly this was to prove to be its swansong. During the late summer it was announced by the NCB that both Writhlington and Kilmersdon collieries would be closed in September 1973. This left only the Somerset & Dorset Railway Circle at Radstock.

The final train load of coal from Writhlington Colliery passed through Radstock North to the GWR line and thence back across the GWR crossing into the West yard to the accompaniment of detonators on 16th November 1973, and the gates were ceremoniously closed for the last time.

The shunter was still kept in Radstock locomotive shed but, here after, was only used to shunt the West yard. Within a week the shunter was gone and the train locomotive undertook all shunting. Clearly time was running out for the Somerset & Dorset. There was no immediate rush to recover the track out to Writhlington; indeed it was retained because

Another view of the Great Western Society rail tour on 5th March 1966. This time working wrong line at Radstock on the down leg of the trip.

Ken Marchant

investigations were being made for the recovery of part of Writhlington Colliery's tip. This was not proceeded with at the time. On 16th October 1975 the Somerset & Dorset Railway Trust (formerly S&DR Circle) removed its last rolling stock hauled by Class 33 No. 33019 over to the West yard before proceeding at a later date to the West Somerset Railway. Contractors moved in soon after to lift the remaining track and demolish the station building. The site was cleared for redevelopment by the early part of 1980.

Motive power used on this section:

Class	No.	Noted
35	D7029	19/10/66
35	D7005	8/12/67
08	D3182	8/12/67
08	D3185	29/12/67
35	D7001	12/6/68
35	D7031	13/6/68
47	47.185	1973
33	33.019	16/10/75

Just ten years later and the last track on the S&DJR is lifted at Radstock.   *Ken Marchant*

The Somerset & Dorset Railway Trust at Radstock 1970–1976

Just prior to the closure of the Somerset & Dorset a number of genuinely interested people met to constitute a society called The Somerset & Dorset Railway Circle, specifically to collect, collate and record as much as possible of the history of the railway, without actually becoming physically involved in preservation.

With the introduction of a monthly 'Question & Answer' newsletter, membership grew rapidly and, of course, with the influx of new blood came inevitable agitation to become involved in practical preservation. At the 1968 AGM two very important proposals were put forward, firstly that the Circle should consider preserving an S&DJR locomotive, namely a 7F Class 2-8-0 from Barry scrapyard, and

secondly the Circle should investigate the possibility of setting up a museum in a former S&DJR station building. Protracted negotiations resulted in the purchase and return of S&D 7F No. 53808 to Radstock in 1970. Prior to this event considerable time and effort had been devoted to finding a suitable home for the Circle's proposed preservation activities. Such a site should be connected to BR and have covered accommodation for No. 53808. It should also be within reasonable travelling distance for a majority of members, with a long term aim of being able to operate the locomotive and any other stock located there. Therefore, the Circle elected a sub-committee for this purpose and investigated the possible use of a number of sites including Avonmouth, Bristol, Binegar, Evercreech Junction, Templecombe, Bath Green Park, Glastonbury, Highbridge and Radstock. Initially an attempt was made to lease Evercreech Junction with a long term objective of purchasing the site. Unfortunately this was not acceptable to BR and the scheme failed.

A kindly disposed BR official learned of the Circle's plight and knowing that Radstock North station buildings were about to be vacated, suggested that this might fulfil the Circle's requirements. Following favourable discussions a lease of £100 per annum was negotiated; for this the Circle had use of the station buildings and up platform at Radstock North station. The Circle would have to carry out certain repairs caused by rot and vandals as well as the general upkeep of the buildings. Regrettably the lease would only be for eight years as the local council required the site for road realignment after BR had ceased to use it.

The first item of rolling stock to arrive at Radstock was on 15th March 1970 in the form of a Great Northern Railway 6-wheeled brake van. Purchase of No. 53808 was secured when £700 of the £2,500 asking price had been paid in April 1970. The move from Barry to Bristol Bath Road depot was completed on 3rd October where she remained until after the Open Day on 17th October 1970. Then, on Thursday 22nd October, came the day for which the Circle had been waiting so long. Shortly after 11 a.m the final triumphant return of No. 53808 to Radstock took place. The winter of 1970/71 saw regular working parties concentrating their efforts on the station buildings and 53808 was tucked away in Radstock shed. Celebration of the closure of the line that year was marked by the opening of the museum, complete with a special first day cover for stamp collectors.

Serious consideration had to be given to the way in which the project would be financed and its ability to attract the general public, as well as railway buffs. The unexpected but timely arrival of *Cranford 2*, an operational 0-6-0 Bagnall saddle tank at Radstock and a visit from David Shepherd on Sunday 15th August 1970, who was looking for a new home for his locomotives due to the failed Longmoor Project, created a completely new and exciting development. *Cranford 2* was steamed within ten days of arrival and on Saturday 14th August the sight and sound of steam returned to Radstock. During the autumn of 1971 the operation was to be restricted to the remaining section of the up line. It was not until 1971 that official sanction

was given for the use of the whole 1½ mile section of line from Radstock to Writhlington.

Discussions continued between the Circle and David Shepherd's Longmoor Group. Initially the Longmoor Group liked what they saw and subject to satisfactory negotiations with BR it was agreed to form The Radstock Steam Trust with the object of purchasing the land, track and buildings at Radstock, eventually to administer the operation of the railway. A proposal that a committee of six persons be formed to administer the setting-up of the Steam Trust, also that the newly formed body should seek charitable status. This was approved at the Circle's AGM on 9th October 1971.

Unfortunately, David Shepherd's negotiations with BR proved fruitless, due to the National Coal Board's reluctance to declare their intentions regarding the two remaining pits at Radstock. Consequently, BR were in no position to sell land and track which, quote "is to remain operational in the foreseeable future". They also made it clear that they were only prepared to sell after the whole section closed, thus dealing with one large parcel of land. So reluctantly, under these circumstances David Shepherd and the Longmoor Group withdrew from the Radstock Project because, in his opinion, the future of the North side was too uncertain. This announcement was obviously a disappointment to Circle members, but with the financial success of the Steam Open Days, the arrival of more locomotives and rolling stock, also the probability of BR's continued presence at Radstock for a while longer, this all gave an air of optimism to the project.

The optimism proved to be well founded as the Radstock Project grew in popularity, this being helped in no small way by the increasing collection of locomotives and rolling stock brought together over the next two or three years. During the spring and summer of 1972, regardless of the success of the Steam Days, arguments prevailed as to the Circle's future at Radstock and of the possibility of 53808 being hired to the newly formed West Somerset line for a season when her restoration was completed. But, by the autumn most people's resolve lay with the Circle's efforts at Radstock. With the now increasing collection of stock came the thought that they could benefit from becoming a registered charity and on 2nd December 1972 an EGM was called to approve the committee's proposal to achieve such status. The meeting duly approved the motion and thus The Somerset & Dorset Railway Museum Trust was born on 3rd January 1973, although at this stage the Circle was not to be wound up.

In December 1971 a formal rental agreement had been signed to enable the Circle to use Radstock North station buildings as a museum and sales area. Unfortunately matters concerning the locomotive depot were not so simple, for although the Circle had permission to use one road and the inspection pit as well as install an electricity supply, BR still stabled their diesel shunter in the other road. Thus it was to the Circle's financial advantage that they had an arrangement whereby they were charged rental on each piece of track that their items of stock occupied, rather than an overall rental on the redundant sidings. Satisfactory negotiations regarding this matter remained unresolved.

To enable all interested parties to discuss the future of the Circle's activities thoroughly, a meeting was arranged at Radstock, and re-convened in the Norton Radstock Council Chambers between officers of the Circle, BR, the County Surveyor, the Clerk and Planning Officer for Norton Radstock Council. The outcome was that BR did not know when coal mining would cease in North Somerset, but would be prepared to sell the trackbed to the Circle at a negotiated price. In principle the County Surveyor and Planning Officer had no objection to the Circle's proposed preservation scheme, though, as had been feared, the Circle would lose the station area and rail connection with BR. Although the Circle were not certain of the time scale involved, now at least it was possible with the right planning and finance to save a small part of the beloved Somerset & Dorset Joint Railway.

Christmas 1972 should have proved to be the high point of the year, ample motive power and rolling stock should have led to a financially rewarding series of Santa specials. Unfortunately BR had other ideas, with the result that they refused the necessary authority for any further locomotive movements by the Circle over BR metals. This was said to be no reflection on their previous behaviour, just a general directive on privately-owned steam locomotive movements on BR track. BR did make one concession to allow several steam hauled brake van trips to Writhlington on Christmas Eve 1972.

After the success of the Christmas trips the New Year was full of optimism for a better season of trips to Writhlington. This was encouraged by another concession on the 22nd April as 'a special occasion' and was repeated on 29th April. These events were soon followed by another letter from BR stating that there were to be no further steam operations at Radstock as it was not one of the approved steam routes.

On 16th May 1973 came the news that had been expected for the past few years – the NCB were to close the two remaining collieries in the North Somerset Coalfield. Writhlington and Kilmersdon were finally to close down on 30th September 1973. With the imminent closure of the collieries came the first indication from BR that in all probability they would be declaring the Radstock section of the S&DJR non-operational with the departure of the last coal train. This announcement opened up a new and exciting development as far as the Trust was concerned in the form of its steam operation. BR had indicated that if there was no physical connection with the rest of the system, it might be possible to come to some arrangement regarding the use of the sidings occupied by the Trust's locomotives and rolling stock. So the final chapter of steam operation at Radstock had begun, not quite in the fashion that the Trust had hoped; still a compromise was better than nothing. After the withdrawal in the spring of 1973 of the BR shunter stabled at Radstock shed, the Trust found themselves the sole occupants of the depot site. Following negotiations BR allowed the Trust to steam their locomotives for engineering purposes, but not unfortunately to carry passengers. Thus it was to transpire that from the autumn of 1973 every open day just happened to coincide with the steaming of locomotives for engineering purposes, and this situation continued until the final Christmas open day in 1974.

Work continued at a steady pace on 53808 with some mention of it being able to attend the Stockton & Darlington 150th Celebrations in 1975, but it would have been towed in the cavalcade. The idea was dropped due the expense involved. During 1973 and 1974 a number of Trust members, still confident of the eventual success of the project, purchased further rolling stock. Even another steam locomotive arrived on site regardless of the steam operation ban.

The Radstock Project had to look further ahead than just running one and a quarter miles of track from a small market town to a disused colliery. A series of meetings followed in which the idea for a mining and industrial museum was agreed upon, with Writhlington Colliery to become the central exhibit. The visitor would therefore board a vintage train at Radstock and travel to Writhlington behind a steam locomotive, view the mining museum and the Trust's railway museum. As time and money allowed further amenities would be added. With this in mind an EGM of the Trust was convened in December 1973, which duly gave its backing to the

formation of a limited company to undertake negotiations with BR and the NCB. The Somerset &
Dorset Light Railway Company was formally incorporated as a private company on 4th January 1974.
The new company lunched an initial £1,000 share
capital issue which as things turned out, was over
subscribed by £55. The directors of the new company were all Trust members, each with an important skill to aid the project in its difficult objective.
During 1974 negotiations were held with all the
concerned parties, support coming from a variety of
interested individuals and organisations.

During the summer of 1974 some light relief
from the rounds of negotiation came in the form of
celebrations to mark the centenary of the opening of
the Bath Extension in 1874. At an open day on the
7th July David Shepherd very kindly presented one
of his Nine Elms prints, and personally autographed
the prize in a draw to raise funds for 53808.

During 1973 and 1974 inflation climbed steeply,
this in turn caused a huge leap in land and scrap
metal prices at a time when the Trust could ill-
afford such an increase. The negotiated purchase
price had been set at £54,000 for land and track in
May 1974 and one has to add to this a monthly
interest cost of £400 until a deposit of £12,000 had
been paid, a time limit of 1st August 1974 being
mentioned. Under these conditions the Trust had to
act fast. On 21st June a company EGM was called
to approve the resolution to increase the share issue
to £16,000. By 27th August the situation was looking grim as only £3,225 had been taken up. BR
wanted an additional £500 payment that month to
give the Trust more time to raise the deposit. It had
been hoped to launch a public company in the
autumn, but the Trust was advised that the time
was wrong and that they should raise more money
to finance it. An attempt was made to raise this
money by a covenant scheme; unfortunately this
failed.

The situation was now becoming desperate with
the directors of the company making appeals for
money and help, as well as writing begging letters
to anybody they thought could help, even to Sir
Richard Marsh for a stay of execution, but all to no
avail. On 2nd February 1975 a meeting was held at
Radstock for members of the Trust and company to
discuss the situation, this being that the Trust could
no longer financially support the Radstock Project
and alternative arrangements would have to be
made for the locomotives and rolling stock based at
the site. There followed a meeting with the BR
Estates Department in Bristol on 20th March 1975,
at which the company made its impossible position
clear and declared that it had no further interest in
Radstock North station or the track and trackbed up
to Writhlington.

In the event of the Project failing in its objective,
the Trust committee had made a contingency plan
which involved the newly formed West Somerset
Railway. All members of the Trust, whether owners
of stock or just grass roots members, wished to
remain together wherever the Trust may have been
based.

By late Spring 1975 all the Trust's locomotives
and rolling stock had been made ready for the
move. During May and June a large amount of
stock departed by road. All remaining items were
moved from Radstock North to the West yard on
16th November, Class 33 No. 33019 was used to
move this stock which then continued the journey
to the West Somerset by lorry. The last item
departed in February 1976. Some Trust members
returned in June 1976 to remove the three-way
point from outside the depot for re-use at
Washford. The company ceased to exist in
December 1976 and was therefore struck off the
companies' register. After the move to Washford
the Trust has gone from strength to strength with
many successes to its credit. Amongst these the one
to bring the greatest pride and joy must have been
the restoration of 53808 to her former glory, and
the locomotive now carries out regular turns on the
West Somerset Railway. The museum at Washford
has grown over the years, with the addition of
archived data being made available to members.
The reconstruction of the interior of Midford signalbox and restoration of Burnham signalbox, both
at Washford, along with other large and education-
ally worthwhile exhibits to the site form a worthy
memorial to the S&DJR.

Highbridge–Bason Bridge Creamery 1966–1972

The original intention to retain the branch as far as
Glastonbury did not come about because by the
time of final closure C. & J. Clark's Shoes had
transferred their business to road haulage. Only a
little under two miles were retained to a point a few
hundred yards beyond the road level crossing at
Bason Bridge, in order that the private sidings of
the large Unigate Creamery could be served. In
1970 this factory was one of the most important
creameries and milk reception centres in Britain,
and there seemed then that there would be abso-
lutely no chance of this section of the S&DJR
closing.

S&DJR 7F No. 53808 is about to travel for the very last time on home metals on 16th November 1975.

The S&DRT Collection

After closure to passenger traffic in March 1966 this part of the branch was quickly altered to the status of a long siding, all signal arms and siding connections (except those at the creamery) being removed. Highbridge crossing (which took the S&D over the main GWR line on the level) had to remain in order that access to the branch could be retained, as was the relevant trap siding that protected the GWR main line from over-running S&D trains. This was controlled from the adjacent Highbridge crossing (GWR signalbox). By 1969 the branch, or long siding, was worked under the control of the signalman, without a train staff. The disc signal from the S&D line to the GWR goods shed site was replaced by a 3ft signal arm of typical GWR origin but mounted on the same bracket.

It seemed that this part of the S&D had a long and busy future in its original state for many years to come, but it was soon apparent that the route of the proposed M5 motorway would cross the line just to the east of the old Highbridge Locomotive Works (much of which was still standing in 1966 despite having been disused since the 1930s). The proposed route of the motorway hereabouts was the subject of a Ministry of Transport enquiry which was held on 21st July 1970, being conducted by an independent engineer, Mr Arthur Floyd.

If the motorway was allowed to sever the line it would place Unigate in a very difficult position. In 1969 Unigate used 1,238–3,000 gallon rail tank wagons, all of which left the Bason Bridge Creamery full for London. If road transport had to be used it would have meant an expenditure of £100,000 on road vehicles with up to 15 extra 32-ton road tankers being required to replace the daily train service. This factory was dealing with 17 million gallons of milk every year at this time, taken from some 600 farms all around the West of England.

At the public enquiry Unigate presented the plan for a bridge to take the line over the motorway. Despite the considerable cost of this it was not impossible to engineer. Nine objectors made their points during the enquiry which lasted a day and a half, but opinion was that any change in the route would have serious effects on a number of properties in the area and the decision stood. Unigate's plan to have the line bridged over the motorway was not approved so the future of this part of the S&DJR was sealed after they had lost the subsequent appeal on the decision. Meanwhile milk traffic continued to flow along the line in ever increasing quantities.

In the construction of the M5 motorway further to the north great use had been made of pulverised fly ash, a waste material from the industrial steel producing areas of South Wales, which was transported in long train loads using hopper wagons to a point as near to the motorway site as possible. This was at Puxton near Weston-super-Mare and it involved constructing a special discharge siding system. By the middle of 1970 plans were well advanced for the commencement of construction on the section of motorway past Highbridge, and in order to accommodate the necessary fly ash it was announced that a further discharge area would be constructed. It soon became obvious that the preferred site would be on the line of the S&DJR at Highbridge.

Despite its temporary nature to lay in such a terminal was no small task, and in order to accommodate the new complex it was planned to demolish part of the locomotive works buildings. This was commenced in 1970 although money was not wasted in demolition of those parts of the works on land not required! The site was cleared sufficiently by December 1970 to enable construction work to commence. Meanwhile construction work on the motorway itself was also starting in the area. On 14th November 1970 what would appear to be the only enthusiasts special traversed the Highbridge–Bason Bridge Creamery line when the Wirral Railway Circle and Great Western Society (Bristol Group) included it in their 'Somerset Rambler II'. The 3-car dmu spent some time at both Bason Bridge and Highbridge station before proceeding to Bath.

The siding had to be capable of taking the largest locomotives then in service on the Western Region, so it was decided that a completely new junction between the S&D and Great Western main line would have to be made. Until this time the original connection through Highbridge GWR goods yard and goods shed was still in use. In consequence the original level crossing that the two railways used finally came to an end, but not before construction of a completely new bridge to take the B3139 road across the planned new junction had been completed. The Bason Bridge line was connected directly into

the down main line by a point facing to down trains, controlled by Highbridge crossing signalbox.

The entire former S&DJR station at Highbridge was also demolished to make room for the new connection. The branch line itself was then repositioned for a considerable length, to a point well beyond the site of the locomotive works by moving it completely about 100 yards to the north of its original formation and connecting it into the new junction spur. Beyond the works the newly repositioned line regained its former course to Bason Bridge. The reason for moving the line was to enable an elevated discharge siding to be built more-or-less on the original trackbed. Construction of this was a large task indeed for it meant ramping a completely new siding up to a height of some 25ft, which was reached at a point somewhere near the site of the former locomotive depot. The new discharge siding then ran across a substantial steel bridge structure which was to act as the actual discharge point for the hopper wagons. From here the line then descended back down to ground level to rejoin the original branch. The entire siding formed a long loop line. Additionally a short 'cripple siding' was laid in on the site of the former station and the whole branch was protected by a new GWR type home signal mounted on a typical GWR solid metal mast just adjacent to the new road bridge. The pulverised fly ash (PFA) control office of BR was situated on the former S&DJR platform No. 5 which was the only part of the former station not to be demolished.

By April 1971 preliminary works on the motorway were well in advance of the schedule, also by this time work on the new fly ash sidings was almost complete. The first train from South Wales arrived on 27th April 1971. The discharge was effected by running the train slowly up the ramped discharge loop, and as each hopper wagon reached the discharge bridge the under side doors of the wagon were released and the contents allowed to fall through the bridge to the ground below. From there it was transported the short distance by road to the site of construction. During the whole of this time normal milk traffic continued to be worked along the branch.

Although Unigate lost its appeal to retain the branch, arrangements were made to temporarily bridge the motorway whilst it was under construction and secure its railhead until a time when final construction would hold up its completion. It was agreed to maintain the branch into 1972, and to do this the line had to be ramped up over the motorway

Highbridge depot soon after track lifting had been completed on 12th January 1967. The buildings would remain a further four years before the whole site was cleared.

Chris Handley

(Before) Highbridge station just after the rationalisation in late January 1967.

Chris Handley

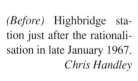

(After) Four years three months later, the station, goods yard, depot and most of the old Highbridge Works had been demolished to make way for a pulverised ash terminal, for the construction of the M5 motorway.

Chris Handley

by some 3ft to form the temporary crossing. At Highbridge, where the new link to the branch from the main line was opened on 4th April 1971 (having been installed from December 1970), the old crossing had become redundant from that date although in situ for some time thereafter.

Towards the end of 1971 the Western Region started to withdraw a number of its diesel-hydraulic locomotives, many of which had been working the milk traffic from Bason Bridge. As a result the Western Region's Chief Civil Engineer authorised the use of BR/Sulzer Class 25 and Brush Class 31 diesel-electric locomotives over the line.

The PFA contract was essentially a short-term operation which was due to last for no more than six months and came to an end on 21st August 1971 when the final 1,000 tons of ash were delivered. In all 750,000 tons were transported from Aberthaw to Highbridge for the M5 construction. The PFA siding – minus discharge ramp – and a short length of the branch remained in use as p.w. sidings until 28th June 1976. These sidings were finally lifted in the early 1980s.

Construction of the motorway was now getting into an advanced state but still the branch was as busy as ever with milk traffic and it was to remain so for the next twelve months. By the end of Summer 1972 it was becoming obvious that the line would have to close soon. BR finally announced the closure to take effect on and from 2nd October 1972. In fact the date came and went and still the milk trains trundled back and forth to Bason Bridge. It was being worked on a day-to-day basis for another week or more before the very last train left Bason Bridge for Highbridge, working as it did so, all the remaining rail vehicles at the former place back to Highbridge. Unigate very reluctantly lost its rail connection.

As a footnote, this large creamery was eventually sold to another concern and was closed in 1987.

Motive power used on this section: Classes 08, 14, 22, 25, 31 and 35.

Broadstone Junction–Blandford 1966–1969
At 10 miles 71 chains this was by far the longest section of the S&DJR to remain in use after March 1966. From this date only the down main line was used on the double track section between Corfe Mullen Junction and Blandford. On 25th July 1966 Corfe Mullen Junction, Bailey Gate Crossing, Bailey Gate station and Blandford station signalboxes were all reduced to ground frames. All signals were then ignored and the line operated on the

'One locomotive in Steam' principle except for occasional variations when more than one locomotive was required on the line at the same time! This would happen when very long and heavy trains of military vehicles had to be shunted into Blandford Camp, and the train locomotive would not be able to use the north end crossover to run round the train. As a result a light engine would work up to Blandford some 15 minutes after the Army special and draw the train back and into Blandford Camp, and by so doing release the train engine. It is not clear whether both locomotives then worked back down the line together or not.

For a majority of the time after general closure, the line up to Blandford was controlled by the signalman at Broadstone Junction signalbox which remained in use, although once the train was on the line he had no other control over it. Broadstone Junction signalbox remained open because it also controlled all the freight using the former LSWR line as far as Ringwood as well as the S&DJR. Then following the opening of the Bournemouth freight concentration depot on 13th February 1967, freight movements along the LSWR line were confined to occasional Army specials up to West Moors and the line took up the status of a long siding. This status was not applied to the S&DJR until 7th May 1968 when all the S&D ground frames were officially closed. After this all freight movements for either West Moors or Blandford were controlled from Poole, though Broadstone Junction signalbox did not officially close until 18th October 1970 and must have been used to control the points at the junction for both freight traffic and demolition trains.

After March 1966 Blandford continued to receive both freight and parcel traffic and at that time was one of the few surviving stations in Dorset which still retained these facilities. Until the opening of the Bournemouth freight depot Blandford's yard was assured a good business and Mr Harold Whiting, a former S&DJR employee, was retained permanently to run the station. (He became one of the last former S&DJR men to see service on the line.) Trains consisted of up to 40 wagons, both box and open wagons, bringing in coal, fertiliser and general merchandise. The procedure at Blandford was simple. With all traffic using only the down line, the train would draw into the down platform and after the locomotive had run round its train via the up line it would proceed to remove the empty wagons from the goods yard and marshall them into the up platform. Then the loaded wagons were drawn out of the down platform and shunted into the appropriate siding before the locomotive coupled onto the empty wagons for the return trip to Poole via Broadstone.

There was further traffic at Bailey Gate where the creamery still relied to some extent on rail delivery of milk tanker wagons. This traffic initially ran separately from traffic to Blandford but as the years passed it was sometimes combined as a single trip. Additional extra traffic was generated by the Army

in connection with its Blandford Camp, mostly in the form of military vehicles but there is no record of any troop specials.

During the remainder of 1966 the regular daily freight service operating to Blandford was as follows:

Arrive Blandford	08.00	Monday to Friday
Depart Blandford	10.00	Monday to Friday

Class 47 No. D1986 about to depart from Blandford Forum with the LCGB special on 3rd November 1968. The Class 74, No. E6108, which had powered the train up the line was still attached to the rear for the return trip.
Peter James

Class 33 No. D6517 arrives at Blandford Forum station with a fertiliser train from Avonmouth on 17th December 1968.
Peter James

No. D6517 is seen shunting the large number of wagons still using Blandford goods yard on 17th December 1968.

Peter James

A view south as No. D6517 shunts a coal wagon later in the day. It is interesting to note that all the station fixtures are still in place even though closure had been announced and track lifting undertaken.

Peter James

No. D6517 is making up its return working of empty vans the same day. Full wagons in the down platform are still to be shunted. Note the up line has already been lifted south of the station.

Peter James

Class 33 No. D6511 is running round its lengthy train on 19th December 1968. This freight traffic was terminated on 2nd January 1969.

Peter James

Milk trains to and from Bailey Gate ran in the afternoons, Monday to Friday and also at weekends when required.

It was not long before the railway enthusiasts' specials started to run over this section, commencing on 21st May 1966 when the British Young Traveller Society 'Hampshire Explorer' travelled up to Blandford, the four-coach train being headed by the Southern Region's BR Standard Class 3MT 2-6-0 No. 77014. As far as can be deduced this is the only member of this class to have ever travelled over any part of the S&DJR. The engine, like all such specials, had to travel back tender first, and it was also notable that this train made use of the up platform at Blandford although only the down line (and platform) were officially in use.

On 11th June 1966 'West Country' Pacifics made a welcome return, if only in a temporary nature, when No. 34012 *Launceston* ran a nine-coach special for the employees of the local brewery, Hall & Woodhouse. It took its train to Brighton. Just under a month later, on 7th July 1966, there was a lot of activity at Blandford when the normal freight was supplemented by a special train of military vehicles. This was hauled by Class 4MT 2-6-4T No. 80032. To shunt this train no less a locomotive than 'West Country' No. 34040 *Crewkerne* arrived from Bournemouth and spent most of the day there. Of course this engine was no stranger to the Somerset & Dorset.

On 16th October 1966 the LCGB included the line as part of its 'Dorset and Hants Rail Tour'. Even though the train consisted of only five coaches it would appear from photographs that no less than three locomotives were involved; BR Standard Class 3MT 2-6-0s Nos 77014 and 76026 were at either end of the train between Broadstone Junction station and Blandford station, and the return trip. From Broadstone the rail tour travelled to Wimborne and back. Then, for some unknown reason, the train was taken away from Broadstone Junction station by 'West Country' No. 34023 *Blackmore Vale*. Where the two 3MTs went to after their short trips is also unknown.

Indications that the Southern Region planned to run down their existing services to Blandford came on 20th December 1966 when BR announced that the parcels depot at Blandford would close from 2nd January 1967.

The major freight traffic continued, mainly in the hands of steam power. Much of the traffic was hauled over the line by BR Class 4MT 2-6-4Ts but LMR Ivatt Class 2MT 2-6-2Ts were also sometimes used as was the occasional 'West Country' on the

normal freight turns. None were new to the line as all had been allocated to Bournemouth or Eastleigh prior to closure.

A big downturn in business took place on 13th February 1967, when the new Bournemouth freight concentration depot began to take over a great deal of Blandford's business, after which the local freight manager who controlled the line, reduced its traffic to 'CBP' (Carted By Public) or complete wagon loads only. This had a drastic effect and it reduced the freight handled to one or two particular products only. By the middle of 1967 about the only regular traffic to come up the line was coal and the occasional bulk order such as fertiliser from Avonmouth, though large consignments of raw materials were occasionally delivered to the Hall & Woodhouse brewery, normally after the hop picking season. 1967 was the last year that such traffic used Blandford yard, after which road transport was used.

If the freight traffic was dwindling the same was not the case for the specials. On 25th March 1967 the Manchester Rail Travel Society ran their 'Hants & Dorset Branch Flyer' over the line, advertising in the process that this would be the last steam hauled tour over the line. This turned out to be the case as the Southern Region withdrew steam during that July. Motive power was as advertised, an Ivatt 2MT, No. 41320. Coming from Bournemouth the train was booked to arrive at 15.05 with a 15.20 departure time. In the event it did not arrive at Blandford until 15.18 and departed again at 15.36.

With the reduction in freight after February 1967 the regular daily freight train was discontinued and a twice-weekly train substituted to run only if required. Usually it did, and it often brought about 40 loaded wagons to the railhead each week to keep Harold Whiting busy. But then at the end of the year all the remaining Army traffic for Blandford Camp was withdrawn and diverted to Wool instead. At this time milk being delivered to Bailey Gate was being used to make cheese and this meant a reduction in milk trains. In consequence they were only run as required by the creamery who arranged with Poole station when they had any traffic to be forwarded by rail.

After February 1967 the freight service timetable had been rearranged to run as required as follows:

| 07.40 | Poole | – | Blandford |
| 09.30 | Blandford | – | Poole |

This service ran normally once or twice a week until mid-1968 when it officially became a twice-

Specials on the Blandford line

Class 4MT 2-6-0 No. 76026 heads the LCGB 'Dorset and Hants Rail Tour' on its trip to Blandford, crossing bridge No. 196 just south of Blandford on 16th October 1966.

John Scrace

Class 3MT No. 77014 was coupled to the other end of the LCGB rail tour and is seen here on the return trip just north of Spetisbury Halt.

John Scrace

When the LCGB 'Dorset and Hants Rail Tour' arrived back at Broadstone Junction station the two 2-6-0s were replaced by Bulleid Pacific No. 34023 *Blackmore Vale*.

John Scrace

On 25th March 1967 the last steam hauled rail tour ran to Blandford behind Class 2MT 2-6-2T No. 41320 with the MRTS 'Hants & Dorset Branch Flyer'. The train is depicted just north of Bailey Gate with No. 41320 working bunker first.

John Scrace

The MRTS rail tour is caught again on the return trip at Broadstone Junction station.

John Scrace

weekly service run on Tuesdays and Thursdays. From dieselisation in July 1967 the trains were invariably in the charge of Class 33s. Starting in June 1967 the Southern Region engineering department made regular visits to the line whilst removing signalling, unused sidings and from Spring 1968 the up main line was gradually lifted back towards Bailey Gate. From mid-1968, when the freight service had officially become twice-weekly, another daily freight working from Bournemouth to Wimborne would work onto the S&D to handle any milk traffic for Bailey Gate when this was required. If necessary this train would also work right up to Blandford on Mondays, Wednesdays and Fridays but how often this happened is not clear. At weekends milk traffic was scheduled on Saturdays by a

Class 08 0-6-0 shunter and on Sundays by a Class 74 Bo-Bo electro-diesel. In the event it seems that the electro-diesels worked all the weekend traffic into Bailey Gate Creamery as no Class 08 shunters appear to have been seen on this part of the S&D until July 1968, and even this was an unconfirmed sighting on an engineering department train.

On 13th June 1968 most unusually a Matisa track recording machine worked the line from Poole, later working back to Broadstone Junction and up to Wimborne. Almost certainly this was a crew training exercise but presumably they checked the track as well.

On 15th June 1968 yet another special ran for the employees of Hall & Woodhouse powered by Class 33 No. 6540. The nine-coach train departed from

Blandford at 07.40 and travelled to Kew, arriving at 11.05. Its night-time return barred it from the S&D and passengers returned from Poole by coach. By this time milk traffic to Bailey Gate on weekends was becoming very spasmodic and they did not run at all on the weekends of June 15/22/29 and July 6/13/20. Also from June the times of the regular freights changed and most reports indicate that trains did not reach Blandford until around 11.30 and that they only stayed about an hour.

On 3rd November 1968 the LCGB ran their 'Hampshireman' tour which was hauled up the line to Blandford by electro-diesel No. E6108. Motive power was unusual, as Class 47 No. D1986 was coupled to the rear of the train for the return journey to Broadstone Junction. Although probably not realised at the time this was to be the last special to run to Blandford and the death blow to this part of the S&DJR came quite suddenly at the end of the year when the Southern Region announced that all freight facilities at Blandford and Bailey Gate would be withdrawn on and from 6th January 1969. This decision may have come about due to the opening of a rail served fertiliser depot that had been constructed at Gillingham during 1968. The last scheduled freight out of Blandford actually ran on 2nd January 1969 and was hauled by Class 33 No. 6513, leaving just a few odd wagons to be collected on 6th January. The track was then left to rust until the track lifting contract commenced almost twelve months later. It is almost certain that a train traversed the line after closure to show prospective contractors what would be involved with this track lifting contract.

Motive power used on this section:

Date	Type			No.	Train worked
21/4/66	4MT	2-6-4T		80011	Poole–Blandford freight
22/4/66	4MT	2-6-4T		80146	Poole–Blandford freight
21/5/66	3MT	2-6-0		77014	BYTS 'Hampshire Explorer'
11/6/66	7P	4-6-2		34012	Hall & Woodhouse Excursion
7/7/66	4MT	2-6-4T		80032	Special military freight
7/7/66	7P	4-6-2		34040	Military freight shunter
16/10/66	3MT	2-6-0		77014	LCGB 'Dorset & Hants Rail Tour'
16/10/66	3MT	2-6-0		76026	LCGB 'Dorset & Hants Rail Tour'
16/10/66	7P	4-6-2		34023	LCGB 'Dorset & Hants Rail Tour'
5/11/66	4MT	2-6-4T		80013	Poole–Blandford freight
26/2/67	Class 33			D6551	Bailey Gate milk
25/3/67	2MT	2-6-2T		41320	MTRS 'Hants & Dorset Flyer'
11/4/68	Class 33			6515	Poole–Blandford freight
13/4/68	Class 74			E6016	Bailey Gate milk
4/5/68	Class 74			E6012	Bailey Gate milk

Date	Type	No.	Train worked
11/6/68	Class 33	6515	Poole–Blandford freight
15/6/68	Class 33	6540	Hall & Woodhouse Excursion
13/8/68	Class 33	6534	Poole–Blandford freight
15/8/68	Class 33	6540	Poole–Blandford freight
5/9/68	Class 33	6521	Poole–Blandford freight
17/9/68	Class 33	6520	Poole–Blandford freight
23/9/68	Class 33	6583	Poole–Blandford freight
17/10/68	Class 33	6514	Poole–Blandford freight
22/10/68	Class 33	6513	Poole–Blandford freight
24/10/68	Class 33	6531	Poole–Blandford freight
29/10/68	Class 33	6525	Poole–Blandford freight
31/10/68	Class 33	6528	Poole–Blandford freight
3/11/68	Class 74	E6108	LCGB 'Hampshireman' to Blandford
3/11/68	Class 47	D1986	LCGB 'Hampshireman' to Poole
5/11/68	Class 33	6513	Poole–Blandford freight
7/11/68	Class 33	6538	Poole–Blandford freight
19/11/68	Class 33	6580	Poole–Blandford freight
21/11/68	Class 33	6532	Poole–Blandford freight
3/12/68	Class 33	6532	Poole–Blandford freight
5/12/68	Class 33	6536	Poole–Blandford freight
10/12/68	Class 33	6535	Poole–Blandford freight
12/12/68	Class 33	6526	Poole–Blandford freight
17/12/68	Class 33	6517	Poole–Blandford freight
17/12/68	Class 33	6531	Diverted Wimborne train
19/12/68	Class 33	6533	Poole–Blandford freight
19/12/68	Class 33	6511	Diverted Wimborne train
24/12/68	Class 33	6507	Poole–Blandford freight
31/12/68	Class 33	6522	Poole–Blandford freight
31/12/68	Class 33	6511	Poole–Blandford extra freight
2/1/69	Class 33	6513	Poole–Blandford freight (Last Train)
6/1/69	Class 33	Unknown	Collected remaining wagons

Poole–Broadstone–Wimborne line

4/4/74	Class 33	33015	Poole–Wimborne freight
8/6/76	Class 33	33111	Poole–Wimborne freight
2/5/77	Class 33	33107	Poole–Wimborne freight (Last Train)
3/5/77	Class 33	33012 + 2 x 4-TC	Lea Valley Railway Club Special

Mangotsfield–Bath (Green Park) 1966–1971

Although not strictly part of the S&DJR, this line's fortunes were to remain inter-related with those of the S&D, so its fate is included.

Immediately after closure to passenger traffic on 6th March 1966 freight traffic continued to work normally and all the signalboxes (except Bath Junction) remained in use right up to Bath. Motive power for most trains was provided by Bristol Bath Road depot. In late 1967 it was decided that to maintain a freight only line with double-track and full signalling was now unnecessary. On 6th May 1968 single line working was introduced using the down line as far as Kelston Wood where a serious problem had occurred with the embankment due to a very bad storm, which meant the up line would have to be used into Bath.

The branch was reduced to single track in 1969 when all redundant track was lifted and all signalling was removed before becoming a long siding. After this, level crossing gates were worked by hand by the train crews. Ordinary freight traffic was, meanwhile, gradually pared away until only full wagon loads would be accepted at Midland Bridge depot and coal to the gas works. As a result of the singling of the Mangotsfield–Bath line any additional train workings to or from Bath Midland Bridge yard now had its locomotive worked in or out by double heading a regular service; many different combinations of locomotives were noted as a result.

Early December 1966 saw a Class 14 diesel-hydraulic locomotive moving an 'out of gauge load' from the gas works over to Midland Bridge goods yard. This train consisted of five other wagons plus a large steam crane. The large load was most likely a redundant part of the gas works which was finally seen being cut up in the Stothert & Pitt works yard some weeks later. Access to the Stothert & Pitt Engineering Ltd yard was maintained as considerable traffic still originated from here, such as scrap metal, parts of cranes and road rollers. Reams of paper were brought in by rail to a large goods shed in the Midland yard for a nearby printing works and some timber traffic also used the Midland yard. Steam power was still to be seen in the Midland yard for a couple of years after 1966, in the form of a self propelled crane which ran on its own section of track in front of the goods shed.

Occasional specials could be seen on the line, one being the 'Cheddar Valley' special which ran into Bath on 16th November 1968, consisting of a three-car dmu, for the LCGB (Bath Branch). A more unusual special visited between 25th and 30th April 1970. This was a Cider Exhibition train consisting of the five Bulmer's-owned Pullman coaches and a BR restaurant car. The train was hauled very appropriately by diesel-hydraulic Class 43 No. D847 *Strongbow*. Bath (Green Park) was busy on this day as another LCGB special was also due. A Class 42 with a ten-coach special used Bath (Green Park) to run round its train several times, during a filming session for the television series 'Softly Softly' which was carried out between Bitton and Weston.

Conversion of the Bath area to natural gas was scheduled for mid-May 1971 and on completion

Bath Gas Works closed down. This led to the withdrawal of the works' two industrial diesel shunters. By this time the coal traffic up to Twerton Bakery had long since ceased (closing in November 1967), so now there were few requirements to bring coal into Bath along this line. Deprived of this traffic BR wasted very little time in paring away the remaining business at Midland Bridge yard. Regular freight traffic ceased to be run over the line from the end of May 1971 with official closure taking place from the beginning of June 1971. A few wagons remained at Bath for a week or two longer before they were collected and taken away.

The yards at Bath were used for the next twelve months to store vast numbers of condemned box vans. Mainly banana vans, these wagons would be worked in over several weeks until every available piece of track was fully occupied, stored for a few months and then worked back out again for breaking elsewhere. Locomotives used on these trains included Class 52, 47, 35 and 25. The final workings out of Bath were in mid-April 1972.

In preparation for the January 1966 closure of the S&D, locomotives had been stored at Bath (Green Park) depot and eventually withdrawn. Most of these locomotives never turned another wheel in revenue earning service. When a bus operator withdrew his application to run a replacement bus service some of the stored locomotives were used again until they either failed or the new closure date was reached, after which they were withdrawn again. One however was steamed again – in fact this locomotive was probably to become the very last active steam locomotive on the Western Region. It was steamed during the week following closure, and despite its official withdrawal, was used to shunt the shed and Midland Bridge goods yard. On 12th March 1966 she was chalked up to be re-lit again on 14th March, and it is believed that Ivatt 2-6-2T No. 41283's last day in steam was 17th March 1966. The next day she was towed by 'Peak' No. D15 to Bristol for disposal, along with all the other locomotives at Bath depot. The large number of redundant steam locomotives required several 'Peak' and 'Hymek' class locomotives to be used on 18th March 1966. Some of these steam locomotives were displayed at the Bristol Bath Road depot open day on 30th April 1966, including Nos 80043, 3681 and 48760 before going to South Wales for scrapping. It is known that BR Class 4MT No. 76026 hauled Nos 75072 and 75073 over the S&D from Bath to Ringwood on 4th March 1966, being noted and photographed at Moorewood. All three locomotives were cut-up during April at Ringwood. These were the only redundant locomotives to be hauled over the S&D for disposal at the time of closure or after.

After closure to passenger traffic in 1966 four or five freight trains continued to use the line daily and this situation existed for at least the remainder of that year. Some of these working were as follows:

    11.45 Bath Midland Bridge to Portishead
    13.05 Bath Midland Bridge to Stoke Gifford
    15.15 Stoke Gifford   to Bath Midland
                            Bridge

As the years went by the number of freight trains fell drastically until no more than one train a day was required.

Motive power used on this section

Class	No.	Date	Notes
08	D3195	25/4/68	Bath Midland Bridge yard
	4029	25/4/70	Bath Midland Bridge yard
25	7510	31/5/71	Last regular freight out of Bath Midland Bridge yard .
35	D7043	18/3/66	With withdrawn steam locomotives
	D7085	30/12/66	Bath Junction
	D7019	19/8/67	Bath Midland Bridge yard
	D7015	8/2/68	Bath Midland Bridge yard
	D7007	15/2/68	Bath Midland Bridge yard
	D7011	27/6/70	Bath Midland Bridge yard
43	D847	25/4/70	Cider Special
44	D15	18/3/66	With withdrawn steam locomotives
45	D53	7/3/66	Bath Midland Bridge yard
	D34	25/5/66	Bath Junction
	D66	29/5/68	Bath Midland Bridge yard
47	D1614	1967	Bath Midland Bridge yard
	D1725	20/1/67	Bath Midland Bridge yard
	1613	1/2/69	Double-heading with No. D1002
52	D1069	15/6/68	Bath Midland Bridge yard
	D1002	1/2/69	Double-heading with No. 1613

LMS 8F 2-8-0 No. 48706 (and BR 4MT No. 80043) arrive back at Bath (Green Park) station on 6th March 1966 with the final Farewell Special.

Ken Marchant

The Last of the Many at Bath (Green Park) Depot

BR Standard Class 4MT 2-6-4Ts Nos 80043, 80041 and 80037 on 11th March 1966. Note the 8F in the S&D coaling stage at Bath, due to a lack of space elsewhere after closure.

Alan Newman

General view from Bath station signalbox on 14th March 1966 of the Midland Railway depot and assorted engines.

Alan Newman

Class 2MT 2-6-2T No. 41283 is shunting 8F 2-8-0 No. 48760 ready for departure on 14th March 1966. No. 41283 may well have been the last active steam locomotive on the Western Region when its fire was finally dropped on 17th March 1966.

Alan Newman

Exodus Day from Bath (Green Park) Depot on 18th March 1966

Ivatt 2-6-2Ts Nos 41307 and 41290, LMS 0-6-0T No. 47506 and Class 2MT No. 41223 await their turn to depart from Bath beside the Midland depot.

Alan Newman

Class 45 No. D15 about to depart from Midland Bridge goods yard with Nos 73001, 80043, 48444 and 92243 to Bristol Bath Road depot open day and then to a scrapyard in South Wales.

Alan Newman

Class 35 'Hymek' No. D7043 is about to depart from the Midland depot with Nos 80037, 47276, 41249 and 41206.

Alan Newman

4

Timetable of Track Lifting and Rationalisation

There were four principal contracts tendered for the dismantling of the Somerset & Dorset Joint Railway main line and branch line, namely:

Evercreech Junction–Bason Bridge.
Writhlington Colliery–Bath.
Blandford–Radstock.
Blandford–Broadstone Junction.

January 1967   –   October 1967
July 1967   –   June 1968
February 1967   –   July 1968
December 1969 –   October 1970

In addition to the main contracts, there were several smaller contracts for rationalisation and track lifting

placed over the next twelve years. These consisted of:

Highbridge station and depot
Bath Green Park station and depot.
Midsomer Norton–Radstock.
Mangotsfield–Bath Midland Yard.
Highbridge–Bason Bridge Creamery.
Radstock–Writhlington Colliery.
Wimborne–Holes Bay Junction.

November 1966 –   February 1967
October 1966   –   May 1967
1969
May 1972   –   September 1972
December 1972 –   February 1973
May 1976   –   August 1976
October 1977   –   July 1978

Mention should be made at this stage of the two permanent way gangs who remained after closure of the line. Their purpose was not only to still maintain the track but also to inspect the main line every two months (no confirmed reports of them on the branch line), the S&DJR having a six month period of grace when a case for reopening could be made. The gangs were based at Radstock and Templecombe, their duties involving clearing and repairing culverts and minor stream bridges to prevent flooding of the line; to remove rubbish and obstacles dumped on the track and to report any vandal damage to trackside fixtures and station buildings. The Radstock gang was responsible for

the line from Twerton Co-op siding to Evercreech Junction, while the Templecombe gang covered Evercreech Junction to Blandford. The line south from Blandford was covered more regularly by the Broadstone Junction gang. The Templecombe gang was seen just north of Shillingstone station on 31st October 1966, with Wickham trolley No. DS3057 repairing a damaged culvert. The Radstock gang was noted twice during 1967, firstly at Midford station with an inspection trolley on 13th February. The following month they were retrieving telegraph wires at Wellow station (it would appear they travelled up from Radstock by lorry!). This gang also undertook a great deal of the work involved with rationalisation of the trackwork in and around Radstock and as far as Writhlington Colliery.

After the passage of the last trains on Sunday 6th March 1966 the main line south of Radstock lay dormant for several months, though several reports speak of a train or trains which travelled the length of the main line. The purpose was said to be to collect lineside and station fixtures, but it is much more likely that these fixtures would have been collected by lorry. These activities are said to have occurred in April or May 1966. The only confirmed passage over the main line in this period occurred on Sunday 18th September, when Type 3 Class 35 'Hymek' No. D7039 worked a train from Bristol via the North Somerset Line to Radstock and then down to Evercreech Junction. It returned to Bristol by the same route. This train was unique in being the *only* train after closure to use the up line south of Midsomer Norton over the Mendips. The purpose of this train was to show prospective contractors what was involved and enable them to place their tenders with BR for the contracts on offer. The train consisted of the 'Hymek' and an inspection saloon.

Before covering the actual dismantling operations on the S&DJR mention must be made of the alterations that took place at Templecombe, the station closing on the same day as the S&DJR, 6th March 1966. From the following day preparations were made to single the Salisbury to Exeter main line of the former London & South Western Railway. The actual process of singling was at the end of April 1967 but not before a change in plans ensured that the double track would remain between Templecombe (exclusive of the station) and Yeovil Junction westwards. Nevertheless the former goods yard and S&DJR lines were no longer required into the station and in addition steps were taken to reduce the 60-lever signalbox frame to just 16. When this took place the junction between the LSWR line and the S&DJR had its points disconnected from the frame, clipped and locked. Demolition trains working the southern most part of the main track lifting contract gained access here and each working necessitated that these points were unclipped and worked by hand, when required. All these trains worked out from Yeovil Junction.

Demolition of the main line of the S&DJR commenced one mile to the north of Blandford on the single track section. It is not clear why this location was chosen for the commencement of work as the

mile of track remaining was never used again, unless it was thought to be useful as a long siding for Blandford goods yard should things become very busy, or it could be that this location was the boundary between the Southern and Western Regions.

It was the responsibility of BR to provide all the necessary wagons and motive power on an operation which was to become, at times, very complex. For the first three months all trains were brought onto the S&DJR via Templecombe Upper, before reversing down to the Junction signalbox and then proceeding locomotive first to the station nearest the railhead. The passing loops at the intermediate stations on this section enabled locomotives to run round their trains and push the wagons down to the railhead. Empty wagons were accommodated in any remaining sidings at the four stations on this section of line, plus additional wagons were held at Templecombe Lower yard.

The contractors developed a system whereby they worked from a fixed point close to the railhead, then, at a convenient time they would move further up the line to the next suitable base, normally a station which allowed them vehicular access to the line. Any goods yards being vacated would then be lifted in advance of the railhead reaching the area. The method of track lifting involved only around a dozen contractors plus BR train crews. The contractors supplied their own caterpillar crane and a converted bulldozer fitted with a device rather like forklift prongs to load sleepers into the open wagons. This was also used to drag the rails out of their chairs and place them ready for the crane to load them onto bogie bolster wagons.

Depending on the location the contractors would either travel to their base each day by road or set up temporary facilities and live on site. The gang was split into two, those clearing redundant sidings and passing loops ahead of the advancing railhead and those lifting the running line. The advance party would also cut down any signals they encountered. The rail was first removed from the chairs and loaded by crane onto a single bogie bolster wagon hauled by the locomotive. Once this wagon was full it would be drawn back to the contractor's base and replaced by open wagons that were loaded with sleepers, complete with their chairs, by the bulldozer. These would be re-united with the bogie bolster wagon and formed into a train which departed each day to Yeovil. Once double track was reached to the north of Templecombe the methods of track lifting changed in as much as the up line rail and sleepers could be lifted directly into wagons on the down line. The down line was then lifted in a similar manner to the single track section.

An occasional train had worked south from Radstock in the first few weeks of January 1967, before the running of four successive trains in one week in early February. These were apparently trial workings in preparation for the loss of the Templecombe connection. As became the norm the down line south of Midsomer Norton station was used. The up line between Radstock and Midsomer Norton had to be used as the down line had been slewed over to form the connection with the Bristol & North Somerset line. From this time until 7th May 1967 no train worked over the Mendips in either direction.

The Templecombe permanent way gang with PW trolley No. DS3057 at the south end of the Shillingstone station loop on 31st October 1966. The reason for their presence here was to clear a nearby culvert, probably No. 181A

Chris Handley

The view from Binegar down distant signal on 25th May 1968. Note the method used to remove the rails from the sleepers.

Peter James

Hymeks on the S&D

Class 35 No. D7005 at Radstock North station with the regular coal train to Portishead Power Station from Writhlington Colliery on 8th December 1967.

Peter James

Class 35 No. D7033 enters Chilcompton Tunnel on an up train of retrieved rails and sleepers on 17th February 1968.

Peter James

Class 35 No. D7008 at Shepton Mallet station, backing onto a loaded train on 27th March 1968. Note the up starter signal.

Timetable for Track lifting from Blandford to Radstock

The contract for the section of main line from Blandford to Radstock was placed with W. R. Arnott, Young & Company, dismantling contractors of Bilston in Staffordshire, early in December 1966. The contractors arrived in the Blandford area to start preliminary work in January 1967, whilst the track lifting and demolition commenced in February and was intended to take about a year. However, this estimate would be exceeded by some five months as the contract would prove a greater undertaking than originally expected. During this period the Somerset & Dorset would reverberate to the strange sound of diesel locomotives, sometimes in pairs, fighting the severe Mendip gradients with their heavy loads through summer and winter.

February 1967

Track lifting commenced on 4th February just over a mile to the north of Blandford station. By 18th February the railhead had advanced northwards to a point just south of bridge No. 189 France Farm Bridge about one mile south of Stourpaine & Durweston halt. The pace of track lifting for the first two months was rather slow as the weather was bad and on several occasions work was suspended due to problems getting to the railhead. The contractors also found themselves short of wagons to remove the lifted materials. Both BR and the contractors had to gradually formulate a system that was viable for both companies if progress were to improve.

March 1967

Further delays with the work, which by this time was well behind schedule, after more problems due to the quantity of rolling stock available. By mid-March locomotives were running round their trains at Sturminster Newton station and pushing the stock to the railhead just south of Shillingstone. It was at this time that a member of the already unreliable Type 2 Class 22 diesel-hydraulic locomotives suffered a derailment and was stranded blocking the line for some three days.

6th May 1967

The railhead had still only advanced just to the north of Shillingstone station due to various problems. May 6th would be the last day on which trains could reach the S&DJR via Templecombe Upper station. On Sunday 7th May the connection with the Salisbury to Yeovil line was removed at Templecombe as the layout was remodelled and the line to Gillingham was singled throughout.

8th May 1967

Commencing on this date all demolition trains would work out from Bristol travelling via the Bristol & North Somerset line to Radstock, there gaining access to the S&DJR via the spur which was put into use on 7th March 1966. Using the extensive facilities of the goods yard at Radstock all trains reversed here, gaining access to the up main line which was then used as far as the south end crossover in Midsomer Norton station. Here all trains would cross to the down main line which was in use exclusively for running purposes. All incoming trains now worked down as far as Evercreech Junction where the southbound trains were scheduled to cross the previous day's now northbound train with loaded wagons. Bristol and Yeovil crews changed trains at this location. Radstock provided an S&D conductor for the Bristol crews, while a

Templecombe man served the Yeovil crews. Previous to this Yeovil crews were in sole charge of all trains. These services commenced from Yeovil and all dismantled materials were distributed from Yeovil either for re-use or to be scrapped, in future this would be undertaken at Bristol. Once the demolition trains started to run, a strict 15 mph speed limit was imposed on the line.

The new diagram called for two locomotives to be on the line at the same time and on each weekday a train was scheduled to depart from Radstock North at approximately 10 am to travel southwards towards the railhead, then just north of Shillingstone. The train, when full, was hauled back to Templecombe where it was stabled overnight in the security of the old S&DJR Upper platform (Platform No. 3). The locomotive remained attached. The following morning the loaded train then proceeded northwards towards Evercreech Junction to await the arrival of the next empty train from Radstock, which arrived at approximately 12.30 pm. Since only the down line was in use these two trains made Evercreech Junction their regular crossing point, although all signals were disregarded, as

Class 22 No. D6331 approaches Chilcompton station from the south on 12th May 1967. This was just five days after the Templecombe connection had been severed.

Peter James

these were to be cut down as the contractors passed them whilst track lifting. Of course, basic line safety precautions were still taken, detonators being placed on the line at strategic locations to ensure that only one train at any one time could be in the Radstock North to Evercreech Junction, Evercreech Junction to Templecombe and Templecombe to contractor's railhead sections.

It was because the locomotives had to stay overnight at Templecombe Upper station that the generally unpopular North British Type 2 Class 22 diesel-hydraulic locomotives were used instead of the favoured Type 3 Class 35 'Hymeks', the former being 'Cold Starters' whereas the latter needed to have their engines warmed prior to starting up.

June 1967
The railhead was now at Sturminster Newton. With the improved weather and availability of more rolling stock the track lifting operation was moving much quicker and the contractors made up time. A number of these trains were very heavy and it was not unusual for them to be divided on the return trip north. Such an event took place on 29th June when the train, in the charge of No. D6324, had to be divided just to the north of Evercreech New when 16 wagons of concrete sleepers and four bogie bolster wagons of rails proved too much for a Type 2 locomotive on the steep Mendip gradients. The locomotive would work the first portion through to Midsomer Norton before returning to collect the

remainder. This could have proved very dangerous as only the second portion of the train had a brake van at the rear. A coupling failure could have lead to many heavily loaded wagons running away on the steep gradients, but fortunately this never happened. At Midsomer Norton station the two portions were reunited and the complete train was then worked down to Radstock, here again the train had to be divided, as it was far too long for the locomotive to run round it in Radstock North station, before departing along the North Somerset line.

At Midsomer Norton the points into Norton Hill Colliery were permanently clipped to set the road into the colliery yard. Once a train had used the run round facilities in Midsomer Norton station these points were also set to allow any runaway wagons to have a straight road into the colliery yard. This was very important as any wagons getting onto the down line north of Midsomer Norton were on a dead end track that would have them derailing onto the connection with the Bristol & North Somerset line. It was around this time that the extensive Norton Hill Colliery railway system was dismantled, but it is unclear whether the NCB or the contractors lifting the main line undertook the work.

July 1967
The railhead was now at Sturminster Newton Bridge No. 171. Despite the pending withdrawal of the Western Region North British Type 2 Class 22 locomotives, No. D6325 appeared on the line on

Class 22 No. D6324 passes through Chilcompton station with a very short train consisting of just one bogie bolster wagon of retrieved rails, and two brake vans, on 14th June 1967.

Peter James

19th July in ex-works condition sporting the new blue livery and was seen several times over the next two weeks.

August 1967

The railhead had passed Stalbridge station by the early part of August and the Dorset/Somerset border had been reached by the 12th of that month. By this time an advance party had already cleared Templecombe Lower yard of all sidings and work was well advanced on the lifting of the Upper yard. Surplus wagons now had to be stored on the up line south of Templecombe. For the last two weeks of August Class 22s were displaced by Type 3 Class 35 'Hymeks', but this was to be short lived as apparently these locomotives could be better used elsewhere ('Hymeks' had seen occasional use on demolition trains during February, March and April due to the poor reliability of the Class 22s). Henstridge station had been passed by the 20th and rapid progress was made back to Templecombe Lower halt, being reached by the month's end.

September 1967

The railhead was now at Templecombe, and the pattern of working radically changed. Now, one locomotive was expected to work out and back in a day with a revised crew roster to match. Also Evercreech Junction now began to be used to store surplus wagons for the railhead, this was because Evercreech Junction was one of the few locations to retain a large number of sidings. This practice led to extra empty stock workings and light engine movements. Some of these locomotives may have worked out to the railhead to double-head the now very heavy loads. Double-headed trains first appeared on 4th September but had ceased by 6th October and in keeping with the new arrangements, the North British Type 2 Class 22 re-appeared but now they were to work in multiple and provided observers with the strange sight and sound of double-headed trains hauled by diesels over the S&D! By the end of the first week of October trains had reverted back to single locomotives due to operational problems. This meant that very heavy trains would once again, sometimes, be worked in two portions.

October 1967

Demolition at Templecombe Junction was completed at the end of September. By 9th October work was in progress on the up main line around one mile to the north of Horsington Lane Crossing,

whilst recovery of the down main-line was not quite so advanced, being only a few chains to the north of Templecombe No. 3 Junction at Cheriton Crossing. This was to be the pattern that was now set for the remainder of the double tracked main line because it was easier to recover the up line straight into wagons standing on the down line. In consequence, demolition of the down line always lagged behind that of the up line. The number of available empty wagons awaiting use also had to grow now that the double track had been reached. By the end of October the Wincanton creamery sidings were completely filled with engineering wagons (both open mineral and bogie bolsters) and this was in addition to all those already held at Evercreech Junction.

November 1967

The railhead was now at a point just south of Wincanton station. On 1st November the down working arrived at Evercreech Junction station behind Class 22 No. D6317. The crew were most surprised to find the previous day's up working parked in the up platform (minus the locomotive) as the guard had refused to work forward in the gathering darkness because he did not know the road. It would appear that conductors were only provided for those drivers who were unfamiliar with the road, but not for a guard in the same position. When No. D6317 returned to Evercreech at around 15.30 the guard again refused to take the train forward over an unknown road. It is said to have been a ploy by crews to get rid of the unpopular Class 22s. So now some complicated shunting was necessary to lose this entire train in an already crowded yard. Part of this train was placed in the middle siding which contained Wickham PW gangers' trolley No. B29W from Radstock (which had been there all year and would finally be removed by lorry), and one damaged wagon. The remainder was placed with the wagons already occupying the up line platform. To fit it all in clear of the crossover, the sleepers across the track beside the water column, which were intended to prevent anything from being inadvertently shunted through the level crossing gates, had to be moved back almost to the gates themselves. After all this the locomotive returned light engine to Bristol via Radstock. It is unclear how this huge build-up of loaded wagons was cleared, but one report suggested two light engines worked out the following day and double-headed the load to Radstock, but this is unconfirmed and would have disrupted the normal round trip.

The first Class 08 0-6-0 shunter to appear on the line was No. D4025 on the weekend of 18/19th November 1967. It is seen stabled in the down platform at Evercreech Junction station. A train of loaded wagons stands in the up platform.

Peter James

Class 22 No. D6312 arrives at Evercreech Junction station on 6th November 1967 with empty wagons for the railhead at Wincanton. In the up platform can be seen the previous day's loaded train, minus locomotive.

Chris Handley

Only three months later and Evercreech Junction is itself about to be abandoned now that the final track is being lifted from the down platform. Class 08 No. D3516 has charge of the last ever train to use this station. Note that the Wickham PW trolley, No. B29W, is still on site awaiting collection by lorry!

Chris Handley

Class 22 No. D6317 crosses Five Arches Viaduct on 1st November 1967, working down the line along the up track with empty stock for the railhead at Wincanton station.

Peter James

On 6th November the methods of working and the crew's roster was to change again: now a Bristol crew took the train as far as Cole station returning home via Bruton station as passengers. They had been relieved by a Yeovil crew, who themselves were relieved by another Bristol crew at Cole on the return trip. By this date the contractors had reached the south end of Wincanton station goods yard and were preparing to pull their base camp back to Evercreech Junction at the end of the first week in November. Also by now the creamery sidings at Wincanton station had been removed, though the one remaining goods yard siding through the goods shed was still in situ and was occupied by several empty bogie bolster wagons.

North British Type 2 Class 22s continued to be used, certainly for the first week in November (No. D6312 was noted at Evercreech Junction on a Wincanton bound train on the 6th), but very soon after this date the working arrangements were to change yet again as Evercreech Junction became the contractor's base. Type 3 Class 35 'Hymeks' again took over from the Type 2s (a Class 35 was photographed near Chilcompton Tunnel on 7th

November), whilst a Class 08 0-6-0 diesel shunter was introduced for the first time for use between the contractor's base and the railhead. The idea was to make the round trip from Radstock to the contractor's base quicker as the train locomotive now only had to detach from the empty wagons and couple up to the loaded wagons. Previously this locomotive had to shunt the loaded wagons to form the return working and place the empty wagons where the contractors needed them. The Class 08 shunter would now do all this work and move wagons to and from the railhead when required. The wagons stored at Evercreech Junction would supplement any short fall as the speed of track lifting increased. The turnaround time for the 'Hymek' at the contractor's base was only an hour compared with the previous half day.

From now on there would always be one such shunter available. The first to be noted was No. D4025 which was stabled at Evercreech Junction station over the weekend of 18th/19th November. On more than one occasion the 08 was required to give assistance to northbound trains climbing the steep gradient to Masbury summit as the train engine fought for adhesion on what was by now dubious track conditions. Restrictions on the number and mix of wagons was imposed on trains travelling between Evercreech Junction and Binegar from the end of November.

By 25th November the down line had been recovered to just north of bridge No. 118 which carried the S&DJR over the GWR main line to Taunton, north of Cole. The up mainline had been recovered a further ³/₄ mile back to Bruton road level crossing. The speed of track lifting had substantially increased since the introduction of the Class 08 shunter, but the contract was still some two months behind schedule and slipping further each week.

December 1967
On 7th and 8th December there were no train movements due to a lack of empty wagons and not for the first time this left the contractors unable to work. The revised working arrangements, whereby the diesel shunter could make up the loaded train each day for the 'Hymek', enabled the latter to travel down to Evercreech Junction daily, returning to Radstock in time to take out the regular scheduled afternoon freight to Bristol. Their extra power meant that this could be combined on many trips with the demolition train. ('Hymeks' already had a regular diagram to Radstock which also had a resi-

dent Class 08 shunter). On occasions, when the train of recovered materials was too much to handle with the regular freight, the wagons were stored on the former up main line at Radstock towards Writhlington Colliery to await a special collection. On 29th December Class 35 No. D7031 worked light engine to Evercreech Junction early in the morning to clear some of the many loaded wagons that had built up over the Christmas period.

January 1968
Christmas and the New Year would see the contract slip over three months behind schedule and it was decided that the company's work on the Writhlington to Bath contract should cease for two months with all effort being concentrated on the main contract. At the end of January the contract was four months behind schedule and drastic action was required to assure penalties were not incurred. On 22nd January track lifting was in progress at Wyke Champflower with Class 08 No. D3355 in attendance at the railhead. This, of course, was the original junction (end on) of the Somerset Central and Dorset Central railways prior to the amalgamation on 1st September 1862. The new year would see the first weekend working, when, on Saturday 20th January Class 35 No. D7015 was seen entering Midsomer Norton station at 14.45 from the south, with a loaded train from Evercreech Junction. Weekend working was another way of getting the contract back on schedule as quickly as possible.

February 1968
Between 22nd January and 15th February the contractors had worked their way slowly northwards towards Evercreech Junction itself. At the beginning of February Mr John Eaton, a former S&DJR employee at the junction, made his farewell trip over the line which he described as follows :

"At 9.30 am on Friday 2nd February 1968 the Class 35 'Hymek' No. D7013 from Bristol slowly pulled into Radstock West station and coupled up to the demolition train consisting of five empty wagons with a brake van at each end. From the West yard, with me aboard it then proceeded to the ground frame on the Bristol & North Somerset line which was released by electric token and the train set back on the down line of the S&DJR, through the platform to the up line after the points had been set and the crossing gates opened by hand. (The signalbox had been demolished.) Cont. p. 65

No. D6317 pauses at Evercreech Junction station and words are exchanged concerning the previous day's up working which is now stabled in the up platform for collection at a later date.

Peter James

At Cole station the Bristol crew hand No. D6317 over to a Yeovil crew.   *Peter James*

No. D6317 arrives at Wincanton station and makes use of the goods shed siding and two creamery sidings to shunt its train.

The railhead is just south of the station on 1st November 1967. Empty stock is left at various locations around the station and the loaded train is made up in the up platform.

All Peter James

By mid-afternoon No. D6317 has completed all the necessary shunting and is ready for the return trip to Bristol via Radstock. The crews will again be changed at Cole, where the Bristol men will relieve a Yeovil crew.

Peter James

Class 22 No. D6341 is seen at Moorewood working north on 20th July 1967.

Peter James

On 20th August 1967 No. D6341 is at Evercreech Junction station after working light engine from Bristol. The purpose of this, and other, light engine movements may have been caused by the lifting of Templecombe goods yards. The railhead was at Henstridge station by this date.

Michael Gates

It was now 10.05 am as we headed for Evercreech Junction, where we were to pick up the loaded wagons brought in from the working site to the station for collection by the demolition train, which would then haul them back to Radstock.

When we reached the 'Five Arches', where the Bristol & North Somerset line (GWR) passes under the S&DJR, the ganger in charge of the train placed a red flag and three detonators on the track for our protection, warning any other train that might work into this section of our presence. As we passed the derelict Norton Hill Colliery I observed with regret how lifeless and forlorn it looked with the line which used to connect the colliery sidings to the S&DJR completely removed. No sign of the bustling activity of former times.

Class 08 No. D3805 is seen at the railhead on 12th March 1966 at bridge No. 97. The purpose of the 08 shunter was to work from the contractor's base to the railhead as often as necessary. At the contractor's base the 08 would make up the daily train for Bristol and relieve the incoming locomotive of its empty wagons.

Peter James

Having collected all the loaded wagons from the railhead No. D3805 travelled back to Shepton Mallet over Prestleigh Viaduct.

Peter James

Class 35 No. D7008 is seen crossing bridge No. 48 at Midsomer Norton station on 27th March 1968, working wrong line as the down line had been slewed over to the North Somerset line. Note the down signal.

Peter James

Midsomer Norton station, where the station and signalbox windows were all smashed and the one time greenhouse was completely wrecked, this brought another nostalgic pang. Here we crossed over to the down line, the points being padlocked and clipped to ensure that if any wagons were to run away they would be intercepted by the catch point.

At Chilcompton, where the signalbox, crossover road and sidings had been taken out of use before passenger trains ceased, the station was in a similar state to that of Midsomer Norton. The water tower and columns where the Radstock banker used to replenish its supplies on its return from Masbury summit still remained.

Passing the site of Emborough Quarry at Moorewood, closed before the S&DJR, I saw that the signalbox had gone but the crossover road and sidings still remained, padlocked and clipped.

Binegar station was in better shape, only one broken window in the signalbox, crossover points again clipped.

Masbury summit and the two Level/50 incline posts gone, so into Masbury Halt where the shelter on the down side and the station name board were still intact and the stationmaster's house occupied. The signalbox, ground frame, sidings and crossovers all gone.

On to the site of Winsor Hill, where the signalbox and points on the up side to the sidings remain as they had been left over twenty years before.

At Shepton Mallet the station buildings and signalbox were smashed, the condition of the station being similar to that of Midsomer Norton. The water column and water tower on the down line still remained, the crossover roads and siding connections had gone. They were taken out before closure.

Over Prestleigh bank to Evercreech New. Again similar to Midsomer Norton, the lime kiln flattened, tiles removed from the roof, signalbox, sidings and crossover had gone before closure.

Finally to Evercreech Junction where, after rounding the curve we saw the remains of the North signalbox, burnt out on the last night of passenger services. The down sidings on the branch to Bason Bridge had been taken out. Only two roads remained in the up sidings. Here wagons were waiting to be loaded. On reaching the station the diesel pushed the wagons up the middle road where they were uncoupled. The locomotive now went over to the up line to pick up the loaded wagons, which, when done, it backed onto the brake van in the middle road and regained the down line for the return trip to Radstock.

Everything was intact at Evercreech Junction, where, as at Binegar, a diesel shunter was kept to take the wagons to the work site or to marshall them for the train to Radstock. Two crossover roads were to be taken out at Evercreech Junction and relaid at Shepton Mallet and siding connections to be made to the sidings still left in for the diesel shunter and run-round purpose. Unless this was done the crossover at Binegar would had to have been used, entailing a journey of nine miles to haul wagons out and take loaded ones back from the work site, when the track had been lifted past Evercreech Junction.

Would this have been the scene if the S&D had dieselised rather than closed down. A Class 35 on a down freight to Evercreech Junction but unfortunately No. D7008 is arriving at the contractor's base on 27th March 1968 with empty wagons for retrieving rails and sleepers.

Peter James

Another view of No. D7008 at Shepton Mallet station on 27th March. Class 08 No. D3805 is seen shunting wagons for D7008's return trip.

Peter James

Class 08 No. D3505 is just south of Masbury on 30th April 1968 with a train of bogie bolster wagons being loaded with rails by the contractor's crane.

Peter James

At Binegar station on 18th May 1968 the contractors are busy lifting the track through the station and demolishing the buildings. The ex-Station Master, Norman Downs, is seen coming over to speak to the photographer. The Class 08 was by now No. D3001, which is stabled at the north end of the station after its day's work.

Peter James

Another view of Binegar station on 22nd May 1968 with the signalbox now a heap of debris on the up platform and the down line rapidly being lifted.

Peter James

The following day Class 08 No. D3001 waits just to the north of Binegar station whilst its wagons are loaded. Over the following week the Mendip Stone Works sidings on the left would be removed.

Peter James

The weather, typical of February, varied as we proceeded, there being drizzle from Radstock to Binegar and heavy rain at Shepton Mallet, but by the time we reached Evercreech Junction it was dry.

The guard told me that on the previous Monday, returning through Winsor Hill Tunnel the 'Hymek' pulling 21 loaded wagons had begun to slip, only succeeding in keeping going with great difficulty."

By the second week of February, track lifting was in progress at Evercreech Junction between the station and the actual junction with the branch a quarter of a mile further north. The down main line had been temporarily terminated at the level crossing and a train with three open wagons, four bolsters and two brake vans, in the charge of Class 08 No. D3516, was in the down platform, clearly one of the last, if not the last train, to serve this station. In the station goods yard stood the Wickham PW gangers' trolley No. B29W and on one of the sidings off the up main line near the remains of the North signalbox was a long rake of empty bolster wagons with yet another long rake stabled on the up main line. This consisted of several bolster wagons, many open wagons and no less than four brake vans. John

Eaton mentioned in his account the reason for reinstallation of crossover facilities at Shepton Mallet and this in turn reflects on part of the orchestrated run-down of the S&DJR by the Western Region in the early 1960s. This involved the progressive track rationalisation which reduced the line's capacity and adaptability by degrees. Nowhere was this more apparent than at Shepton Mallet, this location had lost its run-round facilities and most of its sidings which were out of use from early July 1964 and subsequently removed. In consequence it became impossible for locomotives to run-round their trains anywhere on the nine miles between Binegar and Evercreech Junction.

The implications of these alterations on the final demolition of the line would probably have been lost at that time, but as track lifting moved progressively northwards it became clear that the removal of the run-round facilities at Shepton Mallet may have been rather premature. By the end of January it had been realised that as soon as the crossovers had been lifted at Evercreech Junction the shunter would be required to work both loaded and empty trains on a round trip of anything up to 18 miles between the railhead and Binegar. Much of this would involve propelling wagons down the 1 in 50 gradients without the benefit of a brake van leading (although one was invariably marshalled between the locomotive and wagons) and right through the worst winter weather. As a result, it was decided to recover enough pointwork and track from Evercreech Junction and use these materials to re-instate the run-round facilities at Shepton Mallet station. Since only the down line was in use this would also allow the shunter to gain access to the goods shed through which passed the only remaining up siding. This in turn would become a temporary locomotive shed.

The task of relaying the run-round facilities was put into the hands of the civil engineering department from Bristol. By early February they had recovered all the track that was required from Evercreech Junction, using a train of bogie bolster wagons. The engineering train itself consisted of a diesel crane, wagon, mess coach and brake vans, all in the charge of Class 35 'Hymek' No. D7045. The train worked out from Bristol to Radstock via the Bristol & North Somerset line and over the Mendips to Shepton Mallet on 11th February. Reinstatement of the pointwork at original locations was properly ballasted and soon completed. Having thus regained some of its former dignity Shepton Mallet station became the contractor's base from the 15th, and probably had the distinction of seeing the last track relaying on the S&DJR, (Radstock–Writhlington section apart). The train of empty bogie bolsters lingered at Shepton Mallet for some while and was noted still there on the 27th, shunted well out of the way on the up line to the south of the station. The engineering train returned to Bristol by the same route as the outward journey on 16th February in the company of No. D3355 which was due for a service and re-fuelling at Bristol mpd. Class 08 No. D3516 was its replacement at the railhead.

On completion of this work the contractors moved their base back to Shepton Mallet station and Evercreech Junction was abandoned, Class 35 No. D7033 working the very last train out of Evercreech Junction station on 17th February. Class 08 No. D3516 was now to be stabled in Shepton Mallet's goods shed each night. During those final days of clearance at Evercreech Junction a local farmer, Mr Charles Joyce, acquired many items from the contractors. Pride of place went to the unusual station clock which had one face in the booking hall and the other onto the platform. With the help of the former Stationmaster Harold White the clock was mounted in a wooden crib the depth of the old station wall, and the clock is said to have kept perfect S&D time into the early 1980s. Of the other items he acquired, most appear to have remained exactly where the contractors put them in his farm yard. Amongst these were a pair of crossing gates, yard lamps, several station name boards (one became a drip tray for his Rover 90), many sleepers and lengths of rail. The drip tray was finally saved by the Shipley Model Railway Society and is now on permanent display in their clubroom.

March and April 1968
Demolition proceeded apace during March and April with the result that the contract was now almost on schedule. Between Saturday 9th and Tuesday 12th March over one and a half miles of both lines were lifted. Firstly back to Evercreech New, where the goods yard had already been lifted, then over Prestleigh Viaduct and through Cannards Grave and finally into Shepton Mallet station itself. There the newly installed crossovers, so carefully relaid only six weeks previously were unceremoniously ripped up never to be relaid again. The lack of sidings at Shepton Mallet station did not hinder the contractors as the up line, to north and south of the station was used to store wagons. The siding behind the down platform was still in situ, but unfortunately not connected to the main line. On 12th March Class 35 No. D7006 arrived at Shepton Mallet with just two empty wagons, clearly it was BR's inability to supply a sufficient quantity of wagons that hampered the speed of the track lifting operation on this section of the line. On this date the railhead was a mile to the north of Evercreech New, where the up line was being dismantled and loaded into adjacent wagons. On 27th March Class 35 No. D7008 was at Midsomer Norton station, using, for the first time during this contract, the north end crossover. Previously only the south end crossover had been used but one of these points had been damaged and there was no logic in repairing it. Shepton Mallet was cleared and abandoned during early April and the contractor's base moved over the Mendip summit to Binegar. Shepton Mallet station was not completely demolished when the track was lifted, though the signalbox, footbridge, water tower and signalling department buildings were removed. The remaining structures were removed over the next four years and only the platforms remained by 1973.

Winsor Hill Tunnels were reached during mid-April and caused some delay due to their restrictive bores prohibiting the use of the contractor's crane. This also saw the final removal of the long since

A Journey Up the Line with No. D7008 on 27th March 1968

The train departs from the contractor's base at Shepton Mallet station and passes over Charlton Road Viaduct. The empty wagons on the up line are being stored in case of any shortfall in the daily empty stock working.

Peter James

Passing north through Winsor Hill Tunnel. Note that Winsor Hill signalbox is still intact 20 years after closure. Also, that Hamwood Quarry sidings are in situ and connected to the main line 28 years after closure.

Peter James

Just about to pass over the summit at Masbury and under bridge No. 69 – Oakhill Road Bridge. From this angle the change in gradient is very clear.

Peter James

A final view of No. D7008 as it waits at Chilcompton station on its return from Shepton Mallet station.

Peter James

On 17th May 1968 Class 08 No. D3001 is seen heading towards Binegar with two empty bogie bolster wagons.

With track lifting and demolition under way at Binegar station the contractors moved their base back to Moorewood. On 23rd May 1968 Class 08 No. D3001 has its work cut out shunting a huge number of wagons, both empty and full.

Peter James

Class 08 No. D3506 is on bridge No. 56 with the up line lifted back to Chilcompton station. This is on 13th June 1968.

Peter James

Just six days later, and track lifting is taking place to the north of Chilcompton, at bridge No. 51. These two views of No. D3506's train being loaded with rails and sleepers show the pace of track lifting.

Both Peter James

abandoned Hamwood Quarry sidings, having been closed on 23rd January 1943 but even the connection with the up main line had remained in place whilst these sidings disappeared under a blanket of foliage. The stone constructed Winsor Hill signalbox was also still intact at this time. Work then proceeded apace up to Masbury Halt during the latter part of April. During this period Class 08 shunter No. D3805 was replaced by No. D3505, being seen at Binegar station on the 28th. The wooden superstructure of Binegar signalbox was then being demolished but the remaining buildings would survive a few weeks longer. During April there was a purge on the remaining permanent way huts between Masbury and Radstock, with many being simply set alight and then the minimal brickwork knocked down when the contractors finally passed them lifting the track.

May 1968

Between the 7th and 9th May Masbury Halt was cleared of track and abandoned. No demolition work was carried out here as the station was in occupation, though the signalbox had been closed in July 1964 and was soon demolished. By 14th May the down line had been lifted from Masbury Summit, and only two days later the mile of track north to Binegar station had been removed. Progress was quick because sufficient wagons had been amassed at Binegar and Moorewood to keep the contractors satisfied, and as a result by the 16th contractors were working only just to the south of Binegar station and by the middle of the month they had reached it. Class 08 No. D3001 was now the resident locomotive and at the end of each day's work was located in the down refuge at the south end of Binegar station.

On the 16th work was concentrating on the up line to the south of the south end crossover facility. The following day work was delayed when the south end crossover at Moorewood required the attention of the contractors having seized up through lack of use; the contractors had so far only used the north end crossover at this location. By the 18th the down line ended just south of the south end crossover and the down refuge was still intact but no longer used by the locomotive. The up line had been lifted back to the north end crossover. On the 20th the down refuge and south end crossover along with most of the down line through the station was lifted and until the 25th the locomotive was still berthed by the down home signal before being stabled back at Moorewood.

The contractor's base was moved north to Moorewood from 23rd May. Fortunately the crossover facilities were still in place at Moorewood allowing this location to be used rather than working out of Radstock. The last 'Hymek' to reach Binegar station and use the remaining crossover facility was on the 17th May, number unknown.

At Moorewood the empty wagons were being stored along the up main line for almost a mile in the southern direction and for some distance north. Due to this severe lack of space and the numbers of wagons needed, a serious attempt was made to use the sidings in the Emborough Stone Works which were still intact. Unfortunately the large quantity of barbed wire behind the gates made access impossible. Progress slowed as the number of wagons available diminished even though many were held at Radstock and more frequent trips from Radstock to Moorewood and Binegar were made.

During late May Binegar station was demolished and the remaining down line was lifted. The private sidings just north of bridge No. 65 Binegar Station Bridge, on the down side were lifted on 24th and 25th May. Moorewood's inability to hold adequate wagons for all this work had the consequence that by 27th May the difference in the track lifted from the up and down lines was two miles. The up line remained in situ to just north of Binegar station, whilst the down line was clear of Nettlebridge Viaduct. For the first and only time during this contract the down line was lifted before, and well ahead of the up line. This was because the newer flat-bottomed rail and concrete sleepers used on the down line between Binegar and Moorewood were required for re-use on the Milford Haven branch.

June 1968

Work ceased for the Whitsun Bank Holiday. After this work was concentrated on lifting the up line, so by 7th June both lines were just to the north of Nettlebridge Viaduct. Also on this day a bogie bolster wagon had derailed on the north end crossover at Midsomer Norton station (very few wagon derailments occurred during the complex track lifting period). The contractor's caterpillar crane came down to Midsomer Norton along the up line to re-rail this wagon as this was the best way to get trains moving again, but this prevented any possible use of the up line due to the damage caused by the crane's journey. This incident also meant that no work could be carried out for over two days due to the absence of the crane and the inability of trains to reach the railhead.

June 9th was a sad day for the S&DJR as it was on this day that the last demolition train ran over the line in the charge of a Class 35s 'Hymek', No. D7045, as the railhead had reached Moorewood and the contractor's base was moved back to Midsomer Norton station. From then on all trains would be in the sole charge of Class 08 shunters. These would be stabled back in the Radstock shed each night, the Class 35s going no further than that location to pick-up the demolition trains. From 10th June the Class 08 shunter worked two daily trips out to the railhead, first to collect the loaded wagons and take them to Midsomer Norton. From there the empties were propelled up to the railhead, then returning to Midsomer Norton to collect the loaded wagons again and take them down to the awaiting 'Hymek' at Radstock.

On 11th June the last train passed under bridge No. 58 Coal Lane Bridge, towards Moorewood, waiting just to the south of this bridge whilst being loaded with rails which were taken directly to Radstock and further empty wagons were then propelled up to the railhead for loading. The up line was now north of this bridge and the down line was rapidly lifted during the day. The following day Class 08 No. D3001 returned to Bristol for servicing and re-fuelling, its replacement was No. D3506, which arrived with a conflat wagon fitted with automatic vacuum brakes. This would be used in addition to the two brake vans on loaded trains that were left in Midsomer Norton station whilst the locomotive propelled empty wagons up to the railhead. Concerns had been voiced on several occasions about these heavy loads being left on a steep gradient with sometimes only one brake van to stop them running away. Loaded trains were left in the up

platform with only the clipped north end crossover to impede them should the brake van fail in its task.

The conflat wagon was coupled between the locomotive and the empty wagons at Radstock and remained so coupled as the locomotive worked light engine to the railhead. It was coupled to the leading wagon of the loaded train and was therefore suitably positioned to do its job at Midsomer Norton whilst the locomotive propelled the empty wagons up to the railhead. It would also appear that the problem with the south end crossover had by now been resolved.

June 13th saw a great deal of activity at Radstock North with no less than four locomotives moving about the yard and station. Class 08 No. D3506 arrived at Chilcompton at 11.45 with the conflat wagon to collect the loaded wagons after leaving a train of empty stock at Midsomer Norton station. The loaded wagons were taken down to Midsomer Norton, the empty stock then being pushed up as far as bridge No. 56. No. D3506 returned light engine to Midsomer Norton station at 13.00 and collected the loaded wagons before proceeding down to Radstock. D3506 approached Radstock at 13.30 as Class 35 No. D7031 appeared on the B&NSL with the 12.45 empties from Bristol passing under the North Somerset viaduct as No. D3506 passed over. As the 'Hymek' swung straight across to the S&DJR station with its train, No. D3506 chased after it, if such a thing is possible with a 350hp shunter, whistling to the signalman to keep the crossing gates closed to road traffic so that it could follow the 'Hymek' through the crossing and into Radstock North station!

At Radstock Class 35 No. D7000 was waiting in the S&DJR yard to take over the demolition train,

Class 22 No. D6324 passes through Chilcompton Tunnel and Rock Cutting on the down line with half an up working on 29th June 1967.

Peter James

No. D6324 has now crossed from the down running line to the up line to run round the first portion of its train. Many trains were now so heavy that a Class 22 had insufficient power to haul the complete train over the Mendips. Instead, these trains were split at Evercreech New and worked in two portions to Midsomer Norton. Note the lack of a brake van at the rear of this portion; this could have been disastrous had a coupling failed.

Peter James

Twelve months on and little has changed at Midsomer Norton with Class 08 No. D3506 now working out only as far as Chilcompton station, 13th June 1968.

Peter James

Class 08 No. D3001 shunts the contractor's base at Moorewood, standing on bridge No. 59, 23rd May 1968. Note the Emborough Stone Quarry crushing plant in the background.
Peter James

No. D3001 is still at Moorewood but now this is the railhead, the contractor's base having moved to Midsomer Norton station. Track lifting is in progress on the up line on 10th June 1968, just by bridge No. 58.
Peter James

but had to wait until No. D7031 had set off with the 14.30 coal train to Portishead. The Radstock pilot Class 08, No. D3138 was standing beside Radstock shed until about 14.00 when it left to go and shunt the Great Western yard. With two 'Hymeks' and two Class 08 350hp shunters the S&DJR side of Radstock was a hive of activity that day.

The 14th found the down line lifted as far as bridge No. 54 Green Ditch Lane bridge, while the up line was now ready for lifting through Chilcompton station. The following day the station had been cleared of track and with no sidings to deal with work proceeded northwards at a rapid pace.

On the evening of Sunday June 16th 14 loaded wagons stabled just to the north of Chilcompton station awaiting collection, ran away towards Radstock. These were observed by an ex-railwayman in the village as they entered Chilcompton

Tunnel. He contacted the police who rushed to protect road traffic over the level crossing at Radstock. The runaways could not get that far, of course, as the points leading into Norton Hill Colliery yard were routinely set to provide a trap. As all the track inside the colliery yard had been lifted, the wagons piled up harmlessly, but with a great deal of noise, in the yard. Luckily no one was injured and it is believed that some children were responsible for releasing the wagon brakes.

On 18th June Bristol's breakdown train was in action at Midsomer Norton whilst re-railing the wagons. This train was hauled by a Type 4 Class 47 locomotive but unfortunately its number is unknown. Only one other Class 47 is on record as visiting Radstock North and this did not venture beyond Radstock. The Bristol breakdown train left Midsomer Norton and travelled to Bath Midland Bridge Yard via the Bristol & North Somerset line to deal with a derailed locomotive. On the 19th No. D3506 was at Bridge No. 51 Redan Bridge, whilst sleepers from the up line were being loaded into open wagons. Gradually the train moved north

as far as the south portal of Chilcompton Tunnel. With the up line lifted work started on the down line which was still just to the north of Chilcompton station. June 21st found the contractors busy dismantling Chilcompton station. The prefabricated part of the up platform had been demolished, as had the water tower, the tank being cut-up on the ground. Because of this work, no further track lifting had taken place. In fact no trains were reported between 21st and 25th, not because of work at Chilcompton station but rather industrial action by BR employees. This may be the reason why Chilcompton station was so totally eradicated, unlike most other stations at this time.

Track lifting proceeded very slowly over the next week or so. On Thursday 27th only the second train of the week was sent to the railhead which had still not cleared Chilcompton Tunnel. By the 29th Chilcompton Tunnel was clear and work was proceeding quickly towards Midsomer Norton station. At the end of June an advance party was lifting Midsomer Norton goods yard and a train was seen removing the materials from the yard late on 1st July.

On 17th June 1968, Class 08 No. D3506 is seen at Midsomer Norton station, running round a loaded train before pushing empty wagons up to Chilcompton. Note the use of a conflat wagon to stop any chance of a train running away at this location.

Peter James

July 1968

During the first week of July the contractors reached the southern end of Midsomer Norton station. On 10th July a terrible summer storm caused a great deal of damage in North Somerset. At Pensford, on the Bristol & North Somerset line, along which all trains to Radstock had to pass, the line was washed out. Repairs were considered too expensive and the line was closed from that day. Because the line between Radstock and Mells in the Frome direction was disused, locomotives and wagons at Radstock were temporarily isolated until steps could be taken to inspect, repair and re-open the line to Frome. It was, indeed, fortunate that this short length of line had not already been lifted by this time otherwise the future of the remaining two collieries would have been threatened, let alone the other rail based traffic. As a result of this situation BR could no longer provide any wagons for the contractors and their contract was terminated forthwith, with the railhead just to the south of Midsomer Norton station and this would remain the situation for the best part of the next twelve months.

July 12th saw the very last train movement over the S&DJR in a south bound direction, when Class 08 No. D3505, still trapped in Radstock, busied itself collecting all the remaining wagons up at Midsomer Norton station and bringing them down into Radstock to await eventual removal. It would appear that a Class 35 'Hymek' was also trapped at Radstock but was simply put in Radstock shed until the Frome line re-opened.

The removal of the remaining track between Radstock and Midsomer Norton station was undertaken by BR during 1969 on any occasion when they had staff free to do the work. This work did not involve any rail movements as BR preferred the use of road vehicles. The rails were levered out of their chairs and left at the side of the trackbed before being then loaded onto lorries some time after the sleepers had been removed; the sleepers having been sold to a local wood merchant who collected them in his own lorries.

It is known that a certain amount of the newer flat-bottomed track and concrete sleepers, mostly between Binegar and Midsomer Norton, were re-used. A quantity of these rails and sleepers being used on the Milford Haven branch connection to the Gulf Oil refinery in Pembrokeshire.

Timetable for track lifting from Radstock North to Writhlington Colliery

BR and various contractors nibbled away at the track on this line several times over the years prior to the final closure, although little happened until the demolition of the main line was completed. Thereafter, some track in the goods yard was removed by BR leaving a reduced number of sidings. In June 1970 the redundant up line between Tyning and the crossover facilities to the south of Writhlington Colliery yard were lifted by a local contractor.

The last BR train to use this line ran on 16th October 1973, by which time this was the only tangible remaining part of the S&DJR. Demolition would be delayed for several years partly due to the efforts of the Somerset & Dorset Railway Circle to secure the remaining track as well as the surface workings at Writhlington Colliery, as an example of Somerset's industrial heritage. Also it was thought valuable coal could be retrieved from the slag heaps and if of sufficient quantity the railway would be required to remove it. Unfortunately, this proviso and the fact that the country was sinking into a depression along with a considerable increase in scrap metal prices, meant the S&DRC just could not raise the support and backing necessary to get the project off the ground.

Left with little option they had to relinquish this last tenuous hold on the Somerset & Dorset in 1975, by which time the possible coal traffic was being removed by lorry. BR brought in the demolition contractors during August 1976. From then on all remaining sidings at Writhlington Colliery and the down main line, plus all the track in the S&DJR yard and station were lifted. Also removed at this time was the 1966-built spur with the Bristol & North Somerset line and that part of the B&NSL back across the level crossing to the former Great Western station. Track lifting was completed by December 1976 but many sleepers remained for another year. Also the level crossings – both GWR and S&DJR – were removed and the road resurfaced. The station buildings remained until the local authority redeveloped the complete trackbed site from Tyning to Radstock North station in 1979–80.

Timetable for track lifting from Writhlington to Bath Junction

Demolition of the northern section of the main line was carried out under a separate contract with W. H. Arnott, Young & Co. of Bilston, Staffordshire. Work commenced at a point just north of the Writhlington Colliery sidings north end crossover in July 1967. The crossover facilities were still required for coal traffic, as were the Writhlington Colliery sidings immediately beyond.

With inverted sleepers fixed across both main-lines just to the north of the north end crossover, both lines were severed and lifting commenced northwards, all demolition trains working down from Bath. Like the trains used to the south of Radstock, they were powered by North British Type 2 Class 22 diesels (with odd reports of Type 1 Class 14 D9500 series also being used). One such trip was observed on Saturday 7th October 1967, which arrived back at Bath at 13.30, having departed from Bath between 8.30 and 9.00 consisting of a number of large bogie bolster wagons for rail recovery and several 5-plank wagons for carrying sleepers. At Bath the normal practice was for the locomotive to be detached from the incoming wagons just before Bath Junction, the wagons later being moved to lie alongside the old Midland Railway engine shed for labelling. The rail lengths were destined for Bank Top station, Darlington or 'London Works Oldham' and the chaired concrete sleepers for Fosters of Nottingham. Most wooden sleepers and keys were sold locally for fencing or firewood.

There was a risk of demolition trains hitting obstructions placed on the track through Devonshire and Combe Down tunnels, where children were known to leave old oil cans and other debris across the track. As a result there was a strict 15 mph speed limit imposed on this section. This should have applied to the whole line, but several reports would indicate that this was ignored and speeds could reach 40 mph in places. Just inside the Midford end of Combe Down Tunnel was a large hollowed out room used to store an engineer's trolley. After closure the trolley remained and it is said to have been used to ride through the tunnels; whether it was ever hit by a train is unknown. (How some of these children were not killed is a miracle.) On a lighter note it is said that many a romance started in the tunnels, and then there was the joker who took tape recordings of steam locomotives into the tunnels and scared the pants off everyone in there! Shortly after track lifting two walkers had a shock as they arrived at the south portal of Combe Down Tunnel. They heard a strange noise like a ghost train from within, lights appeared, the noise increased and out steamed an elderly Mini, complete with driver and three passengers. Given the state of the ground, the age of the suspension and the number of occupants, they could not have been more shaken-up if they had been driving over railway sleepers.

It would appear that the main line south of Wellow station was used on several occasions for the storage of withdrawn wagons. These wagons may in fact have been awaiting repairs at the wagon works in Radstock due to a short term storage problem during a very busy period in Radstock yard caused by the presence of demolition trains. On one occasion the wagons on the down line had to be shunted out of the way of a breakdown train. For some unknown reason this train was urgently required at the Bath end of the line but it would have been easier to travel in from Bristol via Mangotsfield rather than take the Bristol & North Somerset line to Radstock and then travel over the S&DJR. It is possible that this train was already at Radstock when summoned by Bath to attend an incident. No reason has been found for this train movement or a precise date but several people confirm seeing it in March or April 1967.

Due to the earlier removal of all sidings and crossover facilities between Bath Junction and Writhlington it was not possible for trains to be shunted, or even for locomotives to run round their trains. As a result all trains were propelled out to the railhead and drawn back down to Bath, and all wagons, both empty or loaded had to be held at Bath. As a result the four miles of single track and five miles of double track would take the best part of nine months to remove, along with one station being demolished. It took a further two months to remove the sleepers between Combe Down and Bath Junction, though one must take into account the fact that this contract was suspended for two months.

Track recovery continued northwards through Shoscombe, Wellow and Midford. The railhead was just to the north of Wellow signalbox by the 2nd November. Midford station and single line track was reached by the 10th December, with Midford station being demolished at the same time. The track past the location of Midford 'A' yard was lifted during the middle of the month and the south portal of Come Down Tunnel had been reached as 1968 commenced.

The tunnels were to cause unforeseen problems for the demolition contractors due to the lack of space in their restrictive and very dark bores. Artificial lights helped but the track had to be moved by hand as the contractor's crane was too large to be used in the tunnels. As a result it was the end of January before Combe Down Tunnel was clear of rails. Work was further delayed when the southern contract was found to be some four months behind schedule. As a consequence all work ceased on this contract for two months whilst

Track lifting in progress just north of Wellow station on 2nd November 1967.
Colin Maggs

Class 22 No. D6321 arrives at the railhead later the same day.
Colin Maggs

everyone was moved south to make up time, otherwise penalties would be due.

Work would recommence again at the southern end of Lyncombe Vale in late March 1968. The restrictive bore of Devonshire Tunnel would again give the contractors problems as they were unable to use a crane to lift the rails from their sleepers. It was also impossible to lift materials into wagons within the confines of the tunnels. So far as can be ascertained the method used was to remove the rails from their chairs and drop them onto the ballast from where the locomotive would drag them out of the tunnel. A caterpillar crane would then load the rails onto bogie bolster wagons brought up by the locomotive. The sleepers would remain in the tunnels until June when they were collected by lorry. These lorries were 4-wheel drive high ground clearance dumpers, the sleepers being lifted out of the ballast by a specially converted bulldozer, similar to that used on the main contract. The lorries gained access to Combe Down Tunnel via Midford goods yard. For Devonshire Tunnel and Bath bank the lorries used Bellots Road.

This track lifting contract was extended in November 1967 when the Twerton Co-op ceased to have its coal delivered by rail. As a result the siding and main line to Bath Junction were no longer required. By mid-May 1968 all the track down to Bath Junction had been lifted. By mid June all the sleepers had been recovered from the tunnels. During June the remaining sleepers were removed from Bath bank, most being sold locally for fencing or fire wood. This contract was completed in early July with the final lorry load of sleepers being removed by Bath Junction signalbox.

Bath City Council wasted little time implementing their plans to improve the congested Lower Bristol Road over which S&DJR bridge No. 1 Twerton Viaduct, passed this being demolished on 4th May 1969 with the road then being straightened and widened. In fact only the three ironwork and steel columned spans were removed in May 1969, the seven or eight brick arches (depending on which side of the bridge you were standing) abutments and part of the embankments on each side of the road being removed on various occasions over the next couple of years.

The Bath Accident Prevention Council had expressed anxiety during the period after closure of the line, especially when demolition trains were using the tunnels, because they had become a playground for local children. Even so, they appear not to have been sealed up for many years as they were both still open to walkers in late 1973. Just who carried out the work of sealing the four tunnel portals is unclear. It certainly took more than one attempt to keep people out. Bath bank and Devonshire Tunnel were purchased by Bath City Council in the early 1970s. This was necessary to allow the demolition of two of the narrow underbridges for road improvements. General landscaping of the bank followed this demolition, which included back-filling up to the north portal of Devonshire Tunnel, both portals being sealed before the back-filling. Bath City Council then made access to the tunnel via a manhole just above and behind the north portal; the purpose of this manhole is unclear but it could be to inspect the tunnel. Also, the Bath Fire Brigade use the tunnel for practising sewer rescues. Wessex Water Authority purchased Combe Down Tunnel on 11th October 1982, but it was still open to brave walkers in 1984. A scene from "Return to Evercreech Junction" was to have been filmed in the tunnel after a preliminary walk of the line in 1984, unfortunately by early 1985 both portals had been sealed with breeze blocks and iron doors. It must be presumed that Bath City Council sealed up Devonshire Tunnel and that Wessex Water undertook the work on Combe Down Tunnel after many meetings and letters from the Bath Accident Prevention Council to both organisations.

Track lifting in progress just north of Midford station in December 1967.
Mike Ware

Timetable for track lifting from Blandford to Broadstone Junction

The Broadstone Junction to Blandford line was to see its last timetabled train run on 2nd January 1969, with a light engine collecting the few remaining wagons from Blandford Yard on 6th January. On and from 6th January the station buildings and line were closed. Thereafter it was to remain dormant for almost a year whilst tenders for track lifting and demolition were placed (the name of the successful tenderer is not known).

By November 1967 all signalling had been removed from the line, although the four signalboxes remained intact but had been downgraded to ground frames simply to control sidings or road crossings. The up line sidings at Blandford were lifted about this time. The up main line was lifted south of the south station crossover to a point about a half mile north of Spetisbury. The yard on the down side of Blandford station was still totally intact and the connection from the north end of the goods shed to the down line was still in place. The down siding between the footbridge and Salisbury Road bridge had been lifted. A couple of sleepers blocked the end of the line just before Salisbury Road bridge. The station buildings, signalbox, and the down water crane were still intact, while the up platform crane had lost its swan-neck. Most of this track lifting would appear to have occurred during the summer of 1968 by the Southern Region Civil Engineering Department.

Work had commenced at the location at which the main contract to Radstock had started in February 1967. Just over a mile of track was lifted back to the Salisbury Road bridge during May and early June 1968. The work south of Blandford continued for a few more months and may only have been terminated when the final decision to close this section of the S&DJR in January 1969 was made, rather than singling back to Corfe Mullen Junction. No information has come to light regarding the locomotives or methods used to undertake this work. It is also unclear whether BR's Civil Engineering Department or the later contractors lifted the short length of track from Corfe Mullen Junction to Carters siding, it had certainly been removed by September 1969.

Demolition commenced with the arrival of the first recovery train on Sunday 28th December 1969, behind Class 33 No. 6519. Dismantling of the line commenced from the Salisbury Road bridge on 30th December 1969.

Although only ten miles of track were involved, recovery and demolition was to be a very slow process, the contractors being served by only one weekly train which worked out from Poole each Sunday morning at around 11.00 and arrived at Bailey Gate at 11.45. Such trains were all worked by Class 33 diesels, though one report mentioned a Class 22. At Broadstone Junction station the locomotive(s) would run round their train and push it to the railhead due to the lack of air brake and the steep gradient from Broadstone to Corfe Mullen Junction. The train's guard was responsible for operating the road level crossing at Corfe Mullen and Bailey Gate, both normally being locked across the track. On arrival at Bailey Gate station the empties were disposed of in the Unigate Creamery sidings, before the locomotive and one brake van proceeded to the down platform. Once the north end crossover had been reversed the locomotive then fly-shunted the brake van onto the up line before setting off light engine to the railhead to collect the loaded wagons. On returning to Bailey Gate the loaded train was shunted back onto the brake van on the up line, before the empties were extracted from the creamery sidings and propelled out to the railhead. On the locomotive's return it was berthed in the down platform whilst the crew had lunch and about an hour later coupled to the loaded train which proceeded back to Poole yard. During the following week the loaded wagons went to Brockenhurst for distribution.

Most of January was spent lifting all the sidings from Blandford goods yard, several of which were set in concrete to allow easy off loading into lorries. It would be early February before work commenced south from Blandford station, with only the down line to be lifted through Charlton Marshall Halt and along to Spetisbury Halt.

These contractors used a lorry based crane to lift the rails and sleepers onto the railway wagons. The lorry could use the up side trackbed as far as Spetisbury as this track had already been lifted. By 9th March 1970 work was in progress at Charlton Marshall. (From Spetisbury a caterpillar crane supplemented the lorry based crane.) This was very slow progress when one considers that they were only lifting single track. Bailey Gate station was largely intact having lost only its up siding and up platform shelter. As soon as work was completed at Blandford station the contractors based themselves at Bailey Gate station which could provide sidings and run-round facilities together with easy vehicular access.

Progress slowed down further once double track was reached south of Spetisbury. By 5th April work was still in progress just south of Spetisbury at S&D

bridge No. 215 Mackeral's Bridge. The up line had been lifted back to just north of S&D bridge No. 217 Cliff Road Bridge, over the busy A350 road. By 12th April a week's concentrated work had lifted the down line from just south of Spetisbury to a point about half a mile towards bridge No. 217. A further week's work had the down line ending about half a mile north of bridge No. 217, while the up line ended just south of this bridge on 19th April.

By 31st May the up line had been lifted back through Bailey Gate station as far as the south end crossover, while the down line ended about half a mile to the north of the station. By now the wooden portion of both Bailey Gate and Corfe Mullen Crossing signalboxes had been demolished although the brick base of Corfe Mullen crossing signalbox is still standing today. Also on this Sunday the first double-headed train was noted at Bailey Gate with Class 33 Nos 6505 and 6544. Double-heading would be the norm for at least the next three Sundays. The need to double-head trains had come about because of the increase in track being lifted after double track was reached. Also a full train of four bogie bolster wagons loaded with rail and 20 open wagons of sleepers were too much for the braking capacity of a single Class 33 on the long descent of Corfe Mullen bank.

Once track lifting in Bailey Gate station itself had made any form of shunting very difficult the method of working on a Sunday was altered. For example on 14th June Class 33 Nos 6514 and 6542 arrived light, and having collected the loaded wagons they returned to Broadstone Junction before pushing the 25 or so empty wagons up to Bailey Gate. The dairy sidings were still usable for a little shunting and these were used to sort out the wagons. The down line ended just north of S&D bridge No. 220 Bailey Gate Station Bridge, and with the exception of the short creamery siding the goods yard had been cleared. The up line was lifted well to the south of Bailey Gate.

The down main line and creamery sidings were still in place on Sunday 21st June. The up line had now been lifted back almost as far as Corfe Mullen crossing. Loaded wagons were scattered along the down line, having been loaded with materials from the up line during the week. Class 33 Nos 6518 and 6549 came out from Broadstone Junction light to gather up these scattered wagons and propel them back to Bailey Gate station, where the load was remarshalled for the return trip to Broadstone. At Broadstone Junction station the loaded wagons were placed in the down 'Old Road' (Poole) platform, before collecting the empty wagons from the up branch (Hamworthy Junction) platform. The locomotives then pushed these empty wagons to the railhead, again wagons were spread along the down line beside what remained of the up line as the locomotives worked back down to Broadstone Junction light engines.

It seems curious now that the south end crossover facility at Bailey Gate station was never used during

Track lifting in progress at Spetisbury Halt on 9th March 1970.   *Peter James*

Class 33 No. 6506 has just pushed its train of empty stock up to the railhead on 5th April 1970, which was south of Spetisbury.
Peter James

On the same day No. 6506 is seen at Corfe Mullen Junction crossing. Note the signalbox is still intact.
Peter James

the track lifting operation to enable locomotives to run round their trains of empty stock, and also to marshal the loaded wagons before the up line was lifted. Right from the first train in December 1969 wagons were always propelled up from Broadstone Junction and full ones hauled down. Even allowing for Corfe Mullen bank's steep gradient this would appear to be a method that could easily have resulted in derailments. It would surely have been easier and safer to use all the crossover facilities at Bailey Gate station? But it would appear that during use as

the contractor's base the north end crossover was in constant use for shunting but never the south. One suggestion is that during demolition of Bailey Gate signalbox this crossover was damaged in some way and could not be used, but this seems most unlikely. It must be remembered that locomotives could run round their trains in the creamery sidings.

By the first week in August the railhead had eventually reached the level crossing gates across the minor road near Corfe Mullen Junction. Just over a week later Corfe Mullen Junction itself and single track had been reached. Corfe Mullen Junction signalbox was demolished around this time. The three miles of single track down to Broadstone Junction station would be completed by 2nd October 1970. All the retrieved materials from this section were delivered to Brockenhurst for redistribution and trains started out from Brockenhurst before calling at Poole each Sunday.

Track lifting and rationalisation between Wimborne and Bournemouth West station

Many people say that this section of line is not part of the S&DJR – true and false. True the S&DJR did not build this section; neither did it build the line from Bath Junction to Bath (Green Park) station. False, without these two connections the S&DJR could not have been a cross country line, linking the industrial north to the south coast.

Changes around Broadstone Junction had been confined to the singling of the 'Old Road' either side of the station, to Hamworthy on 11th December 1932 and to Wimborne on 24th July 1966. A notable event occurred on 11th July 1969, when Class 47 No. 1719 stabled Royal stock at Wimborne. Broadstone's layout remained basically the same until October 1970 but with the lifting of the S&DJR completed, the track layout at the station was simplified as only two sources of traffic used the line to Wimborne and Doulton's sidings. The down Poole and Bournemouth line was taken out of use on 18th October 1970 while the north junction was removed on 13th December the same year. From this date a train to Wimborne came in on the up line, then used

a new slew to get to the Poole and Bournemouth (S&DJR) line briefly before using the down 'Old Road' and slewing across to the up 'Old Road' from the point where this had been singled. The up and down 'Old Road' lines were retained through the station platforms, presumably acting as a run round facility for traffic to Doulton's sidings which was reached by using a short length of the Broadstone to Hamworthy line. This traffic must have ceased by late 1973, as these lines were lifted between November 1973 and January 1974. From then it was just a plain single track with no connections at all through Broadstone station.

Moving out of Broadstone station towards Holes Bay Junction, the line was singled from 18th October 1970 and the redundant track was lifted from 13th December 1970, starting at the Broadstone end. No time scale is known to Holes Bay Junction where a new slew was put in, together with trap points and a ground frame. This meant freight traffic could run directly from Poole yard along the up, London–Weymouth line, then using the new slew gained access to the old up line. The Holes Bay Junction to Wimborne line closed on 2nd May 1977 when Class 33 No. 33107 collected the few remaining wagons at Wimborne. On 3rd May the Lea Valley Railway Society organised a special which ran three trips over the line called 'The Corkscrew Shuttle'. This train comprised Class 33 No. 33012 with a hand written headboard inscribed "The Last Train from Wimborne 3 May 1977 Loco 33012" hauling a 4-TC and all in immaculate condition. Due to the number of people wishing to have a

On 12th April 1970 Class 33 No. 6552 is about to depart with a loaded train to Poole and then Brockenhurst. Bailey Gate station signalbox is still intact, as is the up platform shelter.

Peter James

April 19th, 1970 finds Class 33 No. 6554 pushing its train of empty stock past the site of the junction with the long closed Wimborne line.

Peter James

No. 6554 has now reached the busy road level crossing at Bailey Gate. The crews of the demolition trains had to unlock, operate and then re-lock the two road crossings on this line each time they worked up or down the line.

Peter James

final ride over the line, a second and equally immaculate 4-TC, was supplied for the final run.

There appear to be various dates for the track lifting on this line, from October 1977 through to July 1978. It is unclear who carried out the work or even what locomotives were involved, as the work was rather spasmodic. Wimborne station was clear of track by early January 1978. April 1978 found the trailing points into the up LSWR main line at the former Holes Bay Junction had been removed in late February, so severing the last physical connection with this line. One must presume therefore that all the rails had been lifted as further rail movements were now impossible and that all remaining materials would be removed by road. On 23rd March the River Stour bridge just south of Wimborne was being demolished and at Broadstone Junction station only sleepers, chairs and bolts remained to be collected. The Wimborne station site was cleared for redevelopment in July 1983 and a

Bailey Gate station on 31st May 1970. The signalbox and up platform shelter have been demolished and the station goods yard and the up line north of the station have been lifted. Class 33s Nos 6544 and 6505 are shunting in the creamery sidings.

Peter James

By 14th June the up line had been lifted back to Corfe Mullen Junction. Class 33s Nos 6542 and 6514 continue to use the creamery sidings.

Peter James

On 21st June 1970 Class 33s Nos 6549 and 6518 are hauling a loaded train under bridge No. 223 on their return to Broadstone Junction to collect further empty stock.

Peter Stone

similar fate befell Broadstone Junction station site during August 1984.

Travelling on down the LSWR main line we reach Branksome. This station became the terminus for most of the S&DJR trains after 2nd August 1965, with a bus service connecting to Bournemouth West station. Trains to and from Waterloo continued to use Bournemouth West until 5th September 1965. Also most empty stock from Bournemouth Central was still using the carriage sidings at Bournemouth West. The reason for the change in the S&D trains was to allow alterations to the Branksome to Bournemouth West Junction portion of the Branksome triangle. Initially, the intention was to allow S&D trains to use Bournemouth West station once the alterations were completed, even though the trains would have to use one of the sidings as a route to and from the station. But Bournemouth West station was closed before the work was completed, and from late September all S&D trains terminated at Bournemouth Central. The work was intended to allow the new electric stock to run directly into the old carriage sidings which now form the electric stock maintenance and cleaning depot. Access to these sidings had been from the station end but the new layout would require access from the Bournemouth West Junction end. The track alterations, re-signalling and earthworks took about three months.

As far as the closure of Bournemouth West was concerned the threat had hung over the station from September 1962, when all the north/south expresses ceased to use the S&D. The first mention in local newspapers of the possible closure was on 16th April 1964, and the intention to close was confirmed on 15th July 1964. The original closure date was set for 14th June 1965, to give plenty of time to prepare the site for the new electric multiple-unit depot. However, due to revised procedures for issuing closure notices, the original notice had to be withdrawn. Finally, on 24th August 1965, closure was announced for 4th October 1965. This was somewhat later than originally anticipated and it must presumably have upset the timetable for making track alterations at the carriage sidings.

For the remainder of October empty stock was still stored in Bournemouth West station, until most of the trackwork around the station area had been lifted during the weekend of 30th and 31st October 1965. This included the pointwork leading into the carriage sidings. Also during this weekend the Branksome to Bournemouth West Junction section was reinstated and the Gas Works Junction to

Bournemouth West Junction section was taken out of use. Bournemouth West Junction signalbox was downgraded to a ground frame on 1st November 1965 and then closed on 5th September 1966, although reopened a few months later and still in use today. Strangely, the Gas Works Junction signalbox would not close until 15th January 1967. What little track remained in the station was removed during February 1967. All the station buildings at Bournemouth West remained intact until construction started on the Wessex Way bypass. By April 1970 all the buildings had been cleared and the road was under construction. The remaining land became a coach park in the summer months and in recent years this land has been redeveloped.

Once the new electric unit depot was open, empty stock was shunted into Branksome station and then reversed into the depot. While steam was still in use a locomotive was maintained in the sidings, close to the junction at Branksome, to act as pilot for drawing stock in and out of the various buildings and sidings. The steam locomotive was replaced in June 1967 by a Class 08 shunter.

Branksome depot was closed from 1st January 1963, but locomotives were still stabled there between turns. From this date all staff originally based at Branksome, including S&DJR men, were transferred to the Bournemouth Central depot. The depot had seen a considerable downturn in locomotive activity after the re-routeing of the S&DJR expresses and thereafter it was just used to stable locomotives between turns. Water could still be refreshed but no coaling facilities had been available since before World War II. Branksome depot was officially closed on 5th September 1965. Locomotives were unable to access the depot from 2nd August 1965 because of the track alterations instigated in accordance with the new electric depot. Branksome depot was demolished in 1970 along with Bournemouth West station. Branksome coal yard and Sharpe Jones Pottery sidings both closed on 15th September 1970, and both had been lifted by 29th November 1970.

Timetable of track lifting on the Evercreech to Bason Bridge branch

Dismantling of this line commenced on 30th January 1967, the contract for track lifting being carried out by George Cohen & Sons Co. Ltd of London, with most, if not all, of the rails going to South Wales for scrap. The branch line track was very nearly life expired at the time of closure. The wooden sleepers were sold locally whilst concrete sleepers went for re-use elsewhere.

The track lifting commenced at a point about half a mile from Evercreech Junction North and proceeded westwards. BR provided the contractors with a constant supply of engineering departmental wagons and locomotives, although the contractors were known to have used their own, rather strange looking small diesel locomotive on the Somerset levels. The contractors supplied their own caterpillar crane which was used to load both rails and concrete sleepers into the wagons. The initial contractor's base was at Glastonbury station which had sufficient siding and run-round facilities. All loaded wagons were assembled there, and replaced by empty ones held until required. When enough full wagons were gathered at Glastonbury they were formed into loaded trains and taken back to Highbridge to be worked off the branch. Only Class 03 0-6-0 diesel shunters were used on these branch line workings, short rakes of the empty wagons being propelled to the scene of track lifting, usually once or twice a day. Some of the recovered materials were off loaded from the railway wagons at Glastonbury and conveyed away by road vehicles. Staff working this line had a very tedious task since there were so many level crossing gates to negotiate. Wooden sleepers to be sold locally were removed by the purchaser using a mobile crane and lorries after recovery of the rail.

The railhead was on Pylle bank by the beginning of March 1967, Class 03 shunter No. D2133 being in use on 1st March. The contractors had reached West Pennard by 13th March, at which time diesel shunters Nos D2119 and D2113 were both in use on the line, the former being used as resident pilot at Glastonbury, although on this occasion it had failed. Contractors started demolition work at Glastonbury station in early May but only removed the station footbridge before an offer for the station site was made by a local timber merchant (demolition being completed in 1984). During May the contractors withdrew from Glastonbury and started to use Highbridge as their base, but with all the sidings removed from the S&D station wagons were stored, shunted and removed from the GWR yard.

Work appears to have slowed down drastically during May with very few train movements being

Glastonbury station was the contractor's base in February 1967 being the only station on the branch line with any sidings remaining after closure.

Ken Marchant

In February 1967 the railhead was at Pylle with Class 03 No. D2175 in attendance.

Colin Maggs

noted. According to Industrial Railway Society records T. W. Ward Ltd undertook the remaining track lifting from Glastonbury to Bason Bridge Creamery. There is no explanation for this change of contractor but it is possible that George Cohen & Sons sub-contracted the remaining work to T. W. Ward Ltd. By the early part of June all the track had been lifted back as far as the Eclipse Peat Company near Ashcott and work proceeded rapidly across the remaining Somerset levels. T. W. Ward Ltd used their own Fowler 0-4-0 diesel, No. 421005 for much of this work, but using BR bogie bolsters to recover the rail.

Work was in progress at Shapwick station during mid-July but the contractors did not demolish the station buildings or signalbox. This may have been because the contract was running behind schedule due to earlier delays and BR's inability to supply adequate wagons on a daily basis. Edington Burtle station was cleared and abandoned but the buildings remained intact at the end of August.

Track lifting was all but complete by October 1967, when the contractor had reached a point about 300 yards on the Glastonbury (east) side of the Bason Bridge Creamery. The contractors followed a similar policy to that on the main line of cutting down all signals as they passed them together with the removal of any trackside fixtures that might remain. They would not appear to have undertaken the demolition of any station buildings other than the Glastonbury station footbridge in the May. Bason Bridge station was demolished in November 1968 and in April 1971 Shapwick station and signalbox were removed when the South Drain was widened. West Pennard and Pylle stations have become private dwellings.

The track lifting gang members near Pylle in February 1967.

Colin Maggs

Timetable for track lifting on the Highbridge to Bason Bridge branch line

Closure of this section of the branch was finally effected during the middle of October 1972 as completion of the M5 motorway drew close. The official date was 10th October, but it is known that trains kept on running to the creamery for at least another week or ten days after this date.

Very little time could be wasted after the final train movement as any delay caused to the M5 construction work would have proved very expensive for BR. Track lifting therefore commenced very rapidly and the first rails were lifted during the week commencing 11th December 1972. The Bason Bridge Creamery sidings, run-round facilities and the long headshunt east towards Edington had been lifted by the end of that week, with the wooden sleepers being sold for local use. By 31st December the rails had been removed for the mile or so back as far as the Highbridge side of the M5. Having sold the wooden sleepers they were left in place for the purchaser to collect by lorry when required. Work could now move at a more relaxed pace as the pressure was off. Final track lifting back to the Highbridge station site was completed early in the new year. It is unclear who undertook this work but remembering the timescale involved, it may well have been the BR Engineering Department based at Bristol who were responsible as far as the M5 bridge, after which it could well have been a contractor.

Two very short lengths of track from the new Highbridge Junction were still in situ in June 1982, this being part of the temporary PFA terminal that was installed in connection with the building of the M5 motorway and the stunted branch line.

Timetable for track lifting on the Bridgwater and Wells Priory branch lines
With the exception of the very early demise of the original Templecombe connection in March 1870, and the closure of the Wimborne line on 17th June 1933, the post-war events commence with the lines to Wells and Bridgwater.

The Wells branch closed to all traffic from 29th October 1951. The branch, in later days, commencing from MP 10.37 just to the east of the bay platform at Glastonbury station, rather than having a separate line running parallel with the main branch line. Track lifting commenced at the Wells end of the branch with recovered materials being moved out through Glastonbury yard to Highbridge for final disposal. The track through the bay platform was retained but was removed from a point just to the east of the station, to a position some nine chains before the S&DJR goods yard junction in Wells. This junction was 5 miles 30 chains from Glastonbury. The GWR East Junction was at 5 miles 40 chains.

Following closure, Wells Priory station was used as office accommodation where the area accountancy work for freight traffic was performed for many years. The goods shed continued to be used for 'less than wagon load' traffic until this was transferred to Bristol and delivered from that depot.

All this time there was still a timetabled passenger service over the GWR line from Yatton to Witham, but this finally ceased on 9th September 1963. Freight traffic continued to use the line from the Witham end, being cut back to Cheddar before finally ending on 31st March 1969. Latterly only light stone traffic traversed the branch. The former S&DJR yard at Priory Road continued to be used by the Western Region until 1964, all sidings there being taken out of use on 12th October 1964 and subsequently lifted.

Track lifting and demolition of the Wells branch started on 13th February 1955, and it would appear to have taken until early or mid 1957 to complete the work. Just why a $5\frac{1}{2}$ mile line, with only one halt, should take so long to remove is unclear. The work is believed to have been carried out by the BR Engineering Department in the form of local permanent way gang members lifting the branch as weekend overtime. This would explain the timescale involved, but this is unconfirmed. One of the locomotives known to have been used on this track lifting operation was S&D "Bulldog" 0-6-0 No. 43201 which was photographed at Cemetery crossing in Glastonbury on a demolition train.

Moving on to the Bridgwater branch, which consisted of one station and one halt on its $7\frac{1}{2}$ mile length, from Edington Burtle Junction to Bridgwater North there was also a wharf branch, consisting of a short line leaving the branch line at MP 6.71 and terminating alongside the River Parrett at MP 7.44.

The Bridgwater branch came under threat of closure as early as 1933 due to heavy financial losses. The situation was not helped by the closure of Boards Quarry siding in 1933, this siding was not removed until 1940. Also in 1933 the Cossington station crossover facility was removed due to its poor condition. The wharf branch, from MP 6.71 to 7.44 alongside the River Parrett, ceased to be used in 1909, with the wharf being demolished in 1912 having become unsafe. The disused wharf branch remained in situ until World War II, but with the wartime need for scrap metal the line between MP 7.18 and 7.44 was lifted during January 1942. The remainder of the branch was converted into a long siding and used to store condemned wagons, until lifted along with the rest of the Bridgwater branch in 1955.

Passenger traffic ceased on 1st December 1952. Freight traffic continued for almost two more years but only from Edington Junction to Cossington station. On 1st October 1954 the entire line was closed, except for Bridgwater North station itself, where in order to continue using the S&DJR goods yard and station area, a new short chord line was constructed between the adjacent former GWR Bridgwater Docks branch and the cattle pen siding in the old S&DJR North yard, and which came into operation on 27th June 1954. This small part of the branch now remained in use as a goods station terminating in a headshunt formed from the old S&DJR branch line as far as Castle Fields level crossing at MP 6.70. There appears to be conflicting dates for the final closure of Bridgwater North station, it ceasing to be used as a goods station from 7th July 1962, but it must have closed completely along with the Great Western docks branch on 2nd January 1967.

Track lifting commenced in early October 1955 at Edington. The name of this station then changed from Edington Junction station to Edington Burtle station in recognition of its diminished status. In February 1956 Edington signalbox was closed along with the down platform and the lifting of the passing loop, and all but one siding in the goods yard.

BR supplied all the bogie bolster and open wagons required to remove the recovered materials from the Bridgwater branch, while the contractors used their own small 4-wheel 'Planet' industrial diesel. Track lifting commenced at the Edington end

of the branch with the contractor's diesel working down from Bridgwater to the railhead. Due to its minimal power and traction it could only manage two empty bogie bolsters or three open wagons at a time. Once loaded, only one bogie bolster or two open wagons could be hauled back to Bridgwater. As a result, this 7 mile 25 chain branch line took nearly a year to lift. Unlike scrap merchants contracted to lift the main line, those on the branch lines were very much slower in purchasing and removing bridge ironwork. All the track lifting and demolition was undertaken by a contractor (name unknown). Bridgwater North station was finally demolished between 1st and 8th August 1984.

Track rationalisation at Highbridge

Less than nine months after closure, in March 1966, BR Engineering Department staff had moved into Highbridge. Although the branch line was still retained as far as the Bason Bridge Creamery, all other sidings and facilities were to be removed. BR engineers removed all the points and track serving platforms 1, 2, 3 and 4, together with the complete loop and all the goods yard sidings. Also lifted were the lines giving access to the railway works, motive power depot and turntable. The old Highbridge Works had closed in 1930 as part of a cost cutting exercise by the London Midland & Scottish

A contractor's 'Planet' diesel locomotive in use on the Bridgwater branch on 29th August 1956. Bridge No. 294 near Edington is in the background.

Colin Maggs

Railway. The Works were not demolished but survived until well after the closure of the line, latterly in a very run-down state.

By the middle of January 1967 work had almost been completed, although the turntable was still in situ. Only one siding connection remained, and this was to provide a short spur which acted as a trap point to protect the Great Western main line from the possibility of an S&DJR train accidentally running across the level rail crossing in the Burnham direction. Access between the S&DJR and GWR was very inconveniently through the GWR goods yards and goods shed; a complex arrangement but totally typical where these two companies were involved. A new home signal was erected at this point to control the exit of S&DJR line trains across the GWR main line on the level rail crossing and thence through the goods yard. Highbridge station and its buildings would lie dormant for the next three years.

Subsequently most of this area was redeveloped as the fly ash terminal for use while construction of the M5 motorway was carried out. This temporary layout was subsequently altered back to a single track to maintain the milk traffic to Bason Bridge creamery until October 1972, plus a single short siding.

Track rationalisation at Bath (Green Park) station and locomotive depot

Two months before the announcement by BR that the contracts had been let at the end of December 1966 and before work had commenced at Highbridge, the contractors moved into Bath (Green Park) depot. The extensive sidings which formed Bath Midland Bridge goods yard were to be retained, but some of the adjacent sidings to the main line were scheduled for removal, along with all lines into both motive power depots. The main lines themselves were terminated about 100 yards to the west of the engine sheds and all tracks into Bath (Green Park) station removed. The two sidings which terminated just short of the river bridges, and which ran adjacent to the Midland (smaller) locomotive depot, remained in use. They had previously been used for many years to store locomotives which were out of use or, latterly, withdrawn. Most of the track lifting was completed by February 1967, the recovered materials being transported away by rail to Nottingham via Bristol for sorting into reuseable or scrap. The concrete sleepers were re-used but old wooden sleepers were mostly sold locally.

Two of the main line buffer stops (one actually fitted with buffers, the other without) were removed

Cont. p. 97

The Demise of Bath (Green Park) Depot

Preliminary work commenced at Bath (Green Park) Depot as early as October 1966. The turntable had been cut up by the 30th.

Michael Gates

The view on 30th October 1966 towards the old S&DJR depot just after the connecting pointwork had been lifted leaving only the track round to the Stothert & Pitt's works.

Michael Gates

The S&DJR depot during demolition in April 1967. The site was then redeveloped and used by Stothert and Pitt.

Michael Gates

Two views of the track lifting within Bath (Green Park) station and at the throat of the station. Track was only lifted back as far as the motive power depot entrance at this time, as the goods yard at Bath would remain in use until 1972.

Both Chris Handley

from the station and re-erected at the new termination point of the mainlines. The former 'Boat Road' track beside the locomotive depot, which allowed locomotives to gain access to the S&DJR depot and to the old Riverside branch, (by running down behind the depot to wharves on the River Avon and gain access to Stothert & Pitt engineering sidings), was retained for traffic for a short time. This line was also used by the track lifting trains recovering materials from the locomotive depots. One of the two bridges over the River Avon was removed and is believed to have been re-used at some other unknown location.

Rationalisation and Demolition of the Mangotsfield to Bath Midland Bridge line

Freight traffic for Bath Midland Bridge yard and Bath Gas Works, plus that generated in Bath, was to remain at a similar pre-passenger closure level for almost two years. Even so there was little point in maintaining a double-tracked and fully signalled system simply for a freight only service. This situation remained only until modernisation and rationalisation was considered necessary by Western Region. By early 1968, traffic on the Bath to Mangotsfield line had been reduced by road competition and Western Region policies by some 50%, and with a new signalling system being introduced to the area a decision was made to introduce single line working as soon as possible.

On 5th May 1968 single line working was implemented using the down line as far as Kelston Woods where infrastructure problems necessitated the use of the up line. The up line was cut south of Mangotsfield signalbox and the track was slewed to join the down Bath line, enabling southbound trains to run straight from the down line of the Gloucester to Bristol route to the branch. In June 1968 the Western Region received permission to build a new power signalbox and completely re-signalled the Bristol area, the result of which caused still further rationalisations and closures in the Bristol and Mangotsfield area. On 31st December 1969 it was announced that the line from Yate to Mangotsfield and the branch from there to Bath Midland Bridge yard would be worked as a long siding mainly for the Bath Gas Works coal traffic.

Recovery of the redundant main line track was carried out during 1969. It was already known at this time that the gas works would close when North Sea gas was introduced, and this happened on 28th May 1971. The freight handled at Bath Midland Bridge yard did not now justify the reten-

tion of the line, so it was closed to all regular traffic at the end of May 1971, but the tracks saw some use up to mid-April 1972, simply to store condemned wagons. The track lifting operation commenced on 8th May 1972 from beside the Midland Railway depot, this work being undertaken by Eagre (Scunthorpe) Ltd. Only one locomotive appears to have been used during this contract. BR supplied Class 08 No. 3517 and all necessary bogie bolster wagons, whilst the contractors used their own crane. The Mangotsfield to Bath line track had been renewed in the early 1960s using flat-bottomed rails on concrete sleepers in 60ft panels. This was now lifted directly onto the bolster wagons and transported the short distance to the former Thornbury branch, north of Bristol, to serve the newly reopened Tytherington Quarries. By late-June all that remained in Bath was a small quantity of old bullhead rail, including the pointwork leading onto the S&DJR. This would all be cut up for scrap on site as were the private siding systems of both the Bath Gas Works and Stothert & Pitt engineering works. The remaining track back to Mangotsfield was all recovered by late September 1972. Since this time the trackbed has become a cycleway between Bath and Bristol and shared with the Avon Valley Railway for part of its length.

Rationalisation and track lifting of the remaining sections of the S&DJR

The Dorset Central Railway spur at Templecombe was just about the earliest casualty when the original connection between the DCR and the Salisbury & Yeovil Railway, soon to become part of the London & South Western Railway, became redundant. This 90° trailing connection off the Dorset Central at Templecombe Lower towards the east was closed in March 1870, when a new connection was constructed to the west and Templecombe Upper station was completed. A small portion of the original spur and the point connecting it to the S&YR were lifted but the great majority was retained and converted into a long siding. This siding survived for 97 years until lifted, with the rest of Templecomber Lower yard during the summer of 1967.

Burnham Pier was really more of a slipway than a conventional pier and it still survives. Although it sloped steadily seawards rails were set into the concrete surface forming a long siding beyond the station itself. The pier was probably never intended to take locomotives, more likely the odd wagon may have been taken down by some means to deal with goods delivered by ship to the pier. A small trolley was available for passenger luggage, this being wheeled up to the station. The S&DJR divested itself of the structure to the UDC in 1905, its railway responsibilities now terminating at MP 24.02 – from Evercreech Junction. However, the line had been connected to the nearby lifeboat station and for a number of years this was the preferred means of launching the lifeboat. In 1932 the present esplanade road was constructed and extended across the railway, the lines then being severed. However some of the rails on the pier survived for many years and traces were still visible in the 1960s but by 1989 all trace of these rails had gone.

The Wimborne line (Corfe Mullen Junction to Wimborne Junction) was probably the first true section of the S&DJR to be closed, being the original main line route. This was until the cut-off between Corfe Mullen Junction and Broadstone Junction was constructed in 1884/85 and opened to freight on 14th December 1885 and passenger traffic on 1st November 1886. After this some passenger trains used the Wimborne line until 11th July 1920 and the last through freight train ran on 17th June 1933. Some 78 chains south of Corfe Mullen Junction was Carter's Clay Pit which was served by a single siding on the up side and making a trailing connection going south. This remained open to traffic, with some four chains beyond the siding points being required for a short headshunt. Beyond this point (MP 61.21 from Bath Junction) to Wimborne Junction (MP 63.19) the line was abandoned and lifted at an unknown date. Wimborne Junction was 25 chains to the west of the LSWR station and, of course, marked the true end of the S&DJR.

Not only was this short length of the Wimborne line used to serve Carter's Clay Pit siding but it also served as a refuge for freight trains to clear the main line for the passage of express passenger trains until September 1962. Even after that date a late running freight could clear the line for other trains to pass by using this line. Carter's Clay Pit siding closed on 19th September 1959 although the line to MP 61.10 was subsequently used to store wagons, mostly condemned, for a time. The last consignment of wagons would appear to have been removed from the line late in 1965, no doubt in preparation for the closure of the S&DJR, even though the Broadstone–Blandford line was to remain open. By this time the Wimborne line had become very over-

grown, it last seeing a weedkiller train around 1957. The track remained in situ until 1968, being reported as lifted in the September. It must be presumed that the BR Engineers Department undertook this work at around the time it was singling the line south from Blandford.

Locomotives used on the demolition trains

Blandford to Radstock contract January 1967 to July 1968

Date	Class	No.	Direction	Noted location	Head code
1967	35	D7003		Wincanton station	9Z 05
1967	22	D6331		Radstock North station	
17/02/67	35	D7033		Evercreech Junction	6M 74
03/67	35	D7031		Shepton Mallet station	
04/67	35	D7028		Radstock North station	
08/05/67	22	D6329	Down	Light Engine Templecombe	8H 27
09/05/67	22	D6329	Up	Light Engine Radstock	8H 27
11/05/67	22	D6331	Down		8H 33
12/05/67	22	D6331	Up*	Chilcompton station	8H 33
15/05/67	22	D6333	Down		
16/05/67	22	D6333	Up*	Chilcompton station	
17/05/67	22	D6330	Down		6B 00
18/05/67	22	D6330	Up*	Chilcompton station	6B 00
19/05/67	22	D6331	Down	Evercreech Junction station	9Z 02
20/05/67	22	D6331	Up	Chilcompton station	9Z 02
23/05/67	22	D6331	Down		5Z 07
24/05/67	22	D6331	Up*	Chilcompton station	5Z 07
01/06/67	22	D6323	Down		
02/06/67	22	D6323	Up*	Templecombe Lower	
03/06/67	22	D6337	Down		
04/06/67	22	D6337	Up*	Templecombe Lower	
08/06/67	22	D6340	Down		
09/06/67	22	D6340	Up*	Chilcompton Rock Cutting	
13/06/67	22	D6324	Down		9Z 02
14/06/67	22	D6324	Up*	Chilcompton station	9Z 02
15/06/67	22	D6337	Down		
16/06/67	22	D6337	Up*		
20/06/67	22	D6323	Down		9Z 02
21/06/67	22	D6323	Up*	Chilcompton station	9Z 02
28/06/67	22	D6324	Down		9H 02
29/06/67	22	D6324	Up*	Evercreech New	9H 02
30/06/67	22	D6337	Down	Templecombe Lower	
01/07/67	22	D6337	Up*	Evercreech New	
06/07/67	22	D6320	Down		
07/07/67	22	D6320	Up*		
10/07/67	22	D6331	Down		8H 23
11/07/67	22	D6331	Up*	Chilcompton station	8H 23
12/07/67	22	D6331	Down		8H 23
13/07/67	22	D6331	Up*	Chilcompton station	8H 23
13/07/67	22	D6324	Down		
14/07/67	22	D6324	Up*		
18/07/67	22	D6325	Down	(blue livery)	
19/07/67	22	D6325	Up*	(blue livery)	
19/07/67	22	D6341	Down	Evercreech Junction	8H 22
20/07/67	22	D6341	Up*	Moorewood	8H 22
20/08/67	22	D6321	Down	Wincanton station	9Z 02
04/09/67	22	D6331 +			
		D6311	Up	(double-headed)	8H 22

Date	Class	No.	Direction	Noted location	Head code
07/09/67	22	D6331 +			
		D6323	Down	(double-headed)	8H 20
04/10/67	22	D6315 +			
		D6316	Down	(double-headed)	
06/10/67	22	D6315 +			
		D6316	Up	(double-headed)	
11/67	35	D7003		Wincanton station	5A 02
01/11/67	22	D6317	Down	Wincanton station	8H 23
02/11/67	22	D6321			
06/11/67	22	D6312		Evercreech Junction	9Z 31
17/11/67	35	D7025		Chilcompton tunnel	
18/11/67	08	D4025	Stabled	Evercreech Junction station	
19/11/67	08	D4025	Stabled	Evercreech Junction station	
29/12/67	35	D7031		Radstock North station	
29/12/67	08	D3185		Radstock Spur to B&NSL	
20/01/68	35	D7015	Up	Midsomer Norton station	
22/01/68	08	D3355		Evercreech Junction	
22/01/68	08	D3355		Wyke Champflower	
27/01/68	35	D7039	Up	Midsomer Norton station	10 69
28/01/68	08	D3355			
30/01/68	08	D3355		Evercreech Junction	
02/02/68	35	D7013	Up	Radstock North station	
15/02/68	08	D3516		Shepton Mallet goods shed	
15/02/68	35	D7045		Shepton Mallet	
15/02/68	08	D3516		Evercreech Junction station	
16/02/68	35	D7042	Up	Chilcompton station	
17/02/68	35	D7033	Up	Chilcompton Tunnel	BH 07
27/02/68	08	D3516		Shepton Mallet station	
06/03/68	35	D7015 +			
		D3516	Up	(returning 08 to Bristol)	9Z 07
12/03/68	35	D7006	Down	Charlton Road Viaduct	6C 24
12/03/68	08	D3805	Shunting	Shepton Mallet Yard	
12/03/68	35	D7004		Shepton Mallet station	
27/03/68	35	D7008	Down	Midsomer Norton station	0J 00
27/03/68	08	D3805	Shunting	Shepton Mallet station	
27/03/68	35	D7008	Up	Chilcompton station	3C 10
21/04/68	35	D7028		Binegar station	3C 04
29/04/68	08	D3505	Stabled	Binegar station	
29/04/68	35	D7000	Up	Chilcompton	
30/04/68	08	D3505		¼ mile south of Masbury Halt	
05/68	35	D7029		Binegar station	
02/05/68	08	D3505	Stabled	Binegar station	
14/05/68	08	D3001	Stabled	Binegar station	
17/05/68	08	D3001	Up	Moorewood	
21/05/68	08	D3001		Binegar station	
23/05/68	08	D3001	Shunting	Moorewood	
23/05/68	35	D7043	Down	North of Moorewood	8H 18
25/05/68	35	D7045			
25/05/68	08	D3001		Binegar down distant signal	
07/06/68	35	D7045		Last 'Hymek' to work over the S&DJR	
07/06/68	08	D3001		Moorewood	
08/06/68	08	D3001		Radstock North station	
09/06/68	08	D3001		Midsomer Norton	
10/06/68	08	D3001		Moorewood	
11/06/68	08	D3001		Chilcompton	
12/06/68	08	D3506		Norton Hill Colliery	

Date	Class	No.	Direction	Noted location	Head code
13/06/68	08	D3506		Chilcompton	
19/06/68	08	D3506		Chilcompton Rock Cutting	
12/07/68	08	D3506		Midsomer Norton	

Notes:
Locomotives marked * are confirmed up workings. Therefore one can assume that they worked down the previous day, as the locomotives worked out one day and back the next after the connection with the Salisbury to Exeter line was removed on Sunday 7th May 1967. Thereafter all trains worked over Masbury Summit to Bristol via Radstock.

Writhlington to Bath contract July 1967 to December 1968

1967	35	D7049		Twerton Co-op siding trip
10/10/67	22	D6323	Up	Bath Bank
11/10/67	22	D6323	Down	Horsecombe Vale
02/11/67	22	D6321	Down	Wellow
08/11/67	22	D6316	Down	Bath Bank
18/11/67	22	D6312	Up	Lyncombe Vale
1968	22	D6336		Bath bank (blue livery)
1968	22	D6340		Bath bank
1968	14	Unknown		Lyncombe Vale
26/05/68	08	D3195		Bath Bank

Blandford to Broadstone Junction contract December 1969 to September 1970

28/12/69	33	6519		Blandford station
28/12/69	33	6506		Blandford station
18/01/70	33	6523		Blandford
04/04/70	33	6506		Broadstone Junction station
05/04/70	33	6506		Bailey Gate station
12/04/70	33	6552		Bailey Gate station
19/04/70	33	6554		Corfe Mullen Junction
31/05/70	33	6505 +	double-headed	
		6544 +		Bailey Gate station
04/06/70	33	6514 +	double-headed	
		6542		Bailey Gate Crossing
21/06/70	33	6518 +	double-headed	
		6549		Corfe Mullen Junction

Notes:
Double-heading was resorted to as it was found that the braking power of one locomotive was inadequate for the loads sometimes handled. These were positively the last double-headed trains ever seen on the S&DJR.

Evercreech Junction to Bason Bridge contract January 1967 to October 1967

12/01/67	03	D2119	Bason Bridge station
02/67	03	D2175	Pylle
01/03/67	03	D2133	Steam Bow level crossing
13/03/67	03	D2133	Glastonbury goods yard
13/03/67	03	D2119	Glastonbury goods yard

Mangotsfield to Bath contract. May 1972 to September 1972

08/05/72	08	3517	Bath Midland Bridge Road goods yard

5

Demolition and Redevelopment of S&DJR Land

This chapter covers the period from general closure of the line in 1966 to the present day. After the various track lifting and demolition contracts had been completed the remaining assets were disposed of, with unwanted buildings demolished and that land which was not redeveloped returning to Mother nature. Even in 1994 no less than 14 of the S&DJR's 42 stations still remain, some as private dwellings or, as with Midsomer Norton and Shillingstone, just fortunate not to have been demolished when the track was lifted. Midford station on the other hand is the centre of a serious restoration and preservation project to form an 'on the line' S&DJR heritage centre. Also, of the 380 or so structures that made up the S&DJR's infrastructure some 259 are still standing, from one foot diameter culverts to the 27 spans of Charlton Road Viaduct. Starting at Burnham-on-Sea the reader is taken along the branch lines in words and pictures, and then on a trip from Bath to Bournemouth in 1994 with a brief history of the important locations since closure or the termination of the remaining freight services.

The Branch Lines – Burnham-on-Sea to Evercreech

Very little time was wasted on the Burnham-on-Sea to Evercreech Junction branch to dispose of railway property. The track to Highbridge Wharf and Burnham-on-Sea had been lifted by the end of 1964, while all the station buildings had been demolished by 1967 with the exception of the long excursion platform. The esplanade had long since been extended across the former pier line, but the

pier remains to this day, still in reasonable condition. In fact it is less of a pier, more a slipway. All rails have long since been removed and a road now covers the station site. The tiny Burnham-on-Sea signalbox – more a ground frame hut – was preserved by the Yieldingtree Railway Museum at nearby Bleadon & Uphill station (GWR), but then went to the Dowty Railway Preservation Centre at Ashchurch, Glos. Finally, the box passed into the hands of the Somerset & Dorset Railway Trust and has been totally restored at Washford on the West Somerset Railway.

Highbridge Wharf has been completely infilled since track lifting in 1964. In Highbridge main street where the crossing of the main Bristol to Exeter trunk road was made, the gates were soon removed. The S&DJR goods shed was to remain for a number of years but during the 1980s the site had been redeveloped into a shopping area. The former S&DJR buildings at Highbridge station remained basically intact after the track was lifted in 1966/67 leaving just a single track to Bason Bridge Creamery. The fly ash programme announced in the middle of 1970 caused wholesale demolition of practically the entire station site save part of the concrete No. 5 platform, by December 1970. The locomotive depot and part of the old locomotive works also had to be demolished to make way for the new fly ash terminal. By 1980 the remains of the locomotive works had been demolished, but part of the temporary PFA line was still in place in early 1982. The site of Highbridge station is now the Walrow Industrial Estate.

All the wooden station buildings at Bason Bridge were demolished during November 1968 although the station house seemed to remain in occupation. The only sign of this station now is the overgrown platform. The creamery expanded onto the trackbed, heading towards Edington, but with the loss of its vital rail connection to London the creamery started a slow decline to closure and this was announced in 1985, for 1987. At Edington Burtle the station house also remained in private occupation, the owner taking a large part of the trackbed as his garden. Only the bush-covered platform survived demolition here. Edington Junction station was, of course, formerly the Junction for the Bridgwater branch and with the demise of that line, its facilities had long since been butchered. It had lost its yard and bay platform leaving just a basic railway, even stripped of a passing loop. At this time Edington Junction station was renamed Edington Burtle station in recognition of its reduced status.

Burnham-on-Sea station site in 1993. This was the location of the long excursion platform which remained for many years after the rest of the station had been demolished.

Andy Read

Edington Junction to Bridgwater

Of the 19 bridges on this $7\frac{1}{2}$ mile branch only eight still survive, but it is worth the walk for no other reason than the beautiful Somerset countryside. Board's siding and Quarry has almost been obliterated by infilling to accommodate a civic amenity area. Moving on to Cossington station and stationmaster's house both still exist and are in occupation the latter is now called Manor Farm and farm buildings occupy the site of the sidings whilst a farm track uses the trackbed. Moving on with some difficulty one reaches the site of the short lived Bawdrip Halt, opened in 1923 and constructed of concrete but nothing remains at this location. A bungalow called Essandee is now built on the trackbed at Bawdrip and little of the trackbed and none of the bridges exist on the way to Bridgwater.

Closure of the Bridgwater branch to freight traffic in October 1954 was made possible when Bridgwater North was linked to the GWR branch via the cattle pen siding in June 1954. This line was closed on 2nd January 1967. Since then the goods yard area has become an industrial estate. After demolition of Bridgwater North station in August 1984 the station site has been re-developed as a Sainsbury's superstore.

...and on to Glastonbury

Part of the trackbed to the east of Edington was used to facilitate an improved drainage scheme during 1971. Shapwick signalbox was demolished but the station house, which had been empty for some years, would again be in occupation by 1972. The rest of the station building had been demolished by the time Wessex Water undertook the drainage improvement work. No trace of Shapwick station now remains after the South Drain was greatly widened with a new bridge over it at the point where the signalbox once stood. At Ashcott station the platform and station house remained almost intact for some time. The house is also still in occupation but the platform has now been mostly removed with the trackbed having become a dirt track road.

One of the first stations to be partly demolished whilst the track was being lifted was Glastonbury in May 1967. Only partial demolition had been effected when John Snow & Company, the adjacent timber merchants, took over the complete railway site. They swiftly converted the Wells branch platform into a covered building by boarding up one side with corrugated iron sheeting to enable timber to be stored in the dry. For some strange reason during track lifting at Glastonbury, a horse was stabled in the old waiting room, but for what reason? Otherwise the whole area was soon completely transformed by the appearance of numerous timber stacks around the station. The timber merchants ceased to use the site in the early 1980s and a very dilapidated Glastonbury station was demolished during 1984. Just before demolition a section of the overall station canopy was saved from

Edington Burtle station with only the platform to show its location in this view looking west in April 1993.

Andy Read

Cossington station on the Bridgwater branch in April 1993. The line ran along the other side of the station buildings, which are now a private dwelling.

Andy Read

destruction and re-erected in the town's market place.

All the land and buildings to the west of Glastonbury were sold to the Wessex Water Authority in 1970. This land was used to improve drainage of the Somerset Levels and the trackbed became a private road. The crossing keepers' cottages at Glastonbury Cemetery Lane and Coxley are both still in occupation. S&D bridge No. 266 Dye House Crossing Bridge, is still standing just to the east of Glastonbury. Much of the station and goods yard site was just wasteland used by fly-tippers in 1993. During the early part of 1994 work commenced on the long awaited Glastonbury by-pass. Bridge No. 264 was an early victim, being replaced by a roundabout.

Glastonbury to Wells

The branch line to Wells was an early casualty, closing to all traffic on 29th October 1951. The branch from Glastonbury to Wells Priory Road had only one station on route at Polsham. This station was soon sold off as a private dwelling which it remains to this day. At Wells Priory Road station only a small section of platform remained after the GWR branch ceased to use the station, the GWR branch finally closing on the 12th October 1964 and the track was soon lifted. No date can be found for the final demolition of Wells Priory Road station but the goods shed still remained even after a road had been constructed across the station site in the early 1980s. The goods shed was dismantled in

December 1988 and the small wooden office from the end of the building was saved by the Somerset & Dorset Railway Trust and is now to be seen at Washford. The main structure was dismantled and much of the masonry moved to the East Somerset Railway and used to construct a shop and restaurant at Cranmore. The stationmaster's house at Wells is still occupied.

Twenty one years after the closure of the Wells branch all nine bridges and culverts are still standing, regardless of all the redevelopment in this area. As with the Bridgwater branch and the main branch to Highbridge, the flat terrain on which these lines were constructed means they were very quickly taken back by nature, where man could find no use for the land.

. . . and on to Evercreech

The trackbed just west of the A39 road (Wells to Glastonbury) was quickly sold off and fenced in, whilst at West Pennard the station site was purchased by a local firm who used the goods shed and station for storage and the stationmaster's house as a dwelling. The rather awkward skew bridge, S&D No. 257 West Pennard Bridge, that took the Glastonbury to Shepton Mallet road over the

Glastonbury station site in April 1993 from the location of the station footbridge looking west.
Andy Read

Pylle station building in May 1992, since when the station has been converted into a private dwelling and extended.

railway just to the east of West Pennard station was demolished during the early 1970s. During 1992 West Pennard station was converted into a two storey house. This work required an altered roof line to accommodate the upstairs rooms, also the east end chimney stack was removed as it had become unsafe. The stationmaster's house was still occupied in 1993.

At Pylle station the goods shed roof had fallen in some years before closure (possibly as a result of a fire) although in recent years it has been used as a meat packaging depot, with the result that it was extended across the trackbed. Early in 1994 the goods shed was converted into a five-bedroom house. The adjoining stationmaster's house remains in private occupation. During 1968 and 1969 spoil was tipped into the cutting alongside the adjacent road bridge, S&D No. 243 Pylle Station Bridge, which was eventually demolished, the road then being straightened and widened. The Pylle station buildings still remain and were origi-

nally scheduled to be converted into a new premises for the nearby Fir Tree transport cafe. This was planned in 1971 but was never carried out. However, 20 years on Pylle station was converted into a house with an extension of matching stone and slate roof that looks most appropriate for this fine little station which is now called Tickets.

The remaining trackbed east towards Evercreech Junction North has either been taken over by farmers for grazing land and farm tracks or just taken back by Mother nature. On the main branch line no less than 41 bridges and culverts still remain out of 66 constructed, whilst the fate of twelve is unknown at the time of writing.

The Main Line – Bath to Bournemouth in 1966
Before taking a walk down the main line today, to help get one's bearings let's travel the line in 1966, by train, from Bath (Green Park) station to Bournemouth Central station.

M Ch	
10.54	Bath (Green Park) station. The connections in the station are controlled by three ground frames, Bath arrivals right, Bath departures left; and Bath carriage sidings near the stop blocks. There are two platforms with two carriage sidings between them. On the down platform is a bonded store. While the main station offices are beyond the stop blocks. As we depart the station we pass over the River Avon.
10.14	MR bridge No. 44 River Avon.
9.76	Bath station signalbox, left. Opposite the two motive power depots. Bath Midland Bridge yard is to the left, and note steam crane on its own track. Just beyond to the right is the Bath Gas Works sidings.
9.49	Bath Junction signalbox, right, as we fork off onto the S&DJR line which immediately begins a 180 degree curve out of Bath. The connection here was formerly controlled by two signalboxes – Bath Junction and Bath Single Line Junction.
0.13½	S&D bridge No. 1 Twerton Viaduct (79 yds) at the site of Bath Single Line Junction signalbox, right. There was a ticket platform for up trains hereabouts.
0.31	S&D bridge No. 3 Great Western Railway Viaduct. The line is now well into its long climb up to Devonshire Tunnel.
0.40	Location of May's siding for the Victoria Brick & Tile Company, right.
0.66	At the Co-operative Society ground frame, left, there is a facing connection to the Bath Co-operative Society's single siding.
1.32	S&D bridge No. 10 Devonshire Tunnel (447 yds) followed by Lyncombe Vale.
2.02	S&D bridge No. 15 Combe Down Tunnel (1,829 yds) followed by Horsecombe Vale.
3.21	S&D bridge No. 16 Tucking Mill Viaduct (95 yds) eight arches.
3.51	Midford 'A' ground frame, right, Midford goods yard, left.
3.67	Midford station, consisting of a single platform and a simple wooden structure. Note unique backing signal, with its arm like a flattened X mid-way along the platform. South end is Midford signalbox, right.
3.72	S&D bridge No. 18 Midford Viaduct (170 yds) eight arches. Double track commences just to the south of the viaduct.
5.72½	S&D bridge No. 22 Wellow Viaduct (51 yds) four arches.

Wellow station looking south from the up platform in April 1966.

Michael Gates

Shoscombe & Single Hill halt looking north from the down platform.

Midsomer Norton station looking south from the up platform.

Chilcompton station looking south from the up platform.

Binegar station looking north from the down line.

Masbury halt looking north from the down platform in early May 1968.

Michael Gates

6.14   Wellow signalbox, left, before running into the station; main structure right. The goods yard sidings, right, were controlled by a ground frame.

8.05   Shoscombe & Single Hill Halt, consisting of two concrete platforms only.

8.37   S&D bridge No. 31 Home Farm Viaduct (48 yds) seven arches. We then pass the site of Foxcote signalbox, right, which controlled Braysdown Colliery sidings before Writhlington signalbox was opened.

8.49   Paglinch Crossing.

9.08   Writhlington Colliery siding, left, before passing Writhlington signalbox (formerly called Braysdown). Connections diverge left to Writhlington Colliery. Braysdown Colliery sidings were right.

9.73   A shunting spur and colliery spoil, left, mark the approach to Radstock. Connections to Ludlow Colliery, left, were controlled by Radstock North 'A' signalbox, left. Tyning Incline, a colliery line formerly crossed the line here to reach Tyning Colliery, right. Radstock motive power depot and goods yards are both left.

10.10   Radstock North station, main structures right.

10.14   Radstock North (formerly 'B') signalbox is left, before the level crossing.

10.16   A branch to Middle Pit and Clandown Collieries (44 Ch) right. The line now starts the long drag to Masbury summit with little respite.

10.56   S&D bridge No. 44 North Somerset Viaduct (128 yds) five arches, over the GWR Bristol & North Somerset line and the SCC tramway to Welton. The line is on a high embankment until Norton Hill Colliery sidings.

11.69   Norton Hill Colliery and ground frame controlling the connection, left.

12.00   Midsomer Norton station. Main structure left. Signalbox right, while the goods shed and sidings are left.

13.12   S&D bridge No. 49 Chilcompton Tunnels (separate 64 yd bores).

13.79   Chilcompton station main structure is on the down platform, left. The signalbox was right. The goods yard and sidings used by New Rock Colliery were left.

15.15   Moorewood signalbox is right. The Roads Reconstruction sidings, left, have been lifted.

15.24   Emborough stone works sidings are right.

15.41   S&D bridge No. 61 Nettlebridge Viaduct (67 yds) six arches.

16.38   Approaching Binegar, Roads Reconstruction quarry sidings are left.

16.46   Binegar station, main structures left and signalbox right. Only two sidings and the refuge remain in the goods yard, left. A 3ft gauge line transported barrels of stout from Oakhill Brewery, away left, for transshipment here.

17.55   Masbury Summit (811 feet above sea level). The next eight miles are all down hill to Evercreech Junction.

18.09   Masbury Halt. The main structures and site of demolished signalbox are on the up platform, right. The goods yard was also right. There were formerly private sidings, left, for the Mendipadam stone works and the War Department.

19.27   S&D bridge No. 75 Ham Wood Viaduct (78 yds) six arches. Winsor Hill quarry sidings formerly left. Ham Wood quarry siding in situ, right. The long closed Winsor Hill signalbox is right, between the tracks.

19.52   Entering the single track Winsor Hill 'old tunnel' (239 yds). The up line uses the shorter 'new tunnel' (126 yds).

19.74   Site of Downside quarry siding, left.

20.25   S&D bridge No. 81 Bath Road Viaduct (118 yds) six arches.

20.75   S&D bridge No. 84 Charlton Road Viaduct (310 yds) 27 arches.

21.26   We enter Shepton Mallet (Charlton Road) station; the signalbox is on the down platform, left. There is a siding behind this platform. The main structure is on the up platform, right, as is the goods yard and shed. We pass under the GWR Witham–Cheddar branch. The line now passes into the long deep Cannards Grave cutting which contains four over bridges.

21.51   Cannards Grave.

22.75   S&D bridge No. 95 Prestleigh Viaduct (121 yds) eleven arches.

Evercreech Junction station up platform buildings, looking north.

Cole station looking south from the up platform.

Wincanton station looking north from the south end of the station.

Templecombe depot and Lower yard, looking north, September 1966.

Templecombe Lower halt, looking south through bridge No. 152.

Henstridge station, looking north.

24.30 The goods shed siding (down side, left) and Evercreech L&S Co. siding up side, right, have been removed at Evercreech New station. The signalbox – which was on the up platform – has been demolished. Main structures on down platform, left.

25.12 S&D bridge No. 105 Pecking Mill Viaduct (60 yds) five arches.

25.49 Evercreech Junction. Rounding a sweeping left hand curve the Burnham branch (via Highbridge and Glastonbury) will be seen away right. Just after Evercreech Junction North signalbox, right, the Burnham branch trails into Evercreech North yard (partially removed) right. The goods shed and station yard are behind the down platform, left.

25.73 Evercreech Junction station. Main structures are on the down platform. Evercreech Junction South signalbox is between the station footbridge and the road level crossing, right. The line runs straight now for over a mile towards Wyke Champflower.

26.63 Lamyatt road level crossing – cottage right, before the crossing.

27.11 Bruton road level crossing – cottage right, before the crossing.

27.76 Note the location of the abandoned facing junction with the GWR, curving away right.

28.35 We cross the wrought iron S&D bridge No. 118 Great Western Bridge over the West of England main line, the other end of the spur to the S&D will be seen right.

28.42 Crossing S&D bridge No. 119 Cole Viaduct (62 yds) five arches over the River Brue and a road to Bruton.

28.50 Rattling over S&D bridge No. 120 Castle Cary Road Bridge we enter Cole station, the main structure is left. The signalbox – now demolished – was on the up side far end of the station; although the sidings, left, remain in situ, the connection to the running line has been removed.

28.79 S&D bridge No. 122 Pitcombe Viaduct (60 yds) three arches.

32.76 Having passed through Horsington on a long high embankment we arrive at Wincanton station which has staggered platforms. The main structure is left, while the signalbox is opposite the goods shed on the up platform, right.

34.75 Cheriton crossing.

35.56 We pass the site of Templecombe No. 3 Junction signalbox, right, – closed 12/2/33 – before Horsington level crossing. The crossing ground frame is right, beyond the crossing. There is a facing connection down to the Lower Yard and locomotive depot. As we climb slightly, the line to the Lower Yard, left – on the site of the original alignment – becomes double track as far as Templecombe Junction signalbox.

36.11 Templecombe Junction signalbox (formerly No. 2 Junction) – left, between the main and Lower Yard lines – is adjacent to the junction of the single track to Henstridge and double LSWR line to Templecombe Upper station (which we now traverse). Returning to single track we commence south towards Henstridge.

36.38 To the left are Templecombe depot and the Dorset Central Railway station buildings. The two sidings, left, are on the site of the original platform loop. This originally being controlled by Templecombe No. 1 signalbox, which was just beyond S&D bridge No. 152. There is now no connection to the Lower yard. Between S&D bridge No. 152 and 153 is Templecombe Lower halt, right.

37.12 Common Lane level crossing – cottage right after the crossing.

37.51 Park Lane level crossing.

38.27 Before passing Henstridge station, structure and platform right, note the location of the sidings, right, formerly controlled by a ground frame.

38.29 Just south of Henstridge station we pass over Plott Lane level crossing.

38.44 Marsh Lane level crossing – cottage right after the crossing.

38.61 South Mead crossing.

38.78 We pass from Somerset into Dorset at S&D bridge No. 161 Landshire bridge.

39.45 Drew's Lane crossing.

39.58 The siding, right, which formerly connected with the up loop at Stalbridge was controlled by a ground frame.

39.68 We enter Stalbridge station with the main structures on the up platform, right. Stalbridge signalbox is right, at the end of the up platform just before the road level crossing.

41.53 We cross S&D bridge No. 167 River Lyddon Bridge over the River Lyddon.

Stalbridge station, looking north from the road level crossing.

Sturminster Newton station, looking north from the down platform.

Shillingstone station looking south.

Stourpaine & Durweston halt, looking north.

Blandford Forum station, looking south in October 1966.

Michael Gates

Bailey Gate station, looking north from the up platform.

43.36   Then the S&D bridge No. 171 Sturminster River Bridge over the River Stour. Then through a deep narrow cutting to Sturminster Newton.

43.60   As we enter Sturminster Newton station crossing loop, the water tower is right; there is a connection to the goods shed road behind the down platform, left. The main station structure is on the up platform, right, whilst the signalbox is at the far end of the up platform.

44.49   Crossing the River Stour by S&D bridge No. 175 Fiddleford Mill Bridge.

45.06   Fiddleford crossing.

46.68   The goods yard at Shillingstone station, right, before the signalbox, has been lifted as have the two sidings on the down side, left, before and after the station. The main structures are on the up platform.

48.36½   We pass through the deep Cliff cutting and under S&D bridge No. 184.

48.70   Passing once more over the River Stour on S&D bridge No. 185 Hodmoor Bridge just before the site of Stourpaine loop, closed 18/12/51, and signalbox which closed 24/9/25 becoming a ground frame. All of which were formerly left.

49.53   Stourpaine & Durweston halt, left.

51.60   Mill Dam crossing.

52.25   There is a connection to the goods shed road, left, as we enter Blandford Forum station loop. The signalbox is above the down platform, left, behind which is the goods yard. The main station structures are on the up platform right. Note short up side siding still in situ.

52.46   For the last time we cross the River Stour via S&D bridge No. 198 River Stour Bridge.

54.01   Beyond the third overbridge from Blandford, the platforms of the closed Charlton Marshall Halt are extant left and right. The nameboards are still standing.

55.49   We pass by the platforms of the former Spetisbury Halt. The main structures on the down platform, left, have long since been demolished.

56.75   Cliff crossing.

57.09   We pass over the busy A371 road on S&D bridge No. 217 Cliff Road Bridge.

57.37   Green Lane crossing

58.33   The goods yard at Bailey Gate station – left behind the down platform – is disused. The connections to the milk factory, also left, opposite the signalbox are in use. Station structures are also left.

59.63   Bailey Gate crossing (not a block post) is left, after the road level crossing. The site of Admiralty siding is left, beyond the crossing, the siding was controlled by a ground frame.

60.18   Corfe Mullen Junction signalbox, right, before the road level crossing and before the facing junction for the single line to Broadstone, right. The original route to Wimborne is left, latterly this has only served Carter's Clay Pit siding and the track is now very overgrown.

61.40   Beyond the third overbridge is the site of Corfe Mullen Halt, right.

63.06   We now drop down to trail into the double-track LSWR line, now a freight only line from Broadstone to Ringwood. At Broadstone Junction signalbox, left, we immediately diverge left on to the Poole line. We are now travelling in the up direction.

1.23   Creekmoor Halt.

2.73   At Holes Bay Junction (now controlled from Poole 'B' signalbox) the LSWR link from Hamworthy Junction trails in right, the signalbox was situated in the junction fork.

3.34   Poole 'B' signalbox (formerly West signalbox) is on the down platform, right, at Poole station. At the far end is a road level crossing and Poole 'A' signalbox (formerly 'A' signalbox) also right.

5.20   Parkstone station.

6.45   Branksome station. Branksome signalbox is left, at the junction where the direct line to Bournemouth West diverges right.

6.70   At Gas Works Junction signalbox, right, the line from Bournemouth West used to trail in right.

9.01   Train terminates at Bournemouth Central station as the old S&D terminal of Bournemouth West had closed the previous year.

The Main Line – Bath to Bournemouth today …
Whilst disposal of property was underway on the branch lines a similar fate was taking place on the main line. Bath (Green Park) station became a target for hopeful preservation on architectural grounds and as such was granted listed status. Initially the hopes of saving it were not good as Bath City planners proposed major road improvements through the site once BR abandoned its use of Midland Bridge Goods Yard. This occurred in May 1971 with the last remnants of track being removed by the end of 1972.

In the meantime, BR allowed Bath City Council to make use of the station as a temporary car park in December 1967. In the following year the City Council purchased the site, tarmacked the entire area and made it into a more permanent car park. By now a listed building, it could not be demolished easily, so much soul-searching went into the future uses and this would form a complete book in its own right. Meanwhile, it became more and more dilapidated and by 1974 was looking somewhat forlorn, temporary repairs were authorised by the City Council architect until its fate was finally decided. It would take another five years before this important decision was made in the form of leasing the site to J. Sainsbury for a supermarket and car park, but only after they paid for the restoration of the station building. £1,500,000 later, on 1st December 1982 the restored Bath (Green Park) station was opened by HRH Princess Margaret. The sta-

tion continues to be maintained, having received a fresh coat of paint in 1991.

One of the two wrought iron bridges over the River Avon, just off the platform ends, was removed during the first week of January 1968 for further use elsewhere (location unknown). The remaining bridge still survives in use in conjunction with the Sainsbury's store complex and car park which now occupies the train shed and platform area.

Bath (Green Park) S&DJR locomotive depot and the complete depot site was raised to the ground between October 1966 and May 1967, together with the coaling stage, water cranes and all associated depot buildings. The Midland Railway locomotive depot was not demolished at this time and was still standing in May 1972, its date of demolition is unknown. On 17th December work commenced on the demolition of the Bath station signalbox. The S&DJR depot site was redeveloped by Stothert & Pitt in April 1968, and they ceased business in 1989. The Stothert & Pitt's site is now up for sale which implies further redevelopment of this area. Some short lengths of rail from the works sidings and four wagon bodies remained at the time the site was cleared as reminders of the area's recent past. The low Midland Railway bridge No. 43 Victoria Road Bridge was demolished shortly after track lifting as it impeded the passage of lorries.

The 'Red Bridge' over the Lower Bristol road, better known as S&D Bridge No. 1 Twerton

Bath (Green Park) station in 1967 after purchase by Bath City Council for use as a car park, as can be seen, the ballast was soon replaced by tarmac.

Mike Ware

Bath (Green Park) station in 1989 as a car park for the local Sainsbury's supermarket after they had restored the station buildings.

The former S&DJR and MR motive power depot site had been used by Stothert & Pitt's engineering works until they closed in 1989. The site has since been redeveloped as can be seen in this 1990 view.
Mike Ware

Viaduct, a short distance from Bath Junction on the S&DJR proper, was removed on 4th May 1969. After the closure of the remaining section of line up to Twerton Co-op siding on 3rd November 1967 the removal of the iron work across the road allowed improvements to a dangerous location on the busy Bath to Bristol main road. The abutments and embankments were removed over the next few years. Although the original demolition only involved the iron work it did provoke a bizarre letter to the *Railway Magazine* of September 1969. Headed "Vandalism at Bath":

"Apart from the emotional attitude engendered by this act of wanton public vandalism, the destruction of routeways through our already overcrowded towns is surely atrociously short-sighted.

However long it takes us to realise our mistake in scrapping rail services does not matter half as much as annihilating for all time the means of restoring them. The more routeways that are destroyed now, the greater will be the economic and human cost in restoring them when the time comes, as it surely will, to scrap the motor car."

The trackbed up to Devonshire Tunnel lay derelict whilst plans were being formulated by Bath City Council. The portals of both tunnels would in time be sealed to prevent walkers and local children using them. It would take several attempts to achieve this objective and even today it is possible to enter both tunnels via their south portals which have inspection doors built into the steel plated portions that seal the portals.

Bath City Council purchased Bath bank and Devonshire Tunnel in 1972 to allow them to demolish S&D bridge No. 4 Victoria Brick Company Bridge, and No. 6 Monksdale Bridge, in 1973 as part of their road improvements policy. Then the trackbed from Bellotts Road to Devonshire Tunnel became a 'Linear Park' but with those two under bridges having been demolished much of Bath bank's character had been destroyed. During 1990 and the early part of 1991 S&D bridge No. 8 Englishcombe Bridge, was totally restored, looking now as it must have when constructed in 1873. The deep cutting just before trains dived into Devonshire Tunnel has been infilled along with much back-filling to seal the tunnel portal, making it difficult to recognise now as the 'old' Devonshire bank. The tunnel having been bricked up and back-filled with earth on the north side now forms a very secure shelter in an emergency. Access is now gained through a roof mounted man-hole just above the north portal and Bath City fire service use it to train for sewer rescues. The short section of trackbed in Lyncombe Vale, between the tunnels, is also owned by Bath City Council and has been designated a public walkway.

The north portal of Combe Down Tunnel has been sealed with breeze blocks and iron plates and the south portal with iron plates and an inspection door, which has been forced open in recent years.

Combe Down Tunnel is now owned by the Wessex Water Authority who have no intentions to use it for anything at this time. The land forming Horsecombe Vale was for many years used as a paddock for horses, but was sold at auction late in 1992.

Majestic as the day it was built, Tucking Mill Viaduct towers over all that it surveys, owned until early 1992 by BR, it is now in private hands along with Midford Viaduct. It had been threatened with demolition – but let's hope it never comes to that though expensive repair work is needed to secure its long-term future, as the structure is showing the first signs of the condition that caused the demise of Prestleigh Viaduct. These are cracks in the arches and slight bulging of the piers caused by plant roots letting water and frost into the masonry. The trackbed round to Midford station is overgrown and has areas of rough coppice growing through the ballast.

Midford signalbox was gutted but its empty shell remained when the complete station site was cleared during December 1967 as part of the track lifting contract. The wooden station structure was simply burnt to the ground and the brick back wall of the building was then pushed over to lay against the bank. The shell of the signalbox was finally demolished during the summer of 1968. The wooden remains were knocked down by a bulldozer and then pushed down the bank into the formation of the Somersetshire Coal Canal. In early 1985 a railway almost returned to Midford, in the form of a

The view north from the gutted remains of Midford signal box along the station, showing what remained of the burnt and demolished station buildings in late 1967. The contractors continued to use the trackbed to Combe Down Tunnel as a private road until June 1968.

Mike Ware

The demolition of bridge No. 6, Monksdale Road Bridge in early 1973.

Mike Ware

narrow gauge line. The station area had been cleared of undergrowth and track was being laid towards Tucking Mill and was to have been known as the Tucking Mill Tramway. The group responsible for this undertaking had to vacate the site as the work required planning consent and BR wished to sell not rent the site. The track had been removed by the end of the summer of 1986.

During the 1980s the site occupied by Midford signalbox was fenced off by the local public house

for use as a private car park. The Midford station to Long Arch bridge section was auctioned-off during February 1990. Since then the station site has been transformed with a new platform surface and the trackbed has a fresh covering of ballast as a prelude to the hopeful restoration of all the station buildings and re-laying of track to form a heritage centre.

Midford Viaduct is in good condition having only a light covering of plants on the trackbed and at this time no worrying cracks in the piers, and this viaduct still dominates the tiny village of Midford. Following the trackbed from Midford to Wellow is surprisingly easy as it is mostly clear of heavy undergrowth, which is probably due to the fact that much is used as farm tracks and all the bridges are intact between Midford and Wellow.

Wellow station escaped demolition, although S&D bridge No. 23 Wellow Bridge just to the north of the signalbox did not. Even before the track was lifted in early November 1967, it was announced in the July that the London artist Peter Blake had received planning permission to convert the main station building into a country retreat. It was stated that the building would not be greatly altered except for the addition of a living room, kitchenette and a bathroom. Mr Blake also had the signalbox converted into a studio. The down platform shelter was removed but the repainting of the signalbox, railings and a hut on the up platform had been completed by the summer of 1968. At the same time the trackbed between the platforms was infilled and

Midford station looking north in 1991, after the site had been cleared, the platform resurfaced and the ballast renewed by the Somerset Railway & Industrial Heritage Trust.

Wellow station in December 1967 just after track lifting was completed and before the new owner converted the station into a house.

Mike Ware

Wellow station, looking north in 1990 after conversion into a private dwelling.

Kevin Regan

Radstock North station site in 1990 looking south from the location of bridge No. 38.   *Kevin Regan*

seeded to form a lawn. Wellow signalbox still remains in 1995, the only S&DJR signalbox to survive in its correct location and was up for sale at the reasonable price of just £30,000! The route of the line is quite a problem to follow from Wellow on to Shoscombe as a great deal of the trackbed has been obliterated and returned to farm land, also two bridges have been demolished.

The road bridge, S&D No. 29 Single Hill Bridge under the line to the north of Shoscombe & Single Hill halt was demolished in 1971, at the same time as the halt's waiting rooms and lamp hut. The platform's concrete decking was removed from its precast concrete supports in 1972. By 1985 these supports had also been removed, the area then becoming a paddock for a child's pony, after which it became a garden for a new house. Just to the south the line is clear through Foxcote. On the way down to Writhlington one finds that Paglinch Farm now covers the line. At Writhlington the signalbox was taken down soon after closure. The trackbed through Writhlington Colliery yard and down to the outskirts of Radstock should be easy to follow, since the track was only lifted 19 years ago, if not for the fact that it was used as a private road to clear the slag heaps at Writhlington. Once these slag heaps had been removed the land from Writhlington to Radstock was sold at auction. On the approach to Radstock housing now covers the Tyning area and the former goods yard just to the north of Radstock North station is an industrial estate.

On 27th May 1967, work commenced on the dismantling of the down platform shelter at Radstock North station. On 17th June the demolition of Radstock North signalbox commenced, formerly the 'B' box and this work had been completed by the beginning of July 1967. It was reported at the time that both these buildings had been privately purchased, but then nothing more was heard of them so one must presume they were purchased for their scrap wood value. Further demolition started in November 1969 at Radstock North included a short length of track on the up main line, from the point where the track lifting had ceased adjacent to the temporary spur onto the Bristol & North Somerset line, past the site of the Clandown branch junction to the level crossing gates about 200 yards in length. This work was the continuation of the track lifting from Midsomer Norton to Radstock earlier in the year. At the same time the coal hoist behind the locomotive depot, the ambulance hut, the large water tower, an office building in the goods yard and several other smaller structures were all demolished.

The main station buildings were retained and rented to the Somerset & Dorset Railway Circle at the end of 1969. The Circle would subsequently repair and re-paint all of the station buildings. The remaining mile or so of double track between Radstock North station yard and Writhlington Colliery yard was singled in June 1970 by the removal of the up main line together with the removal of the coaling sidings behind the locomotive shed and two of the goods yard sidings. Nothing remains of Radstock North station, the buildings having been demolished in 1979 and 1980. The site has since been grassed over and used in part as a car park.

Ironically much of the track on the Clandown branch and the whole of the layout of sidings serving the screens at Middle Pit Colliery could still be seen at the end of 1969. Further up the branch the course of the line had become a footpath and a fair amount of the track was easily visible, finally end-

ing about 200 yards from the foot of the old incline up to Clandown Colliery. The incline was still visible, the last few yards at the bottom being incorporated into the garden of an adjacent house as an extension of their lawn.

The trackbed could only be walked from Radstock as far as S&D bridge No. 44 North Somerset Viaduct as access was precluded by brickwalls across the trackbed on both sides. The condition of this structure had deteriorated greatly over the past few years and may well have necessitated its demolition on safety grounds. Fortunately this

Midsomer Norton station, looking north from the up platform in 1990. This is one of the few S&DJR stations to remain almost intact, with only the demise of the signalbox in the mid-1970s and this was on safety grounds.

Andy Read

The clearly defined trackbed just south of Chilcompton Tunnel in 1990, looking north towards the tunnel.

Andy Read

was not the case as Radstock Town Council – who own the viaduct – undertook major renovation work early in 1993 and re-opened it as part of a Linear Park between Radstock and Midsomer Norton. Progress is however hindered by the removal of S&D bridge No. 46 Welton Road Bridge which was demolished in 1982 to allow much needed road widening. In late 1969 a similar fate had befallen S&D bridge No. 48 Silver Street Bridge, just to the north of Midsomer Norton station.

The wrought iron superstructure of bridge No. 48 carrying the line across Silver Street was removed during November 1969. In late 1970 the embankment between the end of the station platforms and the bridge parapet was removed and the area was landscaped and a white fence erected. The removed earth was then used to infill between the platforms. At the same time the embankment to the north of Silver Street Bridge was removed back to the entrance of Norton Hill Colliery and landscaped over. Demolition of Midsomer Norton's station buildings, signalbox and goods shed was stopped in June 1968. Firstly when the demolition contract from Blandford to Radstock was terminated by BR after the Bristol & North Somerset line was washed out due to a storm. Then the local Somervale Secondary School decided they could make good use of the premises. Somerset County Council purchased the complete site but little use was made of the station buildings, although a coat of paint had been applied by January 1970.

In the late 1970s the signalbox was demolished on the grounds that it had become unsafe due to the poor condition of its timber structure, at this time the infilling was removed from between the platforms. In 1988 the station continued to receive preventive maintenance and sported a reclad slate roof and rebuilt chimney stack. During 1991 the exterior of the road side of the station building was restored, along with some work on the interior, and it is hoped that a similar restoration is carried out on the platform side of this building. Both platforms have had work carried out on them and some edging stones have been replaced. The up platform waiting shelter has been partly restored and some new fencing has been erected, and although there is no sign of the signalbox, the foundations of stone still remain. The up starter signal remained at 'danger' whilst becoming entwined with wild roses until 1975 when it disappeared one night! The former goods shed is now used by the local adult education group for various classes. In 1995 the station site is under threat of re-development for housing.

From Midsomer Norton station one can follow the trackbed some distance, but the deep Chilcompton Tunnel cutting has been completely infilled and returned to pasture land again, just as if the railway had never passed this way at all. Chilcompton Tunnel itself is blocked off on the cutting side by the infilling and the two bores used for a farmer's store and a local rifle club range in the other. The trackbed round to Chilcompton station is clear and easy to walk with the exception of the cutting in which S&D bridge No. 52 Baker Robinson Bridge stands, this has been partially infilled and is very overgrown although the bridge is intact. South of this bridge the trackbed now forms part of several gardens.

Chilcompton station site in 1989, looking south.

Binegar station looking north in 1990 after the construction of two houses on the trackbed beside bridge No. 65.

Andy Read

Everything at Chilcompton station, including much of the up platform and some of the down, was demolished at the time of track lifting. The goods yard still remained in use for coal distribution by a local coal merchant, and a timber merchant had made use of the remaining site. Since demolition of Chilcompton's station buildings the site has always had a variety of derelict lorries occupying parts of it. In October 1989 no less than ten refuse collection lorries were there. S&D Bridge No. 53 is most unusual as it has been enlarged no less than three times. It is only wide enough for a cow to pass through on the down side but is wide enough for a lorry on the up side. Can this really account for the three tank traps installed in the bridge during World War II? During the early part of 1991 the complete site at Chilcompton station was being prepared for redevelopment.

The route of the line through to Moorewood and Binegar is reasonably easy to follow, once past the impenetrable undergrowth just to the south of Chilcompton station. Six bridges have been demolished in the two and a half miles to Binegar station. Just before the location of S&D bridge No. 57 Burnthouse Bridge, a recycling plant has been constructed on the trackbed and just beyond this the down line has become part of a paddock. To the south of bridge No. 57 as far as the location of bridge No. 58 Coal Lane Bridge, the slight embankment has been removed and is now grazing pasture. The impression of the siding at Moorewood on the down side can still be seen more than 25 years after the sidings were lifted. There is a total lack of

access to the Emborough stone works site which impedes any chance of viewing Nettlebridge Viaduct. This structure is still standing and is maintained by the owners in superb condition. The trackbed for almost half a mile through the site is clear and level with a good covering of ballast under foot. The gateposts into the Emborough stone works sidings are still standing. These sidings were lifted in 1969 by the current owners and donated by them to a preserved railway, but unfortunately the neatly stacked track was stolen the night before the benefactors were due to collect it.

Nothing remains at Binegar station except part of a platform, all of the station buildings and the signalbox being demolished at the time of track lifting in May 1968. The goods yard continues to be used for local coal distribution, though this may now have ceased. S&D Bridge No. 65 Binegar Station Bridge, just to the north of the station has been removed, only the north abutment remains.

In 1989 two houses were being constructed on the station site, one across the trackbed facing towards Moorewood, the other parallel to the trackbed with the study on the site of the signalbox. According to the owner (who is a local farmer) his new farm house is to be called Beeching's Revenge. At the former goods yard site development is underway for the construction of more farm buildings. After an easy walk from Binegar, with only two over bridges demolished, we reach Masbury Halt. One of the missing bridges being the well known S&D bridge No. 69 Masbury Oakhill Road Bridge, at the summit, which was

Masbury station building in April 1992. Still sound but in need of restoration if it is to survive for many more years. With the exception of the signalbox and down platform shelter Masbury is totally intact.

Andy Read

Winsor Hill Tunnel in 1990. This is the shorter new tunnel constructed for the up line, looking south through the bore.

Andy Read

removed because the ironwork had become unsafe by the early 1970s.

Only the down platform shelter and signalbox at Masbury Halt were removed. The station building has been extended along the platform by Mr Wilfred Couling who has lived there since 1954. The original station building is in need of some restoration work but is basically sound and original. A railway atmosphere still lingers at Masbury Halt. The trackbed is now occupied by a variety of trees planted by Wilfred over the years. Masbury is one of the few S&DJR stations to still have both its platforms totally intact and in good condition. A lot of the trackbed either side of the station and over the summit has been taken back by local farmers, both for farm tracks and pasture land.

The trackbed is easy to follow from Masbury to Winsor Hill Tunnels with only two under bridges missing though most of the land is privately owned. Just to the north of Winsor Hill Tunnels stands S&D bridge No. 75 Ham Wood Viaduct, hiding in a disused tree filled quarry safe from cameras. A close inspection shows this viaduct to be in very good condition, no doubt a side effect of the protection given by the trees against icy wind and rain. Unlike many other S&DJR viaducts Ham Wood does not suffer with trees and large bushes growing on top and its original construction appears to have been of a far higher standard than other viaducts on the line. The down side parapet wall has suffered at the hands of both vandals and BR, who have used concrete blocks rather than local limestone to repair the damage.

Winsor Hill down bore had massive steel doors fitted to it by Rolls-Royce in 1968, which were intended to allow the company to test an Olympus jet engine for Concorde to destruction. The engine was to be run without oil. The experts said it would explode within 20 minutes; as things turned out it ran for two hours and then... After the test (or tests) Rolls-Royce found another use for the tunnel. A small notice on the door stated, 'Danger Keep Out Possible Contamination from radioactive oil. Rolls-Royce (1971) Limited'. The tunnel lining may keep low level radioactivity at bay, but what of the porous Mendips limestone under the tunnel which is riddled with caves? Events at Winsor Hill Tunnels do not end there. In 1981 planning permission was granted by Mendip District Council to the London based Stronghold Engineering & Construction Company for it to build nuclear war shelters in the two tunnels (what would they do with the radioactive oil?). This was to have been the pilot project, to

research and demonstrate the problems of nuclear protection. The work was to have taken five to seven years, but nothing came of the project. In October 1990 a surprised group of walkers found the iron doors on the down tunnel had been removed, but why and by whom? Both tunnels remain in good condition and are basically dry inside. Though Mother nature is encroaching ever more with each passing year on the tunnel portals.

In early 1992 Ham Wood Viaduct, Winsor Hill Tunnels and the trackbed south were sold by BR and the new owner intends them to form a central attraction in a wildlife sanctuary and park. During April 1992 S&D bridge No. 78 Ham Lane Bridge, was demolished, the masonry from the two abutments being heaped on the wide approach to the tunnels. The ironwork across the lane had appeared to be in good condition with no problems. With the bridge gone the embankments on each side have been cut back and gently sloped. This was also the last wrought iron girdered under bridge to survive on the S&DJR main line, most being removed soon after track lifting for their scrap metal value.

The pleasant walk from Winsor Hill to Shepton Mallet station takes you over S&D bridge No. 81 Bath Road Viaduct which has had an interesting history, not least when the 1892 constructed up side collapsed at 10.55pm on 1st February 1946. It is once again the up side portion of this viaduct that threatens its future. When reconstructed in 1947 the builders forgot to include a membrane to protect the piers and arches from rain and frost. As a result the condition of this viaduct is giving concern. Repair costs are estimated at £300,000, of which £100,000 is being offered by BR. This is also the cost of demolition so either way, BR may be paying out £100,000 on this structure in the near future. Mendip District Council are keen to see their local heritage preserved and is working with interested parties to hopefully preserve this structure.

Half a mile south we should reach S&D bridge No. 83 Kilver Street Bridge, over the busy A37 road but this was an early casualty, removed due to the need to widen this busy road in 1969. Strangely the tiny Kilver Street Footpath is still standing a few hundred yards to the north of bridge No. 83, though very overgrown.

The fate of the next structure along the line was rather more unusual, this being the superb 27-arch Charlton Road Viaduct. Built on a sweeping curve and with a change from a falling gradient of 1 in 55 to a rising gradient of 1 in 66 mid-way across just prior to Shepton Mallet station. The BR Estates

Department must have been particularly pleased when, during 1971, Showerings, the 'Babycham' soft drinks manufacturers situated nearby to the viaduct, decided they would purchase it. Below the viaduct at the northern end, Showerings had restored an old landscaped garden which visitors to their extensive bottling and manufacturing plant were taken to sample the local product after the visit, weather permitting. The garden with viaduct as a natural backdrop blended together to form a very pleasant setting which the company did not wish to disturb. Negotiations with BR proved that they were only too pleased to dispose of this liability which was accordingly transferred into Showerings' name for the nominal fee of £5!, plus of course legal fees.

Since this transaction Showerings have spent over £40,000 on maintenance and improvements to the viaduct, including the laying of a waterproof top surface. In the past couple of years Showerings have been taken over by another company that wishes to dispose of the viaduct or gardens. It must be hoped that the future of this important and beautiful structure can be secured before its condition deteriorates. Towards Shepton Mallet station the factory and distribution warehouses occupies the trackbed.

At Shepton Mallet station the signalbox, water tower, footbridge and former signal depot huts were all demolished in mid-1968, all the remaining buildings following at a later date (or dates). In February 1969 the land on which the station and former S&DJR signal department had stood, a total of 13 acres, was put up for sale. By August 1972 all that remained at Shepton Mallet were the two platforms. The site is now occupied by business properties and car parking facilities. Moving south from Shepton Mallet as far as Prestleigh Viaduct the trackbed has now almost all been totally obliterated with infilling and bridge demolitions. Between S&D bridge No. 84 Charlton Road Viaduct and No. 95 Prestleigh Viaduct a distance of exactly two miles, only one bridge remains. This is S&D bridge No. 87 GWR Bridge which carried the former Great Western branch line from Witham to Yatton until closure in September 1969. This bridge and the former S&DJR trackbed is now used by a builder's merchant.

A strange twist of fate at Cannards Grave found the 40-acre site being purchased back from British Railways by the same farming family who had sold the land 100 years previously to the Somerset & Dorset Railway. Amazingly, it took longer to fill the

cutting in with lorry and bulldozer, than men with pick, shovel and wheelbarrow took to dig it out in the 1870s! Three over bridges are now buried in what was Cannards Grave and just to the south, S&D bridge No. 92 Whitstone Lane Bridge, has also been infilled with only the top of the parapet walls to mark its location.

Moving on a mile or so one reaches the site of Prestleigh Viaduct, which from a distance looked as fine as the day it was constructed. This was true of the original up side whilst the newer down side had been deteriorating rapidly over the last five years or so. By 1991 the piers were starting to show a great many cracks in the brickwork, particularly on the outer edge and corners. Two piers were affected by bulging brickwork caused by trees growing on top of the viaduct, the roots of which allowed water access to the arches and piers, this in turn would freeze in the winter months. With the continued expansion and contraction of this water the brickwork started to crack which then allowed more water to get in. The bulging brickwork was on the piers faced with brick when the viaduct was doubled in 1887 and was caused by water getting between the original limestone and the brick facing.

The condition of the viaduct was considered to be 'likely to became dangerous soon' in late 1991 and by mid-1992 it had become dangerous with quantities of brickwork on the ground beside several of the piers on the down side. A local company won the contract from BR to demolish the structure. For two weeks before demolition the contractors were working on the viaduct placing sticks of gelignite in the piers and arches. Demolition took place on Saturday 16th January 1993 and by 8th February not a single stone remained visible of this once huge structure. The 10,000 tons of limestone and brick recovered from the viaduct was recycled by being used as foundations for a local car park. Only a very small length of embankment now remains to the south of the viaduct's location.

The goods shed and lime kiln at Evercreech New station were demolished in 1968. The remainder of the station buildings survived for about another year before they too, were demolished. The former goods yard was then in use as a storage area for some locally based lorries. The station area and goods yard now forms part of a housing estate, while the up platform shelter was purchased and re-erected at the 'S&DJR Memorial Model Railway' track at West Huntspill near Highbridge, where it can be seen to this day. The two miles from Evercreech New to Evercreech Junction is difficult to follow as seven of the ten bridges have been demolished and the remaining trackbed has returned to agricultural use. The most noticeable reminder of the S&DJR in this area is S&D bridge No. 105 Pecking Mill Viaduct, which still straddles the main A371 road. Only the ironwork across the road has so far been removed when it became unsafe. When this structure was widened in 1884/5 to take double

track no effort was made to match the design of the two portions, in fact even the size and shape of the arches are different, let alone the materials used. The often threatened road widening could cause the demise of this otherwise sound and interesting structure.

Evercreech Junction suffered one of the most complete transformations on the whole line. The

Evercreech Junction look-
ing down the site of the
branch line in 1991.

Andy Read

Evercreech Junction sta-
tion down platform build-
ings in October 1990.
Fully restored and now
used for holiday accom-
modation.

Andy Read

down platform buildings escaped demolition in February 1968 and are now a holiday dwelling. All the wooden buildings on the up platform were removed including the signalbox, whilst the footbridge was demolished just after the track lifting was completed in February 1968. At the junction itself the North signalbox, having been gutted by fire after the last regular passenger train in March 1966 was removed, along with the examination hut and turntable. On Monday 23rd November 1968 the level crossing was removed completely and the road resurfaced, the 'official' 5mph speed limit for road vehicles over the crossing (although never heeded and probably not even realised by most road users) being removed!

During the same week the next two road crossings down the line, at Bruton Road and Lamyatt, were similarly removed and resurfaced. Finally, Evercreech Junction station, station yard, goods shed, and much of the land northwards towards the junction itself was sold to a local timber merchant, the trackbed between the two platforms being infilled to form a garden for the new station house, which had been renovated and was finally converted into holiday accommodation. The goods shed was soon converted into a saw mill. The large water tower just to the south of the level crossing survived until the early 1970s. A large number of timber stacks would utilise the former trackbed and goods yard to the north of the station from 1969 to 1980. The area previously forming the junction is now completely unrecognisable. This once busy 24-hour a day operation has now been returned to pasture land and where the 'Pines Express' once proudly passed cows can be seen moving slowly home to be milked.

Moving on south towards Cole, the trackbed is remarkably easy to follow. In recent years a farm out-building has appeared just across the A371 road from Evercreech Junction station. From Lamyatt crossing to S&D bridge No. 113 Cox's Cattle Creep, the trackbed has been obliterated. Further south at S&D bridge No. 115 Wyke Champflower Bridge, the cutting this bridge once passed over has been infilled on the north side but looking south the trackbed is difficult to follow. Between S&D bridge No. 116 Wyke Lane Bridge, and No. 118 GWR Mainline Bridge, the trackbed has all but disappeared, and the ironwork from No. 118 was quickly recovered for its scrap value. It is still possible to see where the stillborn chord was constructed between the S&DJR and the GWR but this was never to see any track laid upon it. A single culvert,

designated S&D bridge No. 116B, is still standing but the unused embankment either side have been removed and the area was returned to pasture land some years ago.

Cole station lost its up platform shelter and signalbox some time before the track was lifted, the box having closed at the same time as Cole goods yards had its connection to the down line removed on 31st May 1965. The substantial looking down platform buildings remained after the track was lifted in mid-November 1967 and has been extended to the rear during conversion to a house. The stationmaster's house is still occupied.

The five-span limestone and brick Cole viaduct survived until 12th September 1984 when, for reasons unclear, it was demolished. The structure proved to be more than a match for Luke Devenish Ltd of Cheddar, their explosives leaving the main piers to be demolished by JCB and hand. Rubble recovered from the viaduct was used to infill the cutting to the south of Cole station and under S&D bridge No. 121 Pitcombe Road Bridge. The road bridge under the line just to the north of Cole station, No. 120 Castle Cary Road Bridge, was dismantled at the same time because the ironwork and one abutment had become unsafe. This demolition contract also included S&D bridge No. 117 Wyke Lane Bridge, which had its ironwork removed on the grounds of safety – or was it the scrap value of the ironwork which brought about their demise? Beyond Cole station and as far as S&D bridge No. 125 Checkers Bridge, the line is broken up by infilling and bridge demolitions.

Shepton Montague was unusual on the S&DJR for two reasons; a long (by S&D standards) straight section, and a tall bridge, S&D No. 127 Rock Cutting Bridge. This stretch of the trackbed is still fairly clear for walkers even though most of the ballast has long since been removed for other purposes, which may well have encouraged the growth of trees and bushes. From S&D bridge No. 131 Plumers Bridge, to well south of Wincanton station little remains to show a railway passed this way.

At Wincanton the up platform shelter was quick to disappear. The goods yard remained in use by a local coal merchant for a time before the large nearby Unigate creamery purchased the station site. The main station building and the gutted shell of the signalbox remained for several more years. In December 1973 the remains of the signalbox were offered to the Somerset & Dorset Railway Trust who removed it to their headquarters at Radstock, where, unfortunately, it gradually rotted away and was never rebuilt. Bridges to the north and immediately to the south of Wincanton station were soon removed during the late 1960s. The fate of S&D bridge No. 134 Union Girder Bridge, is unusual in that the newer down side constructed in 1886 of a single wrought iron girder and timber decked span over both the road and river was removed in 1969, while the far more attractive two-span original structure of Portland stone remained for two more years.

The station site, although owned by Unigate Creameries soon became littered with derelict cars and within a short time had all the appearances of a scrapyard. Thus it remained with the trackbed between the platforms gradually becoming filled with spoil from local building sites. It is unclear when the station buildings were finally demolished or perhaps they fell down, as photographs in the mid 1970s showed them to be in very poor condition. By 1989 all the buildings had gone and those parts of the station site not redeveloped by the creamery were sold off for housing. A short length of the up platform did remain until 1990 when this was removed during the final redevelopment but not before the Swanage Railway removed the concrete lamp posts for re-use at Swanage. The station site is now part of a large housing estate with no trace of its former use, though one of the new homes does have the two trees that appear in many S&D photographs. To the south of the town the new Wincanton by-pass now obliterates the path of the

line, but from south of the by-pass the trackbed can still be followed to Templecombe Junction.

No. 2 Junction signalbox at Templecombe was demolished between November and December 1967. With closure of Templecombe Upper station in 1966 all the station buildings except the Southern-style signalbox were removed. The same was not the case for the former S&DJR buildings in the lower yard, where the engine shed, constructed in the 1950s, and former Dorset Central Railway offices survive to this day and are part of the Plessey Group of companies. The site of the No. 2 Junction and the trackbed towards Templecombe Upper and Wincanton became just waste land used, until recently, by fly-tippers. By 1992 the area occupied by the Junction and Lower yard had been redeveloped as an industrial estate. The spur up to Templecombe Upper station is now part of the access road to the industrial estate. Templecombe Upper station was reopened in October 1983 and has since received a modern BR station structure for passengers.

The tiny Templecombe Lower halt situated between S&D bridge No. 152 Coombe Throope Lane Bridge and No. 153 LSWR Mainline Bridge, had no structure to demolish and simply became overgrown, becoming a perfect home for a local badger family. In the late 1980s bridge No. 152 was partially bricked up and the halt became part of a local resident's garden. It is now possible that Templecombe Lower Halt may become the northern terminus of the 2ft gauge Gartell Light Railway.

Wincanton station site in 1990 shortly before it was redeveloped for housing. The station building had been demolished some years before having become unsafe. Nothing remains in Wincanton to show a railway once served this town since all the bridges in this area have also been demolished.

Andy Read

Templecombe Lower halt, looking north. The platform is on the left and may one day see trains again, as the 2ft gauge Gartell Light Railway hopes to extend as far as here.

Andy Read

The southern end of the narrow gauge Gartell Light Railway near Henstridge station in August 1991, with Lister 4-wheel diesel locomotive *Andrew*.

Kevin Regan

From S&D bridge No. 153 LSWR Mainline Bridge, to Common Lane crossing the trackbed is difficult to walk being used by farmers as a road between their fields, and elsewhere it is very overgrown. This is a great shame as all the bridges are still intact, in fact between Templecombe and Blandford only seven out of the 39 bridges had been removed by 1995. At Common Lane the crossing keeper's house is still occupied and just beyond is a real delight, the Gartell Light Railway on the trackbed. The railway has been constructed by the Gartell engineering company and extends about one mile south to Park Lane near Henstridge. It is planned to extend the line north to Templecombe in the coming years.

All the wooden buildings on Henstridge station platform were removed during 1968. The only visible sign that a station was once here is the remains

The Henstridge station site, looking north in 1992.

Andy Read

of the platform. The former goods yard is a scrapyard, and it may well have been the owners of the scrapyard who demolished the station buildings. Just to the south of Henstridge station can still be seen the road crossing gates in the dense undergrowth that covers the trackbed. At Stalbridge station the signalbox and down platform shelter had been demolished by November 1967. The up platform station buildings and the station house would survive rather longer albeit in a very derelict state. Today nothing at all remains of the station and on the site stands the steel stockholder's offices of Yeovil Steel. Embedded in a road that runs through Stalbridge station goods yard site can be found rails that crossed the road whilst forming the longest siding.

Sturminster Newton signalbox, down platform shelter and water tower had all been removed by mid-1968, although the yard was still in use as a coal distribution point by local coal merchants. This again is a station of which very little remains today and the land is used as a road and car park. The Sturminster Newton goods shed shows the location of the station and is still in use after passing through several owners since BR, including being used as a council roadworks signs store. The white factory building beside the goods shed has also survived and both are now a carpet warehouse. All the remaining station buildings and platforms had been removed by the early 1970s. S&D Bridge No. 173 Butts Dong B3091 Road Bridge, at the north end of

the station site was demolished by Dorset County Council in 1974 as part of a road improvement scheme. The long cutting to the north of the station as far as S&D Bridge No. 171 Sturminster Newton River Bridge, was gradually infilled with rubble over several years and then landscaped by local people, who in 1992 erected gates commemorating the railwaymen of the Somerset & Dorset.

At Shillingstone station the signalbox and down platform shelter were removed along with the up platform shelter, soon after or even during the track lifting operation in May 1967. The station buildings were then used as a store along with the yard by a manufacturer of poultry and farm equipment. In 1970 additional storage space was provided by erecting a large shed between the platforms. By 1989 this firm had ceased to use the station buildings and they were becoming derelict. After a decision by Dorset County Council not to use the trackbed through Shillingstone for a bypass the buildings have been fully restored and are again in use as a workshop. The platforms are clear of plant life as the station often forms the centre piece of the Shillingstone Summer Fete. In 1991 a large scale model railway was laid the length of the station trackbed; steam returned to Shillingstone!

It is possible, with great difficulty, to walk south from Shillingstone station all the way to Blandford. The biggest obstacles are the river crossings as few footpath bridges exist close to the trackbed, also the undergrowth is almost impossible to manage at several locations. Of the 20 bridges between Shillingstone and Blandford only two have been demolished and a further two infilled, one of which was in the former Cliff cutting. S&D bridge No. 188 A350 Road Bridge, is more like a short tunnel as the railway passed under the A350 at an angle, the cutting to the south of this bridge is now very overgrown.

Oddly, Stourpaine & Durweston Halt, closed as long ago as September 1956, not only survived the rest of the line's life but shows no sign of being demolished afterwards either as it is still intact in 1994, though very overgrown and superficially vandalised.

At Blandford station the gradual rundown of freight traffic culminated in the complete closure of the line in January 1969, having also seen the rundown of the associated railway properties, commencing with the station house becoming empty by early 1968. In 1975 the house was occupied again and by 1993 had been restored and modernised. The Stour River bridges at Stourpaine, Fiddleford, Sturminster Newton and Bagber had all been cut by 1970 and the metal of the river bridge at Blandford was severed a few months later. It has come to light that the contractors who recovered the ironwork from these bridges only just covered the expenses involved, thus making little or no profit from this pointless contract. A most noticeable surviving bridge was the impressive structure of grey engineering brick that still arched across East Street in

Blandford, close to the town centre. This remained so until 25th July 1978 when competition winner Mrs Stephens blew up the structure. A total of 350lbs of gelignite was used to remove the arches, parapets and the top of the piers, the remainder of this structure was demolished by hand. The rubble from S&D bridge, No. 196 Damory Court Bridge, found its way into Cliff cutting to the north of Blandford. Rush & Tompkins were contracted to demolish S&D bridge No. 200 Blandford St Mary Bridge, in early 1983. A housing estate now stands on the Blandford station site after its demolition in August 1973.

The trackbed north from Blandford is now a linear park with the station footbridge, S&D No. 194, still in place. As for the remaining trackbed northwards (beyond the linear park) towards Shillingstone, this was purchased for £3,000 by a consortium of local farmers organised by Sturminster Newton estate agent Mr Arthur Richards. The trackbed at Nutford Farm, Bryanston and East Farm Hammon became a private estate road: whilst the deep Cliff cutting at France Farm has been completely infilled by a procession of hundreds of lorries carrying rubble and earth from building sites all around the Blandford area. Farmers ceased to use the private road after it was severed by the construction of the Blandford bypass in the 1980s. Between S&D bridge No. 189 France Farm Bridge and No. 190 France Farm Drove the line of the railway has been totally

Sturminster Newton station site, looking south in 1991 from the location of bridge No. 173. The goods shed remains, as a carpet store, on the left to show where the station was.

Andy Read

Shillingstone station, looking north in 1991. This is the only Dorset Central Railway station to survive and is occasionally the centre piece of the Shillingstone Gala. In 1991 a narrow gauge model railway had been laid the length of the platform in preparation for the Gala.

obliterated, and south of the by-pass for about half a mile it has become impenetrably overgrown.

Much of the trackbed south of Blandford remains fairly well defined because of its later closure date, though the mile or so from Blandford station to Blandford St Mary has completely disappeared. Once south of the southern portion of the Blandford by-pass the trackbed is easy to follow. More so after 1991 as this stretch, as far as Bailey Gate, had been used by Wessex Water to lay new water mains. The trackbed in 1992 looked much as it must have done in 1970, just after the track had been lifted. Only five of the 19 bridges between these two locations have been demolished. The walk from Blandford to Spetisbury is most enjoyable at any time of the year.

Unfortunately the line from the Blandford by-pass to Bailey Gate is now under threat from a proposed relief road for Charlton Marshall, Spetisbury and Sturminster Marshall. The buildingless halt at Charlton Marshall was, until the summer of 1988, difficult to find under its blanket of bushes and trees, until local enthusiasts cleared the site and renewed its dignity. They would appear to be maintaining this improved state of affairs as a visit in 1993 found the halt to still be neat and tidy. One of

the concrete Charlton Marshall Halt platform name-boards is now preserved at the $7\frac{1}{4}$in gauge Moors Valley Railway at West Moors.

From 13th August 1934 Spetisbury station became unstaffed and as a result was renamed Spetisbury Halt on 1st December 1939. In September 1956 the halt was closed, along with Stourpaine & Durweston, Charlton Marshall and Corfe Mullen halts. It is not known when the buildings at Spetisbury Halt were demolished, but certainly by the early 1960s they had gone. The platforms, and steps to them have outlived the closure. 1986 was to see the demise of S&D bridge No. 214 Louse Lane Bridge, to the south of Spetisbury. This bridge had been owned by Dorset County Council. The trackbed between Charlton Marshall and Spetisbury is also owned by Dorset County Council along with the trackbed as far as the location of S&D bridge No. 217 Cliff Road Bridge, over the busy A350, and which was demolished in 1974 to allow for road widening.

By 1973 all the station buildings at Bailey Gate had been demolished, the signalbox having been demolished just before the track was lifted in 1970. Even the milk factory had fallen on hard times and

Blandford Forum station in 1989, looking north towards bridge No. 194. On the right is the former Station Master's house.

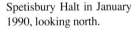

Spetisbury Halt in January 1990, looking north.

This was Bailey Gate station from the location of the now demolished bridge No. 220 looking south in 1992. The bridge was replaced by a roundabout to give safer access to an industrial estate. The up platform was beside the trees on the right.

Bailey Gate crossing, looking south in 1992. The trackbed hereabouts is clearly defined, as is the base of Bailey Gate crossing signalbox with only the wooden portion having been demolished in 1970.

is now in new ownership. In late 1988 the platforms had been demolished and the site was occupied by lorries from the industrial estate with several pre-served World War II army tanks. In April 1992 S&D bridge No. 220 Bailey Gate Station Bridge, was demolished and the road layout altered to allow access to the expanding industrial estate. A small roundabout now resides where bridge No. 220 once stood and a road runs the length of the station site. A road now runs in the opposite direction for some distance using the former trackbed and serves a new housing estate. Appropriately, it is called Railway Drive. Just to the south of the Bailey Gate station was an Admiralty siding of which no trace now remains.

Just a mile further on one reaches Corfe Mullen crossing, where the brick base of the crossing sig-nalbox is still standing. The trackbed round to Corfe Mullen Junction is still clearly visible as a railway trackbed even today. The crossing keeper's house at Corfe Mullen Junction is now a private dwelling and has been completely restored along with about 100 feet of trackbed which is now the garden. The new owner has also restored the south side crossing gates to their former glory. The Carter's Clay Pit site and its siding became a scrapyard before being redeveloped for housing. The Wimborne line ceased

to be used for passenger services on 11th July 1920 and the last freight train ran on 17th June 1933, after which the line was lifted from Carter's Clay Pit back to Wimborne. Fifty years after that track lifting short stretches of this line can still be found and two culverts are still in place.

The site of Corfe Mullen Junction is still clear but the trackbed from here south has reverted back to Mother nature and at the junction site horses can now often be found grazing. In the 2½ miles from S&D bridge No. 223 Corfe Mullen Junction Bridge to Broadstone Junction only three of the 16 bridges have been demolished. The deep Corfe Mullen cut-ting which contained Corfe Mullen Halt has been infilled up to road level at the site of S&D bridge No. 235 Corfe Mullen Halt Bridge, just to the north of the halt. To the south S&D bridge No. 236 Lambs Green Lane Bridge, is still standing though hidden in dense undergrowth. The tiny halt was simply buried when the cutting was infilled and then landscaped over during construction of a nearby housing estate. A visit to this location in 1991 found the cutting had become a boating lake of all things!

Moving to S&D bridge No. 238 Ashington Lane Bridge, at the summit of Corfe Mullen bank, this elegant three span bridge, which once allowed BR

Class 9F 2-10-0 locomotives to pass through its centre arch, has suffered at the hands of fly tippers and official infilling. One can walk down the bank towards the Broadstone golf course with difficulty as the undergrowth is very dense. A visit in 1990 located two telegraph poles still in situ amongst the trees. This section of trackbed is now under threat from more infilling, which will lead to property development, be it housing or industrial. Coming on down to Broadstone Junction itself half a mile of the trackbed is now owned by the Broadstone golf club and as a result general access is not allowed.

Broadstone Junction station is yet another housing estate. With the final closure of the freight only single track to Wimborne on 2nd May 1977, the track had been lifted by July 1978. It was not to be until 1983 that Broadstone Junction station and signalbox were demolished for redevelopment. Some of the station buildings were saved and rebuilt at Medstead & Four Marks station on the preserved Mid-Hants Railway. The remaining trackbed to Holes Bay Junction has been used recently by Wessex Water for a new water mains and is now a footpath and cycle way. Bournemouth West station suffered the fate of many a large terminus station in becoming a coach and car park by 1970. The Wessex Way ring road now crosses the line close to the throat of the station entrance, whilst the location of the station buildings has recently been redeveloped as office accommodation.

Corfe Mullen Junction crossing keeper's house in 1990. The south side gates have been restored by the new owners, whilst the north side gates are also still standing and the track is buried under a layer of tarmac.

Kevin Regan

View south from bridge No. 223 towards the junction in 1992. This location clearly shows its recent past. Horses often graze at this once busy junction.

The Branksome Triangle viaducts in June 1993. Only two sections of this triangle still remain in use since the Gas Works Junction to Bournemouth West Junction section was closed on 30th October 1965. It has been threatened with demolition due to vandals pelting passing traffic with stones. In this view it is clear the viaducts are still in good condition.

Appendix 1

Stations and Halts

Station/Halt	Opened to Passengers	Closed to Passengers	Closed to Freight	Track Lifted	Station Demolished
Bath (Green Park)	7/5/1870	7/3/66	31/5/71	1/67	Restored
Midford	20/7/1874	7/3/66	10/6/63	12/67	12/67
Wellow	20/7/1874	7/3/66	10/6/63	11/67	House
Shoscombe & Single Hill	23/9/1929	7/3/66		10/67	
Radstock North	20/7/1874	7/3/66	15/6/64	8/76	1979–80
Midsomer Norton	20/6/1874	7/3/66	15/6/64	7/68	Restored
Chilcompton	20/7/1874	7/3/66	15/6/64	6/68	6/68
Binegar	20/7/1874	7/3/66	10/6/63	5/68	5/68
Masbury	20/7/1874	7/3/66	10/6/63	5/68	House
Shepton Mallet	20/7/1874	7/3/66	10/6/63	4/68	1970–72
Evercreech New	20/7/1874	7/3/66	1/7/64	3/68	1968–69
Evercreech Junction	3/2/1862	7/3/66	29/11/65	2/68	House
Cole	3/2/1862	7/3/66	5/4/65	11/67	House
Wincanton	11/1861	7/3/66	5/4/65	11/67	Various
Templecombe Lower	17/1/1887	3/1/66		9/67	
Henstridge	31/8/1863	7/3/66	5/4/65	8/67	1968
Stalbridge	31/8/1863	7/3/66	5/4/65	8/67	1967–72
Sturminster Newton	31/8/1863	7/3/66	5/4/65	6/67	1973
Shillingstone	31/8/1863	7/3/66	5/4/65	5/67	Restored
Stourpaine & Durweston	9/7/1928	17/9/56		3/67	Standing
Blandford Forum	31/8/1863	7/3/66	6/1/69	1/70	8/1973
Charlton Marshall	5/7/1928	17/9/56		3/70	
Spetisbury	1/11/1860	17/9/56		4/70	1958–59
Bailey Gate	1/11/1860	7/3/66	5/4/65	21/6/70	Various
Corfe Mullen	5/7/1928	17/9/56		8/70	
Broadstone Junction	1/6/1847	7/3/66	20/9/65	9/70	8/84
Wimborne	1/11/1860	11/7/20	17/6/33	78	7/83
Bournemouth West	15/6/1874	4/10/65		2/67	4/70
Pylle	3/2/1862	7/3/66	10/6/63	13/2/67	House
West Pennard	3/2/1862	7/3/66	10/6/63	13/3/67	House
Glastonbury & Street	28/8/1854	7/3/66	7/3/66	5/67	1984
Polsham	12/1861	29/10/51	29/10/51	1955	House
Wells Priory Road	15/3/1859	29/10/51	13/7/64	1955	By 1984
Ashcott	7/1856	7/3/66	13/7/64	6/67	House

Station/Halt	Opened to Passengers	Closed to Passengers	Closed to Freight	Track Lifted	Station Demolished
Shapwick	28/8/1854	7/3/66	10/6/63	7/67	4/71
Edington Junction/Burtle	7/1856	7/3/66	13/7/64	8/67	Unknown
Cossington	21/7/1890	1/12/52	4/10/54	1955	House
Bawdrip	1923	1/12/52		1955	By 1968
Bridgwater North	21/7/1890	1/12/52	7/7/62	1967	4/8/84
Bason Bridge	7/1856	7/3/66	10/6/63	11/12/72	11/68
Highbridge	28/8/1854	7/3/66	2/11/64	1/67	12/70
Burnham-on-Sea	3/5/1858	29/10/51	20/5/63	2/11/64	By 1967

Two views of the beautifully restored Bath Green Park station, June 1993.
Peter Nicholson

Appendix 2

Closures and Major Changes since 1925

1925
21/9/25   Stourpaine signalbox closed.

1926
13/4/26   Original Bath Junction signalbox closed.

1928
1/4/28   Wimborne S&DJR loop closed and lifted.
          Wimborne single line signalbox closed.
5/7/28   Stourpaine & Durweston halt opened.
5/7/28   Charlton Marshall halt opened.
5/7/28   Corfe Mullen halt opened.
12/28   Double junction to Blandford army camp reduced to a single line junction.

1929
          Pylle signalbox closed and became a ground frame, also the passing loop was lifted.
23/09/29   Shoscombe & Single Hill halt opened.
11/11/29   Clandown Colliery at Radstock closed. (Track lifted 1970/71)

1930
          Highbridge Locomotive Works closed.
          Cattle pens at Evercreech New demolished.

1932
          Burnham-on-Sea station to Burnham pier line closed but used for some years to launch the lifeboat.
11/12/32   LSWR line between Broadstone Junction and Hamworthy singled.

1933
          Middle Pit Colliery at Radstock closed.
          Cow & Gate Creamery siding opened at Wincanton station.
          Cossington Boards Quarry siding closed and Cossington station crossover facilities lifted due to becoming unsafe.
12/2/33   Templecombe No. 3 Junction signalbox closed and soon demolished.
17/6/33   Carter's Siding to Wimborne Junction line closed to freight traffic. Passenger services had ceased on 11/7/20.
19/6/33   Creekmore halt opened.

1934

8/34   Spetisbury station became unstaffed and renamed Spetisbury halt.
28/10/34 Holes Bay Junction signalbox closed.

1938

22/9/38   Masbury station became unstaffed and renamed Masbury halt.

1940

          Cossington Boards Quarry siding lifted.
          Closure of Victoria Brick & Tile works at Bath. May's sidings closed and lifted in the early
          1950s.
23/1/40   Closure of Downside Quarry siding at Winsor Hill.
23/1/40   Closure of Hamwood Quarry sidings at Winsor Hill.

1942

1/1/42   Track lifted on Bridgwater Wharf, scrap went to help the war effort.

1946

8/2/46   Two arches of the up side portion of Bath Road Viaduct collapsed.
8/46   New up side portion of Bath Road Viaduct opened.

1948

          Closure of Windsor Hill Quarry sidings at Winsor Hill.
1/1/48   Control of the S&DJR remained as pre-nationalisation.
2/2/48   Commercial operation of the whole S&DJR system now controlled by the Southern Region.
          Motive power and rolling stock provided by the London, Midland Region.
3/8/48   Winsor Hill Hamwood Quarry signalbox closed.

1949

          Highbridge Wharf closed to shipping, sidings retained for general freight and storage of
          condemned wagons.

1950

1/1/50   Western Region take control of the main line from Bath to Cole and all three branch lines. Motive
          power and rolling stock provided by London, Midland Region to the Southern Region which took
          control of all motive power depots except Bath Green Park.
5/5/50   Templecombe Lower yard closed.

1951

          Radstock East and West signalboxes renamed Radstock North 'A' and 'B' respectively.
27/10/51 Wells Priory Road engine shed closed.
29/10/51 Wells Priory branch closed to passenger traffic.
29/10/51 Burnham-on-Sea to Highbridge closed to local passenger traffic.
29/10/51 Polsham Halt closed to freight and passenger traffic.
2/12/51   Wells Priory signalbox closed.
18/12/51 Stourpaine loop closed and soon lifted.

1952

10/8/52   Spetisbury Halt signalbox closed.
1/12/52   Cossington station closed to passengers.
1/12/52   Bawdrip Halt closed to passengers.
1/12/52   Bridgwater branch closed to passenger services and to freight traffic between Bridgwater and
          Cossington.

1954

19/3/54	Ludlow Colliery at Radstock closed.
4/10/54	Cossington station closed to freight traffic.
4/10/54	Bridgwater branch closed to freight traffic between Edington and Cossington. With this closure Edington Junction station was renamed Edington Burtle station.

1955

	Admiralty sidings at Corfe Mullen closed after many years of disuse.
	Middle Pit Colliery branch closed.
	Several sidings lifted at the north end of Shepton Mallet station yard.
13/2/55	Track lifting and demolition commenced on the Wells Priory branch
10/55	Track lifting and demolition commenced on the Bridgwater branch.
12/55	Wells Priory Road engine shed demolished.

1956

4/2/56	Edington Burtle station crossover facilities, down platform and all except one siding lifted from goods yard.
4/2/56	Edington Burtle signalbox closed and soon demolished.
13/8/56	Braysdown Colliery partially closed.
17/9/56	Stourpaine & Durweston halt closed to passengers.
17/9/56	Charlton Marshall Halt closed to passengers.
17/9/56	Spetisbury Halt closed to passengers.
19/9/56	Corfe Mullen Halt closed to passengers.

1957

	Winsor Hill Quarry sidings and crossover facilities lifted.
4/11/57	Pylle station became unstaffed.

1958

1/2/58	Inter-regional boundary re-located at Templecombe distant signal, from Henstridge. All motive power depots transferred from Southern Region to Western Region control.

1959

	Mendipadam Works sidings at Masbury halt closed.
5/59	Midford 'B' frame closed and siding soon lifted.
15/3/59	War Department sidings at Masbury halt lifted.
19/9/59	Corfe Mullen Carter's siding closed, but retained for wagon storage.
29/10/59	Braysdown Colliery permanently closed.

1960

	The line through the low 'Marble Arch Bridge' became redundant and was soon demolished along with the tramway bridge to Tyning Colliery, leading to the rationalisation of the track layout at Radstock.
5/60	Pylle station goods yard crossover facilities lifted.

1961

5/2/61	Middle Pit Colliery branch and sidings lifted.

1962

	Final inter-regional boundary change, now just south of Shillingstone.
13/4/62	Braysdown Colliery sidings closed and lifted within a year.
25/6/62	West Pennard station became unstaffed.

7/7/62   Bridgwater North goods yard and S&DJR station closed.
8/9/62   Excursion traffic withdrawn on Highbridge to Burnham-on-Sea branch.

1963

1/1/63   Branksome depot closed but still used to stable locomotives.
20/5/63   Burnham-on-Sea station goods yard closed.
20/5/63   Highbridge to Burnham-on-Sea line closed completely, except Highbridge Wharf sidings.
10/6/63   Bason Bridge station goods yard closed (except creamery sidings).
10/6/63   Binegar station goods yard closed.
10/6/63   Masbury halt goods yard closed and lifted that month.
10/6/63   Midford station 'A' goods yard closed.
10/6/63   Pylle station goods yard closed.
10/6/63   Shapwick station goods yard closed.
10/6/63   Shepton Mallet station goods yard closed.
10/6/63   Wellow station goods yard closed.
10/6/63   West Pennard station goods yard closed.
17/12/63 Last school special called at Charlton Marshall halt.

1964

2/64   Midford, Wellow and Chilcompton stations became unstaffed.
4/5/64   West Moors station closed to passengers.
          Wimborne station closed to passengers.
15/6/64   Chilcompton station goods yard closed.
15/6/64   Midsomer Norton station goods yard closed (except colliery sidings).
15/6/64   Radstock North station goods yard closed (except private sidings).
21/6/64   Pylle station ground frame and siding connection removed.
29/6/64   Midford station 'A' frame closed and sidings lifted.
30/6/64   Wellow station sidings and crossover facilities lifted. Goods yard ground frame removed.
1/7/64   Masbury Halt signalbox closed and crossover facilities lifted.
1/7/64   Evercreech New station goods yard closed.
2/7/64   Shepton Mallet station crossover facilities and most sidings lifted.
10/7/64   Binegar station goods yard had four sidings lifted.
13/7/64   Ashcott station goods yard closed and ground frame removed.
13/7/64   Edington Burtle station goods yard closed and siding lifted.
13/6/64   Wells Priory station goods yard closed.
23/8/64   Radstock North 'A' signalbox closed, north end crossover facilities and goods shed sidings taken
          out of use and soon lifted. Radstock North 'B' signalbox renamed Radstock North.
26/8/64   West Pennard signalbox closed, sidings and crossover facilities soon lifted.
7/9/64   Templecombe depot closed but locomotives still stabled there.
10/64   Wincanton station south end crossover facility out of use.
10/64   Ashcott station sidings and Eclipse Peat Company private sidings lifted.
11/10/64 Evercreech New signalbox closed and soon demolished, sidings lifted.
2/11/64   Highbridge East station goods yard closed.
2/11/64   Highbridge East to Highbridge Wharf line closed to freight traffic.
3/11/64   Track lifting commenced on the Burnham-on-Sea station to Highbridge Junction line back as far
          as the S&DJR/GWR crossing.
9/12/64   Moorewood Roads Reconstruction sidings closed.

1965

          Pylle signalbox demolished.
          Remains of Burnham-on-Sea line slewed into GWR Highbridge goods yard.
2/65   Moorewood roads reconstruction sidings lifted.
5/4/65   Bailey Gate station goods yard closed (except creamery sidings).

5/4/65   Cole station goods yard closed.

5/4/65   Henstridge station goods yard closed.

5/4/65   Shillingstone station goods yard closed.

5/4/65   Stalbridge station goods yard closed.

5/4/65   Sturminster Newton station goods yard closed.

5/4/65   Templecombe Upper goods yard closed.

5/4/65   Wincanton station goods yard closed (except creamery sidings).

6/4/56   Sturminster Newton station all sidings lifted.

11/4/65   Chilcompton signalbox closed.

5/65   Shillingstone station down sidings lifted.

16/5/65   Highbridge 'A' and 'B' signalboxes closed.

31/5/65   Cole signalbox closed and siding connections removed.

14/6/65   All freight services between Wincanton and Blandford withdrawn.

18/6/65   Emborough Stone sidings out of use. (Finally lifted 1969)

5/7/65   Moorewood signalbox closed.

7/65   Chilcompton station sidings and crossover facilities lifted.

6/7/65   Henstridge station ground frame closed and sidings lifted.

7/7/65   Stalbridge station most sidings lifted.

8/7/65   Shillingstone station most up sidings lifted.

2/8/65   Bournemouth West station temporarily and partially closed.

5/9/65   Branksome depot out of use, locomotive no longer able to use depot.

5/9/65   Bournemouth West station completely and totally closed.

20/9/65   Broadstone Junction station goods yard out of use 27/10/65.

20/9/65   Parkstone station closed to freight.

20/9/65   West Moors station closed to freight (except Army specials).

3/10/65   Bournemouth West station officially closed.

30/10/65   During this weekend most track was lifted in Bournemouth West station.

1/11/65   Bournemouth West signalbox became a ground frame.

29/11/65   Evercreech Junction station goods yard closed.

1966

3/1/66   Templecombe Lower station closed.

3/1/66   All freight services between Radstock and Wincanton withdrawn, except for Norton Hill Colliery.

3/1/66   Wincanton station creamery sidings closed.

11/2/66   Norton Hill Colliery closed.

28/2/66   Wimborne station closed to freight (except some CBP).

5/3/66   Evercreech Junction North signalbox burnt down.

7/3/66   Broadstone Junction station closed to passengers.

7/3/66   Creekmoor halt closed.

7/3/66   Evercreech Junction South signalbox closed.

7/3/66   Glastonbury & Street station goods yard closed.

7/3/66   Midsomer Norton station private sidings closed.

7/3/66   Shepton Mallet signalbox closed.

7/3/66   Spur to connect S&DJR to the B&NS line brought into operation.

7/3/66   Stalbridge signalbox closed.

7/3/66   Templecombe Upper station closed and soon demolished.

24/7/66   LSWR line between Broadstone and Ringwood singled.

25/7/66   Corfe Mullen Junction, Bailey Gate crossing, Bailey Gate station and Blandford station signalboxes became ground frames.

5/9/66   Bournemouth West ground frame closed but re-opened within months.

12/9/66   Bath (Green Park) Station signalbox closed.

1/10/66   Demolition contractors start preliminary work at Bath (Green Park) S&DJR locomotive depot.

1967
January
Writhlington signalbox demolished.
2/1/67   Track lifting at Highbridge station, goods yard and locomotive depot.
2/1/67   Track lifting inside of Bath (Green Park) station and locomotive depot.
30/1/67   Demolition contractors start preliminary work on 'The Branch'.

February
4/2/67   Track lifting commenced on the Blandford to Radstock contract with Shillingstone station being used as the contractor's base.
18/2/67   Remaining track lifting at Bournemouth West station.
18/2/67   Railhead at France Farm (1 mile south Stourpaine & Durweston halt).
3/2/67   Work started on the track lifting of the 23-mile branch line from Evercreech Junction North to Bason Bridge Creamery.
13/2/67   Branch railhead at Pylle station.

March
Bournemouth West Junction to Gas Works Junction track lifted.
Railhead at Stourpaine and Durweston halt.
1/3/67   Branch railhead at Pylle bank.
13/3/67   Branch railhead at West Pennard station.

April
Railhead just north of Cliff Bridge Cutting.

May
Railhead at Shillingstone station and Templecombe Junction now the contractor's base.
Demolition of Bath (Green Park) S&DJR motive power depot completed during the month.
Branch railhead at Glastonbury station.
7/5/67   Connection at Templecombe Upper between S&DJR and LSWR main line removed, all demolition trains now work in from Bristol via Radstock on the Bristol & North Somerset line.
27/5/67   Work started on the demolition of the down platform shelter at Radstock North station, being completed in early June.

June
Railhead at Sturminster Newton station.
Branch railhead at Ashcott station.
17/6/67   Work started on demolition of Radstock North 'B' signalbox, by 21st the upper half of the box had gone, brick-built lower portion would remain for some time before being demolished.
30/6/67   Cole signalbox and up platform shelter demolished.

July
Railhead near to Sturminster Newton bridge No. 171 over the River Stour.
Track lifting commenced on the Writhlington to Bath contract.

August
Railhead at Stalbridge station.
Northern railhead at Foxcote.
Templecombe Upper and Lower yards lifted.

September
Railhead at Templecombe. Wincanton station now the contractor's base.
Northern railhead at Shoscombe & Single Hill halt.
Branch railhead at Edington.

October

        Track lifted at Horsington.

        Northern railhead one mile south of Wellow.

        Track lifting completed on the Evercreech Junction North to Bason Bridge contract during the month.

9/10/67   Railhead at Cheriton Crossing.

November

        Demolition of Templecombe No. 2 Junction signalbox.

        Part of Stalbridge station, signalbox and down shelter demolished.

1/11/67   Railhead at south end of Wincanton station.

2/11/67   Northern railhead at Wellow station.

3/11/67   Twerton Co-op siding closed.

6/11/67   Evercreech Junction now the contractor's base.

10/11/67 Track lifting in Wincanton station and yard.

15/11/67 Railhead just South of Cole station.

19/11/67 Railhead at Cole bridge No. 118 over the GWR main line just north of Cole station.

December

12/67   Midford station demolished.

12/12/67 Northern railhead at Midford 'A' Yard.

17/12/67 Bath (Green Park) station signalbox demolished.

1968

        Winsor Hill down Tunnel used to test Concorde's Rolls-Royce Olympus engine to destruction.

        Evercreech New up platform shelter sold and goods shed demolished.

        Henstridge station and part of the platform demolished.

        Sturminster Newton signalbox, water tower and down platform shelter demolished.

        Shillingstone signalbox and down platform shelter demolished.

January

22/1/68   Railhead at Wyke Champflower.

30/1/68   Northern railhead at north end of Combe Down Tunnel.

February

        Evercreech Junction station up platform buildings, water tower and signalboxes demolished, footbridge removed and goods yard lifted.

7/2/68   Railhead at Evercreech Junction.

17/2/68 Contractor's base moved to Shepton Mallet station.

March

        Railhead at Evercreech New, Cannards Grave was lifted by mid-month.

        Northern railhead at south end of Devonshire Tunnel.

April

        Railhead at Shepton Mallet and contractor's base at Binegar station. Winsor Hill Tunnels passed mid-month.

May

        Northern railhead at Twerton siding. Sleepers still to be retrieved.

7/5/68   Corfe Mullen Junction, Bailey Gate crossing, Bailey Gate station and Blandford station ground frames all officially closed.

9/5/68   Masbury halt cleared of track.

18/5/68 Railhead at Binegar station, station buildings and signalbox demolished.

20/5/68 Contractor's base moved to Moorewood.

June

Track lifting completed on the Writhlington to Bath contract.

Shepton Mallet signalbox, water tower, footbridge and all the old S&DJR signal department huts demolished.

7/6/68   Railhead at Moorewood.

9/6/68   Contractor's base at Radstock North.

21/6/68   Chilcompton station and all other buildings demolished.

30/6/68   Railhead at Chilcompton Tunnel.

July

1/2/68   Midsomer Norton station sidings lifted.

5/7/68   Railhead at Midsomer Norton station (work stopped due to flood).

September

28/9/68   New Rock Colliery closed.

November

11/68   Bason Bridge station buildings demolished.

23/11/68   Evercreech Junction level crossing removed and resurfaced.

23/11/68   Bruton Road and Lamyatt Road level crossings removed and resurfaced.

1969

Emborough Stone Works sidings lifted.

Midsomer Norton to Radstock section lifted and removed by lorry.

6/1/69   Broadstone Junction station to Blandford station section closed.

4/5/69   Road section of Bridge No. 1 over the Lower Bristol Road demolished.

10/69   Bridge Nos 93 and 94 both Herridge's Cattle Creep, demolished.

11/69   Bridge No. 48 Silver Street Bridge, demolished.

28/12/69   First demolition train arrives for Broadstone to Blandford contract.

30/12/69   Track lifting starts just north of Blandford station.

1970

Bridge No. 257 West Pennard Bridge, demolished.

Bridge No. 134 Union Girder Bridge, demolished.

Clandon Colliery sidings lifted.

Bridgwater Port closed.

2/70   Blandford station and goods yard cleared.

9/3/70   Railhead at Charlton Marshall halt.

4/70   Bournemouth West station and Branksome depot demolished.

5/4/70   Railhead reached Spetisbury halt.

20/5/70   Railhead at Bailey Gate station.

4/8/70   Railhead at Corfe Mullen Junction level crossing.

12/9/70   Railhead just to the north of Broadstone Junction station.

15/9/70   Branksome coal yard and Sharp Jones Pottery sidings closed.

18/10/70   Broadstone Junction signalbox closed. Broadstone Junction station to Holes Bay Junction line singled with the track lifted by 13/12/70.

29/11/70   Branksome coal yard and Sharpe Jones Pottery sidings lifted.

12/70   Part of Highbridge works demolished.

12/70   All of Highbridge station, engine shed and yard buildings demolished.

1971

4/71   Shapwick station demolished to widen drainage channel.

31/5/71   Bath Gas Works and Bath Midland Bridge Road goods yard closed.

31/5/71   Mangotsfield to Bath line closed to regular freight traffic.

1972

	Shepton Mallet station site cleared for redevelopment.
20/3/72	Highbridge West (GWR) signalbox closed.
20/4/72	Mangotsfield to Bath line closed to all traffic.
8/5/72	Track lifting starts on the Mangotsfield to Bath contract.
10/10/72	Highbridge to Bason Bridge Creamery line closed.
11/12/72	Track lifting starts on Highbridge to Bason Bridge contract.

1973

	Bridge No. 6 Monksdale Road Bridge, demolished.
8/73	Blandford station site cleared for redevelopment.
9/73	Writhlington Colliery closed.
16/10/73	Last train to Writhlington Colliery.
19/11/73	Radstock to Writhlington Colliery line officially closed.
23/11/73	Radstock North Motive Power Depot officially closed.

Post-1973

1974	Bridge No. 88 Fosse Lane Bridge, demolished.
1974	West Moors station closed to remaining freight traffic.
1974	Bridge No. 173 Butts Dong Bridge, demolished.
1974	Bridge No. 217 Cliffe Road Bridge, demolished.
1974	Sturminster Newton station demolished.
8/76	Track lifting started on the Writhlington to Radstock contract.
2/5/77	Wimborne to Holes Bay Junction line closed.
1/10/77	Track lifting started on the Wimborne to Holes Bay Junction contract.
5/7/78	Wimborne to Holes Bay Junction track lifting contract completed.
25/7/78	Bridge No. 196 Damory Court Bridge, demolished.
1979–80	Radstock North station buildings and Bridge Nos 38 and 40 demolished.
1982	Bridge No. 46 Welton Road Bridge, demolished.
1983	Bridge No. 197 Farquarson Bridge, demolished.
1983	Bridge No. 199 Lock's Bridge, demolished.
1983	Bridge No. 200 Blandford St Mary Bridge, demolished.
7/83	Wimborne station site cleared for redevelopment.
1984	Glastonbury station demolished.
8/84	Bridgwater station site cleared for redevelopment.
8/84	Broadstone Junction station site cleared for redevelopment.
9/84	Bridge No. 117 Wyke Lane Bridge, demolished.
9/84	Bridge No. 120 Castle Cary Road Bridge, demolished.
12/9/84	Bridge No. 119 Cole Viaduct, demolished.
1986	Bridge No. 214 Louse Lane Bridge, demolished.
1987	Bridge No. 99 Evercreech Road Bridge, demolished.
12/88	Wells Priory Road goods shed demolished.
1989	Bridge No. 135 Cemetery Road Bridge, demolished.
1990	Bridge No. 133 Union Bridge, demolished.
1990/91	Bridge No. 8 Englishcombe Bridge, renovated.
1991	Remains of Chilcompton station site cleared for redevelopment.
4/92	Remains of Bailey Gate station site and bridge No. 220 cleared for redevelopment.
4/92	Bridge No. 78 Ham Lane Bridge, demolished.
13/1/93	Bridge No. 95 Prestleigh Viaduct, demolished.
3/93	North Somerset (or Five Arches) Viaduct renovated.
4/94	Pylle goods shed converted to residence.

Appendix 3

S&DJR Main Line and Branch Line Bridges

The 98 miles of S&DJR trackbed – (not track miles) – had no less than 382 structures constructed over or under them. Under structures could be as small as a one foot diameter culvert or as big as Charlton Road Viaduct in Shepton Mallet. Over structures varied just as greatly from the tiny Tyning Arch at Radstock to Combe Down Tunnel at over a mile in length.

The S&DJR was not only responsible for the structures over and under which it ran but also many outlying bridges which had to be constructed to take diverted rivers, streams and roads, and many of these are still in use today.

Not only does the style of bridges on the S&DJR vary greatly due to the two companies involved with its construction between the 1850s and 1870s but also between 1886 and 1902 when a majority of the main line was doubled. It is therefore possible to view a structure from the up side and see a bridge constructed from natural stone, whilst the down side is constructed from brick with a wrought iron handrail parapet. Even stranger is a bridge of masonry on one side and wrought iron girders and timber decking on the other. It is therefore important to view both sides of an S&DJR bridge on double tracked sections before deciding on its construction.

This complete S&DJR bridge list of the main line and three branch lines covers seven factors common to every structure. 1) *Bridge reference number* from Bath to Broadstone, Evercreech Junction North to Burnham-on-Sea, Glastonbury to Wells Priory and Edington Junction to Bridgwater North.

2) *Map reference or references* in the case of tunnels and viaducts.

3) *Mile post readings* to and from the same locations as bridge reference numbers.

4) *Official bridge name* as quoted on the Southern Railway, London, Midland & Scottish Railway or BR Western Region bridge lists.

5) *Type and size of bridge* relates to whether it is an over or underbridge – over being a bridge over the track and an under bridge being one over which the railway travels. Example: culverts and viaducts are always 'under' and tunnels 'over'. The size of a bridge simply relates to the number of spans involved in its construction, not its length or height.

6) *The materials* are the likes of masonry, brick, wrought iron, cast iron and timber, stating which parts of the structure are made of which material.

7) *The current condition* of the structure. This can vary from still standing to demolished, via abutments only, still standing infilled or replaced by a modern structure. Some culverts have been demolished and the stream or flood water being dealt with by a pipe or drainage system.

Bridge names tend to be local names chosen, sometimes illogically, when the line was constructed. Thus some structures have two or more names, whilst others share the same name. Some structures do not have a local or official name other than the type of structure it is. As well as bridges, viaducts, culverts and tunnels this list contains occupation bridges, accommodation bridges, cattle creeps, sheep creeps, cattle droves, non-stream culverts, arches, brooks, tramways, cattle arches, bridleways, footbridges, drove bridges, rhines and flood openings. A short explanation of these various structures is needed to understand their differing uses. An occupation bridge is provided to give access to an area of land severed by the construction of the railway. (They are still constructed under motorways and by-passes to allow access to fields split by the new road.) These structures can also be referred to as accommodation bridges. Different types of occupation bridges appear not to be defined.

Cattle creeps or sheep creeps are under bridges with no right of way, generally of low headroom for access to fields by livestock.

Cattle droves are most often over bridges that take a track or drove over a railway which has crossed its route.

Non-stream culverts are culverts which do not carry a flowing watercourse but are intended to provide a flood relief because the watercourse had been diverted during the construction of the railway.

Flood openings may serve the same purpose as a non-stream culvert. Most S&DJR river bridges have flood arches on either side of the main river arch.

Bridleways and footbridges both serve as non-vehicular routes over or under the railway for the sole use of walkers. Culverts on the S&DJR varied in size from as little as one foot in diameter to ten feet in diameter for No. 263 on the branch near Glastonbury. On the other hand bridge No. 53 under Chilcompton station is big enough on the up side to drive a lorry into but only just large enough on the down side to accommodate a cow. It also has several tank traps from World War II in it!

After parts of a river were used for the Glastonbury Canal, bridges crossing it were called rhine bridges to show the river now followed a man made course.

Tramways can be under or over structures for the sole use of a tramway line. On the S&DJR all the tramways were based around Radstock to serve the collieries after a failed attempt to construct a canal from the Kennet & Avon at Dundas Basin to Radstock, though the Paulton arm was a success. The route of the Somersetshire Coal Canal from Midford to Radstock was purchased by the Somerset & Dorset Railway in February 1871 for £20,000 and formed part of their extension from Evercreech to Bath. In so doing the railway became responsible for all canal constructed structures; several tramway structures still survive at Radstock.

The materials used in a particular bridge may have changed over the years as repairs were carried out. In 1938/39 several bridges were strengthened to take the new LMS 4-6-0 type locomotives, as a result details in the list may prove to lack these changes because the bridge list information dates from well before World War II. The BR Western Region bridge list is almost identical to the earlier LMS and SR lists with only major changes being noted, such as Bath Road Viaduct. Many structures had there original parapets replaced with either brick or wrought iron (WI) handrails, though at least two retained wooden parapets until the railway closed. Where possible information has been checked against photographs taken in recent years, but understandably this is not always possible.

Many of the remaining structures can be photographed from public roads, especially south of Blandford. Whilst others are easily accessible either along the trackbed or across fields, it must be remembered that in most cases both of these options are private property.

Bath Junction to Broadstone Junction

Bridge No.	Map Ref.	Mile Post	Official Bridge Name

Type and Size and Construction. Present Condition

1	736648	0.13$^{1}/_{2}$	TWERTON VIADUCT

11-span public under bridge crossing Twerton Road and Bellott's Road. WI girders and timber decking on steel columns and masonry abutments. Also eight brick arches on masonry piers and abutments faced with brick. WI handrail parapets.

Demolished 4/5/1969 by BCC

2	733646	0.27	TWERTON FOOTBRIDGE

1-span public under bridge crossing footpath to Twerton Cemetery. Old rail decking on masonry abutments faced with brick. WI handrail parapets.

Demolished by BCC

3	733645	0.31	GREAT WESTERN RAILWAY VIADUCT

3-span private under bridge crossing Great Western Railway. Brick arches on masonry piers and abutments lined with blue brick. WI girders and corrugated floor plates over centre arch. Piers buttressed on up side. WI handrails on brick parapets

Still standing

4	733642	0.47	VICTORIA BRICK & TILE COMPANY BRIDGE

1-span private under bridge crossing road to brick yard. Brick arch on masonry abutments. Brick parapets

Demolished by BCC

Bridge No.   Map Ref.   Mile Post   Official Bridge Name
Type and Size and Construction. Present Condition

5   734641   0.55   CLAUDE AVENUE BRIDGE
1-span public over bridge carrying Claude Avenue. Masonry arch on masonry abutments widened on north side with steel trough decking on brick abutments and parapets faced with blue brick.   Still standing

6   737639   0.74$^1/_2$ MONKSDALE ROAD BRIDGE or KELSON'S BRIDGE
1-span private under bridge crossing road to Harding's Brick Yard. Masonry arch on masonry abutments brick lined. Plate steel parapets.   Demolished 1973 by BCC

7   738638   0.77$^1/_2$ OLDFIELD ROAD BRIDGE or Dr ASHFORD'S BRIDGE
1-span private under bridge crossing road to Dr Ashford's land. Masonry arch on masonry abutments with masonry parapets.   Infilled in the late 1940s

7A   739638   1.02   CULVERT
1-span under bridge. Bath Stone abutments and lined. Blue brick faced.   Still standing

8   740637   1.12   ENGLISHCOMBE BRIDGE
3-span public under bridge, was a footpath to Englishcombe Field, now road to a housing estate. Masonry arches on masonry abutments and piers. Faced with blue brick. Blue brick parapets with cast reproduction handrails.
                                                                                            Still standing restored 1990

9   742636   1.22$^1/_2$ MAPLE GROVE BRIDGE
3-span private over bridge carrying roadway to Mr Turney and Dr Hensley's fields. Masonry arches on masonry piers and abutments with masonry parapets.   Still standing

10   744635   1.32–1.52   DEVONSHIRE TUNNEL
North end portal infilled and landscaped, south end portal sealed with breeze blocks. Masonry and brick portals. Tunnel masonry lined.   Still standing

11   749634   1.58   KETLEY'S BRIDGE
1-span private under bridge crossing road to Ketley's Gardens. Old rail decking on masonry abutments, lined with blue brick on north side. WI handrail parapets.   Re-decked 1989 for Walkers

12   750634   1.62$^1/_2$ WATERY BOTTOM BRIDGE
3-span private under bridge crossing public footpath to Bath Hill. Masonry arches on masonry piers and abutments. Blue brick faced with red brick repairs. WI handrails on brick parapets.   Still standing

Bridge No. 3, Great Western Viaduct viewed from the up side in February 1988. Note how the piers have been buttressed to resist the forces of up trains crossing this curving structure.

Andy Read

Bridge No.   Map Ref.   Mile Post   Official Bridge Name
Type and Size and Construction. Present Condition

13   752633   1.73¹/₂   MOGER'S BRIDGE
1-span private over bridge carrying occupation road and public footpath. Masonry arch and abutments, lined with blue
brick. Blue brick parapets.   Still standing

14   753633   2.00   MOGER'S BRIDGE
3-span private under bridge crossing occupation road. Masonry arches, piers and abutments. Lined with blue brick. WI
handrails on brick parapets.   Still standing

15   753633   2.02–3.05   COMBE DOWN TUNNEL
Both portals sealed with breeze blocks and bricks with iron inspection doors. Masonry and brick portals, brick arch in
places remainder of roof natural rock. Natural rock on walls with some blue brick. Repaired in red brick.   Still standing

16   763616   3.21–3.26   TUCKING MILL VIADUCT
8-span public under bridge crossing roadway to waterworks and footpath to Combe Down. Down side, masonry
arches on masonry abutments and piers lined with blue brick. Up side, brick arches on brick piers and abutments. Brick
parapets.   Still standing

17   760610   3.55   LONG ARCH BRIDGE
1-span public over bridge carrying Tucking Mill Lane. Masonry portals, arch and side walls.   Still standing

18   760606   3.72–3.80   MIDFORD VIADUCT
8-span public under bridge crossing Frome to Bristol Road, the Cam Brook, the Somersetshire Coal Canal and GWR
branch line from Limpley Stoke to Camerton. Down side, masonry arches on masonry abutments and piers, lined with
blue brick. Up side, brick arches, piers and abutments. WI handrails on blue brick parapets on both sides.   Still standing

18A   760605   3.76   TWINHOE ROAD OVER CANAL
1-span public outlying bridge, road crossing Somersetshire Coal Canal. Re-decked 1892 with cast iron rather than timber
decking on masonry abutments. Red brick repairs. Steel plate parapets.   Still standing

19   759596   4.46   TWINHOE BRIDGE
1-span private over bridge carrying Lord Temple's Occupation Road. WI girders and corrugated floor plates on masonry
abutments. Steel plate parapets.   Still standing

Bridge No. 15, Combe
Down Tunnel. This is the
south portal in Horse-
combe Vale. The iron
doors were fitted in early
1985.

Andy Read

Bridge No. 16, Tucking
Mill Viaduct, from the
down side. Note the dam-
aged parapet wall caused
by vandals.

Andy Read

Bridge No.   Map Ref.   Mile Post   Official Bridge Name
Type and Size and Construction. Present Condition

20   757594   4.61   TWINHOE BRIDGE
1-span public under bridge crossing Midford to Wellow road. Down side, masonry arch and abutments lined with brick. Up side, brick arch on masonry abutments. Red brick parapets both sides. Repaired with blue brick.   Still standing

20A   756593   4.63   CULVERT
1-span under bridge. Masonry abutments and lining. Faced in blue brick.   Still standing

21   746583   5.63   MORRIS'S BRIDGE
1-span private over bridge carrying Morris's Occupation Road. WI girders and corrugated floor plates on masonry abutments. WI plate parapets.   Still standing some infilling

22   744583   5.72$^{1}/_{2}$ WELLOW VIADUCT
4-span public under bridge crossing Wellow to Hinton Charterhouse road. Down side, brick arches on masonry piers and abutments lined with bricks. Up side, brick arches on masonry piers and abutments, faced in blue brick. Blue brick parapets with coping stones on both sides.   Still standing

23   740582   6.10$^{1}/_{2}$ WELLOW BRIDGE
1-span public under bridge crossing Wellow to Norton St Philip road. WI girders and corrugated floor plates on masonry abutments with red brick repairs. WI handrail parapets.   Abutments only

24   737579   6.30   STORE'S or STORER BRIDGE
1-span private under bridge crossing occupation road. Down side, masonry arch and abutments. Up side, WI girders and WI floor plates on masonry abutments. Up sidings, WI trough girders with heavy timber decking on masonry abutments.   Still standing down side only

25   737579   6.34   THATCHER CULVERT
1-span under bridge. Masonry arch and side walls.   Still standing

26   734576   6.53   STONEY LITTLETON BRIDGE or WELLOW BRIDGE
1-span public over bridge carrying road to Stoney Littleton. WI girders and corrugated floor plates on masonry abutments with red brick repairs. WI plate parapets.   Still standing

26A   731573   6.56   CULVERT
1-span under bridge. Masonry arch and side walls faced in Bath stone, repaired with red brick.   Still standing

26B   731573   6.63   CULVERT
1-span under bridge. Masonry arch and side walls.   Still standing

27   727566   7.38   3ft CULVERT
1-span under bridge. Masonry arch and side walls.   Still standing

28   725565   7.51   STONEY LITTLETON BRIDGE
2-span public over bridge carrying road to Stoney Littleton. Down side, masonry arch on masonry abutments and pier. Up side, brick arch on masonry abutments and pier faced with blue brick. Brick parapets. All repairs in red brick.   Still standing

28A   723564   7.56   CULVERT
1-span under bridge. Masonry arch and side walls with brick lining.   Still standing

29   720561   8.02   SINGLE HILL BRIDGE
1-span public under bridge crossing road to Frome. Down side, brick arch on masonry abutments. Masonry parapet with WI handrail. Up side, WI girders and corrugated floor plates with timber decking on masonry abutments. WI handrail Parapet.   Abutments only since 1971

30   715559   8.31   3ft 6in CULVERT
1-span under bridge. Masonry arch, walls and invert. Widened with brick arch, invert and masonry walls. Facing repaired with red brick.   Still standing

Bridge No. 22, Wellow Viaduct, – down side view in 1990. The widening of this structure in 1891 can be seen clearly.

Andy Read

Bridge No.	Map Ref.	Mile Post	Official Bridge Name

Type and Size and Construction. Present Condition

31   714558   8.37–8.39   HOME FARM VIADUCT
7-span public under bridge crossing road to Bath. Down side, brick arches on masonry abutments and piers lined with blue brick. Up side, brick arches on masonry abutments and piers. Repaired in red brick. Arch over road demolished 9/90.   Still standing

32   710556   8.59   PAGLINCH FARM BRIDGE or PEGLYNCH BRIDGE
1-span private over bridge carrying road to Peglynch Farm. WI girders and corrugated floor plates on masonry abutments with WI plate parapets.   Still standing

33   705554   9.07   WRITHLINGTON COLLIERY or BRAYSDOWN LANE BRIDGE
1-span public under bridge crossing road to Frome. Brick arch on masonry abutments, faced with blue bricks.
                                                                                                                      Still standing

33A   704553   9.07   WRITHLINGTON STREAM BRIDGE
1-span private outlying bridge for sidings to Writhlington Colliery. North side, brick arch on masonry abutments. South side, masonry arch and abutments with red brick repairs. Brick parapets.   Still standing

34   701552   9.30   3ft 6in WOODBOROUGH STREAM (CULVERT)
1-span private under bridge crossing stream. Masonry arch, walls and Invert.   Still standing

35   695550   9.56   3ft CULVERT
1-span private under bridge. Blue brick barrel and facing.   Still standing

36   695550   9.59½   3ft TYNING COLLIERY STREAM (CULVERT)
1-span private under bridge crossing stream from Tyning Colliery. Brick arch, masonry side walls and abutments. Still standing

37   694550   9.71   TYNING(S) ARCH or MARBLE ARCH
2-span private over bridge carrying sidings to Tyning Colliery. Over main line, WI main and cross girders, timber decking with WI handrail parapets on masonry abutments. Over siding, masonry arch and abutments. WI handrail parapets. Structure removed 1960.   Up side abutments only

38   690549   10.08   PUBLIC FOOTBRIDGE
2-span public over bridge carrying footpath. Originally of all wooden construction with additional steps to serve Radstock station. Rebuilt in 1926 of ferro-concrete with no steps to serve the station.   Demolished 1980

Bridge No.   Map Ref.   Mile Post   Official Bridge Name
Type and Size and Construction. Present Condition

39   689549   10.11   RADSTOCK STATION FOOTBRIDGE
1-span private over bridge carrying foot passengers. WI girders and timber decking on timber trestles.
Demolished 1959 by BR

40   688549   10.15   RADSTOCK SUBWAY
1-span public under bridge crossing Bath Road and tramway to Middle Colliery. WI trough girders and timber decking with WI floor plates over tramway on each side of subway. Masonry abutments and WI handrail parapets.
Demolished 1980

40A   688549   10.15   ROAD OVER RADSTOCK BROOK
2-span public outlying bridge for Radstock to Frome road over brook. Originally brick arches on masonry piers. Side extensions to public road bridge constructed to give better access.   Still standing but rebuilt

41   687550   10.19½   CLANDOWN TRAMWAY BRIDGE
1-span public under bridge crossing tramway and footpath to Middle Colliery and Midsomer Norton. WI girders and corrugated floor plates and timber decking on masonry abutments with WI handrail parapets. Red brick repairs.   Still standing

42   687549   10.20   8ft CULVERT
1-span private under bridge. Masonry arch and abutments. Blue brick faced and lined.   Still standing

42A   687550–684554   10.20   CULVERT on CLANDOWN BRANCH
1-span private under bridge for a stream from Clandown Colliery. Masonry arch and walls, almost one mile long.   Still standing

43   686549   10.25½   WELTON TRAMWAY ARCH
1-span private under bridge crossing a public footpath to Welton. Brick arch on masonry abutments with WI handrail parapets.   Still standing

44   681548   10.56–10.61   NORTH SOMERSET VIADUCT or FIVE ARCHES VIADUCT
5-span private under bridge crossing the Bristol & North Somerset branch line, a public footpath to Clandown and a tramway and public footpath to Welton. Down side, brick arches on masonry piers and abutments. Up side, brick arches on masonry piers and abutments. Lined with blue and red bricks. Up side buttressed in red brick. Renovated 1993.   Still standing

44A   681547   10.56   WELLS WAY TRAMWAY BRIDGE
1-span private outlying under bridge for tramway crossing stream. Brick arch on masonry abutments. Blue brick faced. Brick parapets.   Still standing

44B   680547   10.56   WELLS WAY TRAMWAY BRIDGE
1-span public outlying under bridge. Masonry arch and abutments. Blue brick faced.   Still standing

45   679547   10.65   WELLOW BROOK
1-span private under bridge for stream. Brick arch on masonry abutments.   Still standing

46   678547   10.68   WELTON ROAD BRIDGE
1-span public under bridge for road to Welton. Brick arch on masonry abutments and walls.   Demolished 1982 by SCC

46A   669542   11.44½   NORTON HILL COLLIERY BRIDGE
1-span private over bridge carrying tramway and footpath. Steel lattice girders on steel trestles onto masonry abutments and foundations.   Part abutments only

47   668541   11.49   BEAUCHAMP'S CATTLE ARCH
1-span private under bridge crossing occupation road. Down side, brick arch on masonry abutments and walls. Up side, masonry abutments with brick arch and walls.   Abutments only part infilled

48   664537   11.76   SILVER STREET or
                                           MIDSOMER NORTON STATION BRIDGE
1-span public under bridge crossing Radstock to Midsomer Norton road. WI girders and corrugated floor plates with timber decking. WI handrail parapets on masonry abutments. Red brick repairs.   Demolished 11/1969 by SCC

Bridge No.   Map Ref.   Mile Post   Official Bridge Name
Type and Size and Construction. Present Condition

49   652522   13.12–13.15   CHILCOMPTON TUNNEL
2-span public over bridge carrying road to Midsomer Norton. Brick arches on masonry abutments and pier. Lined with blue brick. Masonry and brick parapets above portals. North portals infilled. South portals open.   Still standing

50   649515   13.47   3ft CULVERT
1-span private under bridge. Masonry arch and walls.   Still standing

51   649515   13.51   REDAN BRIDGE
1-span public under bridge crossing road to Midsomer Norton. Down side, brick arch on masonry abutments. Up side, red brick arch on masonry abutments lined with blue bricks. WI plate screens on brick parapets.   Still standing

52   647514   13.61   BAKER ROBINSON'S BRIDGE
2-span public over bridge carrying road to Midsomer Norton. Brick arches on masonry abutments and pier. Faced with blue brick. Repairs in red brick. Brick parapets.   Still standing some infilling

53   643514   14.00   CATTLE CREEP
1-span private under bridge crossing public footpath to Chilcompton and approach road to goods yard. Brick arch on masonry abutments faced with red and blue brick. Widened three times and contains several World War II tank traps.   Still standing

54   639514   14.19   GREEN DITCH LANE BRIDGE
1-span public under bridge crossing road to Chilcompton. WI main and cross girders with timber decking and WI handrail parapets on masonry abutments. Up side, faced with blue brick.   Abutments only

55   637515   14.24   PONTING'S CATTLE CREEP
1-span private under bridge crossing occupation road. Brick arch on masonry abutments. Up side faced in blue brick with red brick repairs. Masonry and brick parapets.   Still standing

56   636514   14.31   BOWN'S BRIDGE
1-span private under bridge crossing occupation road. Brick arch on masonry abutments with brick parapets. Blue brick faced.   Still standing

57   631512   14.62   BURNT HOUSE BRIDGE
2-span public over bridge carrying road to Bath and Wells. Down side, brick arch and pier faced with blue brick. Up side, brick arch partly faced with blue brick. Masonry abutments and brick parapets.   Demolished

Bridge No. 51, Redan Bridge, just north of Chilcompton station. Viewed from the down side. Note extended parapets and side walls in 1991.

Andy Read

Bridge No. 53, Cattle Creep, under Chilcompton station in 1990. This bridge was widened three times and contains World War II tank traps.

Kevin Regan

Bridge No. Map Ref. Mile Post Official Bridge Name
Type and Size and Construction. Present Condition

58   630510   14.75   COAL LANE BRIDGE
2-span public over bridge carrying road from Old Down to Nettlebridge. Down side, brick arch and pier faced with blue brick. Up side, brick arch partly faced with red brick. Masonry abutments and brick parapets.   Demolished

59   625509   15.17   BRISTOL ROAD BRIDGE
1-span public under bridge crossing road to Bristol. Up side, WI main and cross girders with timber decking. WI handrail parapet. Down side, brick parapet. Masonry abutments faced in red brick.   Abutments only

60   623508   15.31   GATE'S CREEP
1-span private under bridge crossing occupation track. No information on construction or materials.   Infilled 9/1925

61   622507   15.41–15.46   NETTLEBRIDGE VIADUCT
6-span public under bridge crossing occupation road. Down side, brick arches on masonry abutments and piers with brick parapets. Up side, masonry arches, abutments and piers. Lined with blue brick. Concrete and WI handrail parapets.
                                                Still standing

62   620502   15.67   PORTWAY BRIDGE
1-span public under bridge crossing road to Gurney Slade. WI main and cross girders with timber decking and WI handrail parapets on masonry abutments. Repairs in red brick.   Abutments only

63   620498   16.06   CHARD'S CATTLE CREEP
1-span private under bridge crossing occupation road. Down side, brick arch on masonry abutments. Up side, masonry arch and abutments. WI handrails on brick parapets. Red brick repairs.   Still standing

64   620497   16.10   TILLET'S LANE BRIDGE
1-span public under bridge crossing road to Gurney Slade. Brick arch on masonry abutments with brick parapets.
                                                Still standing

65   616492   16.41   BINEGAR STATION BRIDGE
1-span public under bridge crossing road to Oakhill. WI girders with timber decking and WI handrail parapets on masonry abutments with red brick repairs.   North abutments only

66   611488   16.78   GOLLIDGE'S BRIDGE
1-span private over bridge carrying occupation road. WI girders and and corrugated floor plates on masonry and blue brick abutments. WI handrails on brick parapets.   Demolished

67   610485   17.14   JAME'S CATTLE CREEP
1-span private under bridge crossing occupation road. Down side, brick arch on masonry abutments. Up side, masonry arch on masonry abutments. Masonry parapets. Repairs in red and blue brick.   Still standing

68   610481   17.33   BINEGAR BOTTOM BRIDGE
1-span public under bridge crossing road to Wells. Down side, brick arch on masonry abutments. Up side, arch cased with one ring of bricks on masonry abutments. Masonry parapets with blue brick coping.   Still standing

69   609478   17.48   OAKHILL ROAD BRIDGE
1-span public over bridge carrying road to Oakhill. WI girders with corrugated floor plates on extended masonry abutments faced with blue brick. WI plate parapets.   Demolished

70   604472   18.07   MASBURY STATION BRIDGE or MASBURY BRIDGE
1-span public over bridge carrying road to Wells. WI girders with corrugated floor plates on masonry abutments. WI plate parapets.   Still standing

71   603470   18.16   4ft CULVERT
1-span private under bridge. Brick barrel with masonry facing.   Still standing

72   604465   18.45   CROSCOMBE BRIDGE
1-span public under bridge crossing road to Croscombe. WI girders and corrugated floor plates with timber decking on masonry abutments. WI handrail parapets.   Demolished

Bridge No. 68, Binegar Bottom Bridge – to the south of Binegar station in 1990. Viewed from the up side.

Andy Read

Bridge No. 70, Masbury Station Bridge, looking north towards the Summit. This was one of the few remaining wrought iron bridges in 1993.

Andy Read

Bridge No.   Map Ref.   Mile Post   Official Bridge Name
Type and Size and Construction. Present Condition

73   604464   18.51¹/₂   CORP'S BRIDGE   Demolished
1-span private under bridge crossing bridle path. Brick arch on masonry abutments.

73A   605468   18.55   CULVERT   Still standing
1-span private under bridge. Masonry lined and faced with brick repairs.

73B   606460   18.61   THRUPE FARM BRIDGE
1-span private over bridge carrying occupation road. WI girders and corrugated floor plates on masonry abutments and
WI plate parapets.   Still standing

74   606459   18.70   SOMERVILLE'S BRIDGE
1-span private under bridge crossing occupation road. Masonry abutments and brick arch with WI handrail parapets.
                                                                                    Part demolished and infilled

75   609454   19.27–19.30   HAM WOOD VIADUCT
6-span private under bridge crossing occupation road. Down side, brick arches on masonry abutments and piers. Up side,
masonry arches, abutments and piers. All cased in blue brick. Masonry parapets with coping stones and repaired with
brick and breeze blocks.   Still standing

76   611452   19.49¹/₂   3ft CULVERT
1-span private under bridge. Brick arch and masonry walls.   Still standing

77   614450   19.52–19.63   WINSOR HILL (OLD) TUNNEL – Down Line
1-span private over bridge carrying road to Croscombe. Brick arch and masonry with brick side walls in places, the
remaining portions natural rock (Lias limestone).   Still standing, both portals open

77   614452   19.54–19.60   WINSOR HILL (NEW) TUNNEL – Up Line
1-span private over bridge carrying road to Croscombe. Brick arch on masonry walls with blue brick portals.
                                                                        Still standing, both portals open

78   616448   19.74   HAM LANE BRIDGE
1-span public under bridge crossing road to Shepton Mallet. WI girders with corrugated floor plates and timber decking
on masonry abutments, repaired with bricks. WI handrail parapets – removed before 1966.   Demolished 4/1992

79   618446   20.08   DAVIS'S CREEP
1-span private under bridge crossing public footpath and occupation road. Masonry abutments with brick arch and parapets.   Still standing

Bridge No.   Map Ref.   Mile Post   Official Bridge Name
Type and Size and Construction. Present Condition

80   620443   20.22   DAVIS'S BRIDGE
1-span private over bridge carrying occupation road and public footpath. WI girders with corrugated floor plates on masonry abutments with WI plate parapets.   Still standing

81   620443   20.25 – 20.31 BATH ROAD VIADUCT
6-span public under bridge crossing road into Shepton Mallet. Down side, masonry abutments and piers with red brick arches. Up side, original brick structure collapsed 1946, replaced by red brick abutments, piers and arches. Lacks water-proof membrane. Brick parapets.   Still standing

82   625438   20.63   KILVER STREET FOOTBRIDGE BRIDGE
1-span public under bridge crossing public footpath. Down side, brick arch on masonry abutments. Up side, masonry arch and abutments. Small brick parapets.   Still standing

83   626437   20.67   KILVER STREET BRIDGE
1-span public under bridge crossing road into Shepton Mallet. WI girders and corrugated floor plates and timber decking with WI handrail parapets on masonry abutments.   South abutment only since 1969

84   627436   20.75 – 21.09 CHARLTON ROAD VIADUCT
27-span public under bridge crossing 3 public footpaths into Shepton Mallet. Down side, masonry abutments with brick arches and piers. Up side, masonry abutments, piers and arches cased in brick. Built on a centre curve with a failing gradient of 1 in 55 and 1 in 130 changing to a rising gradient of 1 in 66 at the mid-way point. Every third pier is buttressed on the down side to resist the lateral forces of fast and heavy trains.   Still standing

85   628432   21.16   CHARLTON ROAD BRIDGE
1-span public under bridge crossing road into Shepton Mallet. WI girders and corrugated floor plates with timber decking and WI handrail parapets. Masonry abutments with red brick repairs.   Demolished by MDC

86   628431   21.24   SHEPTON MALLET STATION FOOTBRIDGE
1-span private over bridge carrying foot passengers. Steel girders and stanchions with ferro-concrete decking and steps.
                                                                             Demolished 1968 by BR
87   628427   21.42   GREAT WESTERN RAILWAY BRIDGE
2-span private over bridge carrying Great Western Railway. Down side, brick arch on a masonry pier and abutment with brick parapets. Up side, WI girders and corrugated floor plates on masonry pier and abutment. WI handrail parapets.   Still standing

88   628425   21.51   FOSSE LANE BRIDGE
2-span public over bridge carrying road to Cannards Grave. Brick arches on a masonry pier and abutments. Pier faced with blue bricks on the up side. Brick parapets.   Demolished 1974 by MDC

89   628421   21.70   NORMAN'S BRIDGE
2-span private over bridge carrying road to Norman's Fields. Masonry abutments and pier with brick arches and parapets.   Cannards Grave infilled

90   628418   22.06   BARTLETT'S BRIDGE
2-span private over bridge carrying road to Bartlett's Brick Yard. Masonry abutments and pier with brick arches and parapets.
                                                                             Cannards Grave infilled
91   628417   22.12   NORMAN'S BRIDGE
2-span private over bridge carrying road to Norman's Fields. Up side, brick abutment, pier and arch. Down side, masonry abutment, pier and arch. Brick parapets.   Cannards Grave infilled

92   628413   22.32   WHITSTONE LANE BRIDGE
1-span public over bridge carrying road to Doulting. Masonry abutments and arch with brick parapets.
                                                                             Still standing infilled
93   631410   22.56   HERRIDGE'S CATTLE CREEP
1-span private under bridge crossing road to Herridge's Fields. Old rail girders and old rail decking. WI handrail parapets on masonry abutments, repaired with brick.   Demolished 10/1969

Bridge No. 95, Prestleigh Viaduct, viewed from the down side in 1991. This viaduct was demolished and cleared in just ten days in January 1993.

Bridge No.　　Map Ref.　　　　Mile Post　　　Official Bridge Name
Type and Size and Construction. Present Condition

94　　　　634408　　　　22.68　　　HERRIDGE'S CATTLE CREEP
1-span private under bridge crossing road to Herridge's Fields. Masonry abutments and brick arch with brick parapets.　　　　　　　　　　　　　　　　　　　　　　　　　　　　　Demolished 10/1969

95　　　　635407　　　　22.75–23.00　　PRESTLEIGH VIADUCT
11-span public under bridge crossing road to Doulting. Up side, limestone and brick abutments, arches and piers. Down side, masonry abutments, piers and arches encased in blue brick. Brick parapets with coping stones.　　　　　　　　　　　　　　　　　　　　　　　　　　　Demolished 16/1/1993 by BR

96　　　　637403　　　　23.16　　　OSBORNE'S CATTLE CREEP
1-span private under bridge crossing road to Osborne's Fields. WI ballast plates with corrugated floor plates and timber decking. WI handrail parapets on masonry abutments, brick repairs.　　　　　　　South abutment only

97　　　　639399　　　　23.47　　　OSBORNE'S CATTLE CREEP
1-span private under bridge crossing road to Osborne's Fields. Down side, masonry abutments, arch and parapet. Up side, brick arch on masonry abutments with brick parapet.　　　　　　　　　　　　Still standing

98　　　　640398　　　　23.52　　　CLARK'S CATTLE CREEP
1-span private under bridge crossing road to Clark's Fields. Down side, masonry abutments, arch and parapet. Up side, brick arch on masonry abutments with brick parapet.　　　　　　　　　　　　Still standing

Bridge No.   Map Ref.   Mile Post   Official Bridge Name
Type and Size and Construction. Present Condition

99   643394   23.73   EVERCREECH ROAD BRIDGE
1-span public under bridge crossing road to Bruton. Brick arch on masonry abutments with brick parapets.

Demolished 1987

99A   643391   24.10   CULVERT
1-span private under bridge. Masonry abutments and lined with brick arch.

Still standing

100   644390   24.14   LOXTON'S CATTLE CREEP
1-span private under bridge crossing road to Harding's Fields. Brick arch on masonry abutments with blue brick parapets.
End of bridge on down side bricked up.

Still standing, part bricked up

101   644388   24.23   LEIGHTON LANE BRIDGE
1-span public under bridge crossing road to Evercreech. WI main and cross girders, corrugated floor plates with timber
decking on masonry abutments with WI handrail parapets.

North abutments only

102   644383   24.46½   WESTON TOWN BRIDGE
1-span public under bridge crossing road to Evercreech. WI main and cross girders with timber decking on masonry abutments. WI handrail parapets.

Abutments only

103   642380   24.74½   PADFIELD'S CATTLE CREEP
1-span private under bridge crossing road to Padfield's Fields. WI main and cross girders with timber decking on
masonry abutments. WI handrail parapets.

Abutments only since 1969

104   640376   25.06   3ft CULVERT
1-span private under bridge. Part brick and part masonry arch. Masonry walls and invert.

Still standing

105   639375   25.12 – 25.15 PECKING MILL VIADUCT
5-span public under bridge crossing Evercreech to Shepton Mallet road. WI girders and corrugated floor plates with timber decking over road. Four brick arches on masonry abutments and piers – up and down sides have different size arches.
Piers on down side faced in blue brick. Road span had WI handrail parapets but was removed during the 1970s. Brick
arches have brick parapets.

Still standing

105A   639375   25.14   TRACK OVER STREAM
1-span private outlying bridge for track to cross diverted stream. Masonry arch and abutments faced in blue
brick.

Still standing

105B   639375   25.14   MAIN ROAD OVER STREAM
1-span public outlying bridge for Evercreech to Shepton Mallet road to cross diverted stream. Masonry arch and abutments faced in blue brick.

Still standing

106   639375   25.17   ALLEN'S BRIDGE
1-span private under bridge crossing road to Allen's Farm. WI main and cross girders with timber decking on masonry
abutments. WI handrail abutments.

Demolished

107   637373   25.27   PARK BRIDGE
3-span private over bridge carrying road to Allen's Farm. Masonry abutments, piers, arches and parapets.   Still standing

108   635371   25.47   GOLLEDGE'S CATTLE CREEP
1-span private under bridge crossing road to Golledge's Fields. Down side, masonry abutments and arch. Up side, brick
abutments and arch with brick parapets.

Demolished

108A   636369   25.50   CULVERT   Demolished
1-span private under bridge. Brick barrel.

109   638366   25.67   MOODY'S CATTLE CREEP
1-span private under bridge crossing road to Moody's Fields. Mild steel corrugated floor plates with timber decking on
masonry abutments repaired with red brick. WI handrail parapets.

Demolished

Bridge No.　　　Map Ref.　　　　Mile Post　　　Official Bridge Name
Type and Size and Construction. Present Condition

110　　　　639365　　　　25.76$^{1}/_{2}$　　　EVERCREECH STATION FOOTBRIDGE
1-span private bridge carrying foot passengers. WI plate girders with timber decking on trestles. WI plate parapets.　　　　　　　　　　　　　　　　　　　　　　　Demolished 2/1968 by BR

111　　　　642362　　　　26.18$^{1}/_{2}$　　　RIVER ALHAM BRIDGE
1-span private under bridge crossing stream. Masonry arch on masonry abutments. Brick parapets.　　　Still standing

112　　　　643361　　　　26.23$^{1}/_{2}$　　　SHEPHERD'S CATTLE CREEP
1-span private under bridge crossing road to Shepherd's Fields and public footpath to Evercreech. Masonry arch on masonry abutments.　　　　　　　　　　　　　　　　　　　　　　　Still standing

113　　　　657348　　　　27.44$^{1}/_{2}$　　　COX'S CATTLE CREEP
1-span private under bridge crossing road to Cox's Fields. Masonry arch on masonry abutments, face of arch in blue brick.　　　　　　　　　　　　　　　　　　　　　　　　　　　　Still standing

114　　　　658346　　　　27.54　　　　MITCHELL'S CATTLE CREEP
1-span private under bridge crossing road to Mitchell's Fields. Masonry arch on masonry abutments.　　　Still standing

115　　　　660343　　　　27.69　　　　WYKE CHAMPFLOWER BRIDGE
1-span public over bridge carrying road to Castle Cary. Masonry arch, abutments and parapets with red brick repairs. This is the only S&D bridge originally built for double track on the Bath extension.　　　Still standing backfilled

116　　　　662342　　　　28.03$^{1}/_{2}$　　　WYKE LANE BRIDGE
1-span public under bridge crossing road to Castle Cary. Red brick arch on masonry abutments and masonry parapets repaired with blue brick.　　　　　　　　　　　　　　　　　　　　　　　　Still standing

116A　　　665340　　　　28.20　　　　CULVERT
1-span private under bridge. Masonry lined on masonry abutments.　　　　　　　　　　　　　Still standing

116B　　　664339　　　　28.18　　　　CULVERT ON G.W.R CHORD
1-span private outlying bridge. Masonry abutments and lined with brick.　　　　　　　　　　Still standing

117　　　　667339　　　　28.31　　　　WYKE LANE BRIDGE
1-span public under bridge crossing road to Castle Cary. Down side, WI main and cross girders with timber decking. Up side, brick arch on masonry abutments. WI handrail parapets.　　　Abutments only since 9/1984

Bridge No. 100, Loxton's Cattle Creep, has been bricked up mid-way through. This is a view of the down side in 1991.

Andy Read

Bridge No. 116, Wyke Lane Bridge, viewed from up side. The red brick arch stands out on this otherwise masonry constructed bridge.

Bridge No.   Map Ref.   Mile Post   Official Bridge Name
Type and Size and Construction. Present Condition

118   668338   28.35   GREAT WESTERN BRIDGE
1-span private under bridge crossing Great Western Railway. Down side, WI main and cross girders with timber decking. Up side, steel girders and mild steel corrugated floor plates with timber decking on masonry abutments. CI plate parapets.   South abutment only

119   669338   28.42 – 28.44   COLE VIADUCT
5-span public under bridge crossing road to Bruton and stream. Brick arches on masonry abutments and piers partly faced with blue bricks. Red brick repairs. Brick parapets.   Demolished 12/9/1984

120   670336   28.50   CASTLE CARY ROAD BRIDGE
1-span public under bridge crossing road to Bruton. Up side, brick arch on masonry abutments faced with blue brick. Down side, WI girders with corrugated floor plates and timber decking. WI handrail parapets.   Demolished 9/1984

121   671334   28.64$^{1}/_{2}$ PITCOMBE ROAD BRIDGE
2-span public over bridge carrying road to Pitcombe. Brick arches on masonry abutments and pier, pier on down side faced with blue brick. Masonry abutments. Repairs in red brick.   Still standing, part infilled

122   672331   28.79 – 29.01   PITCOMBE BRIDGE or PITCOMBE VIADUCT
3-span public under bridge crossing road to Pitcombe. Brick arches on masonry abutments and piers partly faced with blue brick. Brick parapets removed.   Still standing

123   673329   29.08   PITCOMBE CHURCH BRIDGE
1-span public under bridge crossing road to Shepton Montague. Brick arch on masonry abutments. Up side, faced in blue brick. Wooden handrails on brick parapets.   Still standing

124   676325   29.35   SHEPTON MONTAGUE BRIDGE
1-span public under bridge crossing road to Wincanton. Down side, WI main and cross girders with timber decking. Up side, WI girders and mild steel corrugated floor plates with timber decking on masonry abutments repaired with red brick. WI handrail parapets.   Demolished

125   682320   29.75   CHECKER'S BRIDGE
1-span public under bridge crossing road to Wincanton. Brick arch on masonry abutments. Red brick repairs. Brick parapets.   Still standing

126   684318   30.08   THREE ARCH BRIDGE
3-span private under bridge crossing occupation road and stream. Brick arches on masonry abutments and piers. Up side abutments and piers faced with red brick. Masonry parapets.   Still standing

127   686316   30.24   ROCK CUTTING BRIDGE
2-span public over bridge carrying road to Stoke. By S&D standards a very tall bridge. Brick arches on masonry abutments and pier. Partly faced with blue brick. Masonry parapets. Red brick repairs.   Still standing

127A   688313   30.40   CULVERT
1-span private under bridge. Red brick lined and faced.   Still standing

128   689312   30.45   HANHAM'S CATTLE CREEP
1-span private under bridge crossing road to Hanham's Fields. Brick arch on masonry abutments. Brick parapets.   Still standing

129   690310   30.61$^{1}/_{2}$ 4ft CULVERT
1-span private under bridge. Brick arch and invert with masonry abutments.   Still standing

130   693308   31.37   3ft CULVERT
1-span private under bridge. Brick barrel.   Still standing

131   708291   32.29$^{1}/_{2}$ PLUMER'S BRIDGE
2-span private over bridge carrying road to Wolfrey's Farm and public bridle path. Brick arches on masonry abutments and pier. Down side, faced with blue brick and repairs in red brick. Brick parapets.   Still standing

Bridge No.   Map Ref.   Mile Post   Official Bridge Name
Type and Size and Construction. Present Condition

132   709290   32.36$^{1}/_{2}$ VERRINGTON ROAD BRIDGE
1-span public under bridge crossing road to Wincanton. Down side, WI main and cross girders. Longitudinal timbers with timber decking on masonry abutments. Up side, WI girders and mild steel corrugated floor plates with timber decking on masonry abutments. WI plate parapets.   Abutments only

133   710287   32.55$^{1}/_{2}$ UNION BRIDGE
1-span public under bridge crossing road to Wincanton. Brick arch on masonry abutments. Faced with blue brick. Brick parapets.   Demolished 1990

134   710286   32.61   UNION GIRDER BRIDGE
2-span up side and 1-span down side public under bridge crossing road to Wincanton and a stream. Up side, Portland stone arches, abutments, piers and parapet. Down side, WI main and cross girders with longitudinal timbers and timber decking on masonry abutments with WI handrail parapet. Down side removed 1969. Up side demolished along with down side abutments in late 1970.   Demolished

135   710284   32.70   CEMETERY ROAD BRIDGE
1-span public under bridge crossing road to cemetery. Brick arch on masonry abutments with brick parapets.   Demolished 1989

136   710282   32.74   WINCANTON STATION FOOTBRIDGE
1-span private over bridge carrying foot passengers. Originally timber girders, decking and trestles. Girders strengthened with steel channels. Replaced by ferro-concrete structure.   Demolished 1968 by BR

137   710280   33.07   SHERBORNE ROAD BRIDGE
1-span public under bridge crossing road to Wincanton. Up side, WI main and cross girders with longitudinal timbers and timber decking. Down side, WI main girders and corrugated floor plates with timber decking. Masonry abutments faced with blue brick and repaired with red brick. WI handrail parapets.   Demolished 1968

138   710278   33.16   RIVER KYLE or CALE BRIDGE
1-span private under bridge crossing the River Cale. Brick arch on masonry abutments and brick parapets.
                                                       Re-decked 1990 for a road

139   710274   33.39   3ft CULVERT
1-span private under bridge. Brick barrel.   Still standing

140   710271   33.55   3ft CULVERT
1-span private under bridge. Brick barrel.   Still standing

141   710262   34.18$^{1}/_{2}$ GROVE BRIDGE
2-span private over bridge carrying occupation road. Brick arches on masonry abutments and pier. Pier on down side faced with blue brick. Masonry and brick parapets.   Still standing

141A   710258   34.35   CULVERT
1-span private under bridge. Masonry lined and red brick faced.   Still standing

142   709256   34.48   MACKINHILL CATTLE CREEP
1-span private under bridge crossing road to Austin's Farm. Basemer steel trough girders with longitudinal timbers and timber decking on masonry abutments. WI handrail parapets.   Abutments only, part infilled

143   709254   34.64   MACKINHILL SHEEP CREEP
1-span private under bridge crossing track to Austin's Fields. Old rail and timber decking on brick abutments with WI handrail parapets.   Infilled 3/1941

144   709252   34.72   BULL BROOK BRIDGE
1-span private under bridge crossing a brook. Red brick arch and parapets on masonry abutments.   Still standing

145   708246   35.07   3ft CULVERT
1-span private under bridge. Brick barrel.   Still standing

Bridge No. 127, Rock Cutting Bridge, at Horsington, looking north. Elegant but sturdily constructed of masonry with brick arches.

Kevin Regan

Bridge No.	Map Ref.	Mile Post	Official Bridge Name

Type and Size and Construction. Present Condition

146   708242   35.37   HORSINGTON BRIDGE
2-span public over bridge carrying road to Horsington. Brick arches on masonry abutments and pier, pier faced with blue brick on down side. Brick parapets.   Still standing

146A   708242   35.38   CULVERT
1-span private under bridge. Masonry lined and brick faced.   Still standing

147   708242   35.38   6ft CULVERT
1-span private under bridge crossing stream. Brick arch and invert on masonry abutments. Wooden handrail parapets.
                                                                                     Still standing

147A   708238   35.52   4ft 9in CULVERT
1-span private under bridge. Old rail and timber decking on brick abutments and invert with WI handrail parapets.
                                                                                     Unknown

147"S"   708238   35.52$\frac{1}{2}$ TEMPLECOMBE JUNCTION SIGNAL BRIDGE
1-span private over structure for signals. Old rail girders and stanchions with timber decking.   Cut down 1967

147B   709234   35.68   CULVERT
1-span private under bridge. Brick barrel.   Still standing but damaged

148   709232   36.09   PECK'S BRIDGE
1-span private under bridge crossing occupation road. Brick arch on masonry abutments. Brick parapets.   Still standing

149   709231   36.14   3ft CULVERT
1-span private under bridge. Masonry arch on masonry abutments.   Still standing

150   709231   36.16   PECK'S CATTLE CREEP
1-span private under bridge crossing occupation road and public footpath. Brick arch on masonry abutments. Masonry parapets.   Still standing

151   708226   36.42   TEMPLECOMBE BRIDGE
1-span public under bridge crossing road in Templecombe. WI main girders and corrugated floor plates with timber decking, on masonry abutments with red brick repairs. CI plate parapets.   West abutment only

152   710226   36.36   COOMBE THROOP LANE BRIDGE
1-span public over bridge carrying road to Templecombe. Brick arch on masonry abutments, masonry parapets.   Still standing

Bridge No.   Map Ref.   Mile Post   Official Bridge Name
Type and Size and Construction. Present Condition

152A   710227   36.36   COOMBE THROOP LANE BRIDGE
1-span public outlying bridge carrying road to Templecombe. Brick arch on masonry abutments, masonry parapets.
                                                                                                 Still standing

152B   711227   36.38   5ft CULVERT IN LSWR CHORD
1-span private outlying bridge crossing stream. Brick arch on masonry abutments, masonry parapets.
                                                                                                 Infilled, some remains visible

152C   713227   36.40   BEWSEY LANE BRIDGE
1-span private outlying bridge crossing road to Bewsey's Fields. Brick arch on masonry abutments and walls. Masonry
parapets   Infilled, some remains visible

153   710226   36.39   LSWR MAIN LINE BRIDGE or SOUTH WESTERN BRIDGE
1-span private over bridge carrying LSWR main line. Brick arch on masonry abutments and walls. Masonry
parapets.   Still standing

154   710226   36.41   6ft CULVERT
1-span private under bridge. Red brick arch and facing.   Still standing

154A   710226   36.42   CULVERT
1-span private under bridge. Originally brick arch and brick faced.   Infilled, water now piped

154B   712224   36.56   CULVERT
1-span private under bridge. Red brick arch and brick facing.   Still standing

155   712223   36.57   TEMPLE LANE BRIDGE
1-span public over bridge to Carring Road Templecombe. Masonry arch, abutments and parapet.   Still standing

156   716219   37.04   MITCHELL'S CATTLE CREEP
1-span private under bridge crossing occupation road. Masonry abutments and arch. Blue brick parapet.   Still standing

156A   718214   37.34   1ft CULVERT
1-span private under bridge. Brick barrel.   Still standing

157   720213   37.43   EAVIS'S CATTLE CREEP
1-span private under bridge crossing occupation road. Masonry abutments and arch faced in red brick with blue brick
parapets and WI handrails.   Still standing

158   720213   37.44   3ft CULVERT
1-span private under bridge. Brick barrel.   Still standing

159   725203   38.18   SHAFTESBURY ROAD BRIDGE or HENSTRIDGE BRIDGE
1-span public over bridge carrying road to Sherborne. Masonry abutments and arch with brick parapets.   Still standing

160   726200   38.29   3ft CULVERT
1-span private under bridge. Brick barrel.   Still standing

160A   726199   38.32   CULVERT
1-span private under bridge. Originally brick barrel. Rebuilt with a pipe surrounded with stone.   Still standing rebuilt

160B   730194   38.72   CULVERT
1-span under bridge. Red brick arch and lining.   Demolished water now piped

161   731192   38.78   LANDSHIRE LANE BRIDGE
1-span public over bridge carrying road to Henstridge. Masonry arch, abutments and parapet.   Still standing

161A   731192   38.78   CULVERT
1-span private under bridge. Red brick arch and lining.   Still standing

Bridge No. 161, Landshire Lane Bridge, on the Somerset/Dorset border. This over bridge is constructed totally from masonry.

Andy Read

Bridge No. 174, Lord River's Bridge, or Butt's Dong Bridge. A small, simple but rugged structure.

Andy Read

Bridge No.	Map Ref.	Mile Post	Official Bridge Name
Type and Size and Construction. Present Condition			

161B 744175 40.31 2ft CULVERT
1-span private under bridge. Red brick arch and lining with blue brick facing. Still standing

162 747173 40.40 BIBERNE CULVERT
1-span private under bridge crossing stream. WI trough girder with timber decking on blue brick abutments and blue brick parapets. Still standing

163 756168 41.16 KING'S MILL LANE BRIDGE
1-span public over bridge carrying road to Shaftesbury. Red brick arch and abutments. Blue brick parapets. Still standing

164 758167 41.24 4ft CULVERT
1-span private under bridge. Brick barrel. Still standing

165 760166 41.39 GREEN'S BRIDGE
1-span private over bridge carrying occupation road. Brick arch, abutment and blue brick parapets. Still standing

166 762164 41.51 GREEN'S CATTLE CREEP
1-span private under bridge crossing occupation road. Brick abutments faced in blue brick with red brick arch. WI handrail parapets. Still standing

167 763164 41.53 RIVER LYDDON BRIDGE
2-span private under bridge crossing River Lyddon. WI main and cross girders with longitudinal timbers and timber decking. Brick abutments and pier with WI handrail parapets. Abutments only

168 764163 41.61 ANDREW'S CATTLE CREEP
1-span private under bridge crossing occupation road. Brick abutments faced in red brick with blue brick arch and parapets with WI handrails. Still standing

169 768180 42.07 BAGBER BRIDGE
1-span private over bridge carrying occupation road. Brick abutments with red brick arch and blue brick parapets. Still standing

169A 772156 42.48 CULVERT
1-span private under bridge. Brick barrel. Still standing

Bridge No.   Map Ref.   Mile Post   Official Bridge Name
Type and Size and Construction. Present Condition

170   777150   42.71½   BLACKWATER BRIDGE
2-span private under bridge crossing River Divilish. Masonry abutments and pier faced in red brick with blue brick arches and parapets with WI handrails.   Still standing

171   783144   43.36   STURMINSTER NEWTON BRIDGE
5-span private under bridge crossing River Stour. WI lattice girders and WI cross girders with longitudinal timbers and sleeper decking on masonry abutments. Also four brick flood arches on masonry piers and abutments faced with red brick and WI handrail parapets.   Flood arches only survive

172   785142   43.52   WHILE LANE BRIDGE
1-span public over bridge carrying road to Marnhull. Masonry abutments partly faced in brick with blue brick arch and parapets.   Infilled, one parapet visible

173   787142   43.58   BUTT'S POND BRIDGE or BUTTS DONG BRIDGE
1-span public over bridge carrying road to Sturminster Newton. Masonry abutments and arch faced in blue brick. Blue brick arch and parapets.   Demolished 1974 by DCC

174   791141   43.78   LORD RIVER'S BRIDGE or BUTT'S CATTLE CREEP
1-span private under bridge crossing occupation road and public footpath. Masonry abutments and arch faced in blue brick with blue brick parapets with WI handrails.   Still standing

175   800138   44.49   FIDDLEFORD MILL BRIDGE
5-span private under bridge crossing River Stour. WI lattice main girders and WI cross girders with longitudinal timbers and timber decking. Also four flood openings with WI girders and corrugated floor plates and timber decking on masonry piers and abutments, red brick faced. WI handrail parapets.   Abutments only

176   813135   45.35   HAMMOON LANE BRIDGE
1-span public over bridge carrying road to Hammoon. Brick abutments and walls. Red brick arch and parapets.
                                                     Still standing

177   816132   45.54   3ft CULVERT
1-span private under bridge. Brick barrel.   Still standing

Bridge No. 180, Hayward's Bridge, just north of Shillingstone station, slightly knocked about in 1991.

Kevin Regan

Bridge No.   Map Ref.   Mile Post   Official Bridge Name
Type and Size and Construction. Present Condition

178   820127   46.09   RAGVANS DROVE BRIDGE or RAGLAN'S DROVE BRIDGE
1-span private under bridge crossing occupation road. Brick abutments with red brick arch and parapets.   Still standing

178   820127   46.09   CULVERTS IN ABUTMENTS OF 178
2 Single private under spans for streams. Red brick barrels.   Both still standing

178A   821124   46.25   CULVERT
1-span private under bridge. Red brick barrel.   Still standing

179   821121   46.38   OCCUPATION BRIDGE
1-span private under bridge crossing occupation road. Red brick arch on brick abutments and parapets with WI handrails.   Still standing

180   822120   46.46   HAYWARD'S BRIDGE
1-span public under bridge crossing road to Okeford. Brick abutments with red brick arch, walls and parapets with WI handrails.   Still standing

181   823119   46.50$^{1}/_{2}$ 8ft COOKWELL BROOK CULVERT
1-span private under bridge crossing Cookwell Brook. Brick arch, walls and invert.   Still standing

181A   830111   47.10   CULVERT
1-span private under bridge. Brick barrel.   Still standing

182   834105   47.57   HACKER'S BRIDGE
1-span private under bridge crossing occupation road. Red brick arch on brick abutments. Brick facing and parapets with WI handrails.   Still standing

182A   834105   47.58   CULVERT
1-span private under bridge. Red brick barrel and facing with blue brick coping.   Still standing

182B   834105   47.58   CULVERT (Road Over)
1-span public outlying bridge. Masonry abutments, red brick faced and lined. Blue brick coping.   Still standing

182C   835103   47.66   2ft CULVERT
1-span private under bridge. Masonry abutments, red brick faced and lined. Blue brick coping.   Still standing

183   838102   48.04   WARREN'S BRIDGE
1-span private under bridge crossing occupation road. Brick abutments and walls with red brick arch. Abutments faced in red brick. WI handrail parapets.   Still standing

184   844102   48.36$^{1}/_{2}$ CLIFF BRIDGE
3-span private over bridge carrying occupation road. Brick arches on brick piers and abutments. Faced in red brick. Brick parapets with WI handrails.   Infilled, one parapet visible

185   850099   48.70   HODMOOR BRIDGE
5-span private under bridge crossing River Stour. WI lattice main and WI cross girders with longitudinal timbers and timber decking on brick abutments. Also four flood arches on brick piers and abutments. WI handrail parapets throughout.   Flood arches only survive

186   857094   49.32   HEAD LANE BRIDGE or MEAD LANE BRIDGE
3-span private under bridge crossing occupation road. Brick arches on brick abutments and piers faced in red brick. WI handrails on red brick parapets.   Still standing

187   860091   49.53$^{1}/_{2}$ DURWESTON BRIDGE
1-span private under bridge crossing occupation road. Brick abutments with brick arch and walls. Blue brick parapets.   Still standing

Bridge No.   *Map Ref.*   *Mile Post*   *Official Bridge Name*
Type and Size and Construction. Present Condition

188   863088   49.76^1/$_2$ A350 ROAD BRIDGE or STOURPAINE BRIDGE
1-span public over bridge carrying road to Shaftesbury. A long skew angle bridge. Brick abutments and walls with red brick arch and blue brick parapets.   Still standing

189   868082   50.30   FRANCE FARM BRIDGE
1-span private over bridge carrying occupation road. Brick arch on brick abutments and blue brick parapets.   Infilled, one parapet visible

190   876083   50.68^1/$_2$ FRANCE FARM DROVE
3-span private under bridge crossing occupation road. Brick abutments and arches with brick piers faced in red brick. WI handrail parapets.   Still standing

191   879081   51.12   NUTFORD BRIDGE
3-span private under bridge crossing occupation road. Brick arches on brick abutments and piers. Blue brick parapets with WI handrails.   Demolished

192   881073   51.54   MILLDOWN ROAD BRIDGE
1-span private over bridge carrying occupation road and public footpath. WI plate parapets and corrugated floor plates on brick abutments.   Still standing

193   886067   52.11   SALISBURY ROAD BRIDGE
1-span public over bridge carrying Blandford to Salisbury road. Brick abutments faced in red brick with red brick arch and walls. Blue brick parapets and coping stones.   Still standing

194   887066   52.19   BLANDFORD STATION FOOTBRIDGE
1-span public over bridge carrying foot passengers. WI plate parapets with corrugated floor plates on brick abutments.   Still standing

195   888066   52.23   BLANDFORD STATION SUBWAY
1-span private under bridge crossing for foot passengers. Part corrugated floor plates and part brick arch on brick abutments.   Demolished 1973

196   888064   52.32^1/$_2$ DAMORY COURT BRIDGE
3-span public under bridge crossing Poole to Blandford road. Brick arches on brick piers and abutments. Brick parapets. All faced in grey engineering brick.   Demolished 25/7/1978 by DCC

196A   888064   52.32^1/$_2$ CULVERT UNDER BRIDGE 196
1-span private under bridge crossing stream. Blue brick barrel faced in grey engineering brick.   Still standing

197   888063   52.37   FARQUHARSON BRIDGE
3-span private under bridge crossing occupation road. Brick arches on brick abutments and piers with brick parapets.   Demolished 1983 by DCC

198   888061   52.46   BLANDFORD RIVER STOUR BRIDGE
5-span private under bridge crossing River Stour. WI lattice main girders and WI cross girders with longitudinal timbers and timber decking. WI handrail parapets. Also four brick flood arches on brick piers and abutments with red brick parapets one side and blue brick parapets on the other.   Two flood arches only survive

199   888058   52.57   LOCK'S BRIDGE
3-span private under bridge crossing occupation road. Brick arches on brick piers and abutments with brick parapets.   Demolished 1983 by DCC

200   888055   52.75   BLANDFORD St MARY BRIDGE
2-span public over bridge carrying Poole to Blandford Road. Red brick arches on red brick pier and abutments with red brick parapets.   Demolished 1983 by DCC

201   889051   53.15   WARD'S DROVE BRIDLEWAY
2-span private over bridge carrying occupation road and public footpath. Masonry abutments with red brick arches and piers with blue brick parapets.   Still standing, infilled

Bridge No. 203, Charlton Marshall Halt Bridge looking north. This halt is now cared for by local enthusiasts.

Bridge No.	Map Ref.	Mile Post	Official Bridge Name

Type and Size and Construction. Present Condition

202   892046   53.44$^1/_2$ BOYT'S BRIDGE

1-span private under bridge crossing occupation road and public footpath. Masonry abutments with red brick arch and blue brick parapets.   Still standing

203   896044   53.79$^1/_2$ CHARLTON MARSHALL HALT BRIDGE

1-span public over bridge carrying road to Thornycombe. Brick abutments and walls faced in red brick with red brick arch and parapets with blue brick coping.   Still standing

204   897039   54.10   CHARLTON PARK BRIDGE or
HUNTLEY'S CATTLE CREEP

1-span private under bridge crossing occupation road. WI ballast plates with corrugated floor plates and timber decking. WI handrail parapets. All on red brick abutments.   Abutments only since 1972

205   898038   54.15   MIDDLE DROVE BRIDGE

1-span private under bridge crossing occupation road. Red brick abutments and walls with red brick arch and parapets.   Still standing

206   898038   54.19   BASTARD'S CATTLE DROVE

1-span private under bridge crossing occupation road. Red brick abutments and walls with red brick arch and parapets.   Still standing

207   900037   54.26   CHARLTON DROVE BRIDGE

1-span public under bridge crossing road to Thornycombe. Red brick abutments and walls with red brick arch and parapets.   Still standing

208   904033   54.52$^1/_2$ COLONEL BROWN'S FOOTBRIDGE

1-span private over bridge carrying footway to residence. Originally timber girders and decking on brick abutments. Rebuilt on the brick abutments with ferro-concrete decking and parapets.   Still standing

209   906031   54.66   COLONEL BROWN'S BRIDGE

1-span private under bridge crossing road to residence. Brick abutments and walls faced in red brick. Red brick arch and parapets.   Still standing

210   907030   54.77   4ft CULVERT

1-span private under bridge. Brick arch on brick walls and invert.   Still standing

210A   908030   54.78   CULVERT

1-span public outlying bridge. Brick arch on brick walls and invert.   Still standing

Bridge No.　　Map Ref.　　　Mile Post　　　Official Bridge Name
Type and Size and Construction. Present Condition

211　　　　907029　　　54.78¹/₂　　　WEST END BRIDGE
1-span public under bridge crossing road to Thornycombe. Brick abutments and walls faced in red brick. Red brick arch and parapets.　　　　　　　　　　　　　　　　　　　　　　　　　　　　　Still standing

212　　　　910026　　　55.18¹/₂　　　STRANGE'S BRIDGE
1-span private over bridge carrying occupation road. Red brick arch on brick foundations and abutments. Blue brick parapets.　　　　　　　　　　　　　　　　　　　　　　　　　　　　　　Still standing

213　　　　913022　　　55.44　　　SPETISBURY STATION BRIDGE
1-span public under bridge crossing road to Mapperton. Brick abutments and walls faced in red brick. Red brick arch and parapets with blue brick coping and WI handrails.　　　　　　　　　　　　　　　　　Still standing

214　　　　918017　　　55.78　　　LOUSE LANE BRIDGE or LOOSE LANE BRIDGE
1-span public under bridge crossing road to Spetisbury. Brick abutments and walls faced in red brick. Red brick arch and parapets.　　　　　　　　　　　　　　　　　　　　　　　Demolished 1986 by DCC

215　　　　923015　　　56.28¹/₂　　　MACKERAL'S BRIDGE
1-span private under bridge crossing occupation track between fields. Brick abutments and walls faced in red brick. Red brick arch and parapet.　　　　　　　　　　　　　　　　　　　　　　　Still standing

216　　　　928012　　　56.57¹/₂　　　TORY'S BRIDGE
1-span private under bridge crossing track into fields. Brick abutments and walls faced in red brick. Red brick arch and parapets.　　　　　　　　　　　　　　　　　　　　　　　　　　　Still standing

217　　　　934009　　　57.09　　　CLIFFE ROAD BRIDGE or A350 ROAD BRIDGE
1-span public over bridge carrying Poole to Blandford Road. Red brick abutments, walls and arch constructed at a skew angle. Blue brick parapets with coping stones.　　　　　　　　　　　　　Demolished 1974 by DCC

218　　　　944998　　　58.02　　　14ft CULVERT
1-span under bridge. Masonry abutments with brick arch and facing.　　　　　　　　　　　　Still standing

219　　　　944998　　　58.03　　　STURMINSTER MARSHALL BRIDGE
1-span public under bridge crossing road to Almer. Brick abutments and walls faced in red brick. Red brick arch and parapets.　　　　　　　　　　　　　　　　　　　　　　　　　　　　　　Demolished

220　　　　948994　　　58.30　　　BAILEY GATE STATION BRIDGE
1-span public over bridge carrying Sturminster Marshall to Poole road. Brick abutments and walls faced in red brick. Red brick arch and parapets.　　　　　　　　　　　　　　　　Demolished 4/1992 by DCC

220A　　　952992　　　58.50　　　CULVERT
1-span private under bridge. Red brick barrel with blue brick facing.　　　　　　　　　　　Still standing

220B　　　954991　　　58.62　　　CULVERT
1-span private under bridge. Red brick barrel with blue brick facing.　　　　　　　　　　　Still standing

220C　　　956991　　　58.74　　　CULVERT
1-span private under bridge. Red brick barrel with blue brick facing.　　　　　　　　　　　Still standing

221　　　　973982　　　60.08　　　CORFE MULLEN BRIDGE
1-span private over bridge carrying road to fields and brick yard. Brick abutments and walls faced in red brick. Red brick arch and parapets.　　　　　　　　　　　　　　　　　　　　　　　Still standing

222　　　　976982　　　60.21　　　4ft CORFE MULLEN CULVERT
1-span private under bridge. Brick barrel.　　　　　　　　　　　　　　　　　　　　　Demolished 1990

223　　　　977983　　　60.28¹/₂　　　CORFE MULLEN JUNCTION BRIDGE
1-span public over bridge carrying road to Poole. Brick abutments and walls faced in red brick. Red brick arch and parapets.　　　　　　　　　　　　　　　　　　　　　　　　　　　　Still standing

Bridge No. 223, Corfe Mullen Junction Bridge, looking south towards the junction in 1992

Bridge No.	Map Ref.	Mile Post	Official Bridge Name

Type and Size and Construction. Present Condition

223A   983985   60.60$^1/_2$ CULVERT
1-span private under bridge. Brick Barrel.
Still standing

224   987986   60.78   DIGGER'S BRIDGE (Wimborne Line)
1-span public under bridge crossing Wimborne Road. Red brick abutments, arch, walls and parapets.
North abutment only

225   998990   61.50   3ft CULVERT (Wimborne Line)
1-span private under bridge crossing stream. Red brick barrel.
Demolished

226   004991   62.09   4ft CULVERT (Wimborne Line)
1-span private under bridge crossing stream. Red brick barrel.
Still standing

227   005991   62.18$^1/_2$ MERLEY BRIDGE (Wimborne Line)
2-span private under bridge crossing occupation road to fields. Red brick arches on brick abutments and pier. Brick parapets.
Demolished

227A   013988   62.57   CULVERT (Wimborne Line)
1-span private under bridge crossing stream. Red brick barrel.
Still standing

228   017986   63.00   OAKLEY ROAD BRIDGE (Wimborne Line)
1-span public over bridge carrying road to Poole. Red brick abutments, arch and parapets.
Demolished

229   985985   60.68   GLEN LANE'S BRIDGE or GEN LANE BRIDGE
1-span public under bridge crossing road to Corfe Mullen. Masonry abutments and walls with red brick arch and parapets.
Still standing

230   985985   60.69   3ft CULVERT
1-span private under bridge. Red brick barrel with blue brick facing.
Still standing

231   986985   60.76   3ft CULVERT
1-span private under bridge. Brick barrel. North end extended with 2ft CI pipes.
Still standing

232   987985   60.78   GOODCHILD'S BRIDGE
1-span private under bridge crossing occupation road. WI main and cross girders with longitudinal timbers and timber decking on brick abutments with WI plate parapets.
Abutments only

233   989985   61.08   3ft CULVERT
1-span private under bridge. Brick barrel.
Still standing

234   991985   61.18   GOODCHILD'S BRIDGE
1-span private over bridge carrying occupation road to fields. Brick abutments and walls faced in red brick. Red brick arch and parapets.
Still standing

Bridge No.   Map Ref.   Mile Post   *Official Bridge Name*
Type and Size and Construction. Present Condition

234A   991985   61.20   CULVERT
1-span private under bridge. Brick barrel.   Still standing

235   994984   61.38   CORFE MULLEN HALT BRIDGE or PUBLIC BRIDGE
1-span public over bridge carrying road to Lytchett. Brick abutments and walls faced in red brick. Red brick arch and
parapets.   Demolished and cutting infilled

236   996983   61.44   LAMB'S GREEN LANE BRIDGE
1-span public over bridge carrying road to Lytchett. Brick abutments and walls faced in red brick. Red brick arch and parapets.   Still standing

237   998982   61.57   5ft 2in CULVERT
1-span private under bridge. Brick arch walls and invert.   Still standing

238   999979   61.73   ASHINGTON LANE BRIDGE
3-span public over bridge carrying Wimborne to Corfe Mullen road. Brick abutments and arches on brick piers with brick
parapets.   Still standing, some infilling

239   001975   62.14   6ft 10in CULVERT
1-span private under bridge. Red brick barrel and abutments.   Still standing

240   003969   62.49$^{1}/_{2}$ 3ft CULVERT
1-span under bridge. Brick barrel.   Still standing

240A   004972   62.60   GOLF COURSE FOOTBRIDGE
1-span private over bridge carrying golf course footpath. No information.   Demolished/removed 1920s

241   005964   62.74   5ft 8in CULVERT
1-span private under bridge. Brick arch, walls and invert.   Still standing

Evercreech Junction to Burnham-on-Sea

242   634375   0.30$^{1}/_{2}$ PARK BRIDGE
1-span private over bridge carrying road to Allen's Farm and public footpath. Masonry arch and abutments with masonry
parapets.   Unknown

243   618388   1.56   PYLLE STATION BRIDGE
1-span public over bridge carrying road to Shepton Mallet. Masonry arch and abutments with masonry parapets.
                                                                Demolished 1970 by SCC

244   1.68   4ft 3in CULVERT
1-span private under bridge. Masonry arch and walls.   Still standing

245   611389   2.12   LONG CLOSE BRIDGE
1-span private over bridge carrying occupation road. Masonry arch on masonry abutments and parapets. Faced in blue
brick.   Demolished 1960

246   609388   2.22   5ft 2in CULVERT
1-span private under bridge. Masonry arch and walls.   Still standing

247   605386   2.44   PILTON ROAD BRIDGE
1-span public over bridge carrying road to Pilton. Masonry arch on masonry abutments with red brick parapets.
                                                                Still standing

248   2.56   6ft CULVERT
1-span private under bridge. Masonry arch and abutments.   Still standing

249   600385   2.71   OCCUPATION ROAD BRIDGE
1-span private under bridge crossing occupation road to fields. Masonry arch, abutments and parapets.   Still standing

| Bridge No. | Map Ref. | Mile Post | Official Bridge Name |

Type and Size and Construction. Present Condition

250 600385 2.72 6ft RIVER BRUE CULVERT
1-span private under bridge. Masonry arch, abutments and invert. Still standing

251 3.38$^{1}/_{2}$ CATTLE CREEP
1-span private under bridge crossing occupation road between fields. Masonry arch and abutments. Still standing

252 3.69 CATTLE CREEP
1-span private under bridge crossing occupation road between fields. Masonry arch and abutments. Still standing

253 579394 4.29 CATTLE CREEP
1-span private under bridge crossing occupation road. Masonry arch and abutments. Still standing

254 578394 4.29$^{1}/_{2}$ CATTLE CREEP
1-span private under bridge crossing occupation road. Masonry arch and abutments. Still standing

255 4.50$^{1}/_{2}$ 3ft 9in CULVERT
1-span private under bridge crossing stream. Masonry arch and walls. Still standing

256 4.60$^{1}/_{2}$ CATTLE CREEP
1-span private under bridge crossing occupation road. Masonry arch and abutments. Unknown

257 568395 5.05 WEST PENNARD STATION
1-span public over bridge carrying road to Shepton Mallet. Masonry arch on masonry abutments and walls faced in blue brick with brick parapets. Demolished 1970 by SCC

258 5.54 4ft CULVERT
1-span private under bridge crossing stream. Part BH rail decking on brick side walls and part masonry arch and side walls. Repairs in red brick. Handrail parapets. Still standing

259 6.14 8ft 4in CULVERT
1-span private under bridge crossing stream. Up side, mild steel corrugated floor plates and WI ballast plates on masonry abutments. Down side, masonry arch and abutments. WI handrail parapets. Still standing

260 6.32$^{1}/_{2}$ RHINE BRIDGE
1-span private under bridge crossing stream. Corrugated floor plates and WI ballast plates on masonry abutments. WI handrail parapets. Still standing

260A 545400 6.40 3ft 7in CULVERT
1-span private outlying bridge. Masonry arch on masonry abutments. Still standing

260B 542400 6.51$^{1}/_{2}$ 3ft 7in CULVERT
1-span private outlying bridge. Masonry arch on masonry abutments. Still standing

260C 539401 6.68 3ft 7in CULVERT
1-span private outlying bridge. Masonry arch on masonry abutments. Still standing

260D 538401 6.73$^{1}/_{2}$ 3ft 7in CULVERT
1-span private outlying bridge. Masonry arch on masonry abutments. Still standing

261 7.05$^{1}/_{2}$ RHINE BRIDGE
1-span private under bridge crossing stream. Steel corrugated floor plates and WI ballast plates on masonry abutments, repaired in red brick. WI handrail parapets. Still standing

262 7.21$^{1}/_{2}$ 8ft CULVERT
1-span private under bridge crossing stream. Masonry arch on masonry abutments. Still standing

263 7.33$^{1}/_{2}$ 10ft CULVERT
1-span private under bridge crossing stream. Masonry arch on masonry abutments. Still standing

Bridge No.   Map Ref.   Mile Post   Official Bridge Name
Type and Size and Construction. Present Condition

264   511405   8.49   WELLS ROAD BRIDGE
1-span public over bridge carrying Glastonbury to Wells road. WI girders and brick arch filling with timber decking. WI corrugated parapets on masonry abutments.   Demolished 3/1994 by SCC

265   495393   9.73¹/₂   NORTHLOAD ROAD BRIDGE
1-span public over bridge carrying road to Glastonbury. Masonry arch on masonry abutments with brick parapets.
                                                                                          Still standing

265A   493390   10.10   CULVERT
1-span private under bridge. Masonry arch on masonry abutments.   Unknown

265B   492389   10.16   MILL STREAM CULVERT
1-span private under bridge. Masonry arch on masonry abutments.   Infilled 1988/89

266   491389   10.26   DYE HOUSE CROSSING BRIDGE
1-span private under bridge crossing stream. WI trough girders and ferro-concrete decking on masonry abutments. WI handrail parapets.   Still standing

266A   491388   10.26   MILL STREAM BRIDGE
1-span public outlying bridge, Glastonbury to Meare road crossing stream. Originally, corrugated floor plates with WI plate parapets on masonry abutments. Rebuilt WI girders and decking with tarmac covering on masonry abutments. Masonry parapets.   Still standing

267   490390   10.30¹/₂   GLASTONBURY STATION FOOTBRIDGE
1-span private over bridge carrying foot passengers. WI lattice girders on timber trestles with timber decking, uprights and roof.   Demolished 1967 by BR

267A   486392   10.51   ROAD OVER CANAL BRIDGE
1-span public outlying bridge carrying road over canal. Old rail decking on concrete abutments. WI handrail parapets.
                                                                                          Still standing

268   479392   11.05¹/₂   RIVER BRUE AQUEDUCT BRIDGE
1-span private under bridge crossing River Brue. WI lattice girders with mild steel corrugated floor plates and timber decking on brick abutments.   Still standing

269   451395   12.78¹/₂   ASHCOTT CANAL BRIDGE
3-span private under bridge crossing rhine. Timber girders and decking on timber piles with concrete abutments. WI handrail parapets.   Still standing

Bridge No. 264, Wells Road Bridge just east of Glastonbury station in 1991. A wrought iron structure on masonry
abutments. Unfortunately it was demolished in 1994.
                                            Kevin Regan

Bridge No. 265, Northload Road Bridge is a far more
attractive bridge than No. 264, being constructed of stone
but shows how S&DJR bridges can vary.
                                            Kevin Regan

Bridge No. 268, River Brue Aqueduct Bridge. The lattice girders, steel floor plates and timber decking of this bridge have withstood the test of time well.

Kevin Regan

Bridge No.   Map Ref.   Mile Post   Official Bridge Name
Type and Size and Construction. Present Condition

269A   449396   13.09   ASHCOTT ROAD OVER RIVER
1-span public outlying bridge carrying Glastonbury to Meare Road over rhine. Originally, CI and timber girders with timber decking on masonry abutments.   Replaced by modern bridge

270   15.65¹/₂   LOCK BRIDGE
3-span private under bridge crossing South Drain. Timber girders and decking on timber piles with longitudinal timbers carrying the permanent way. WI handrail parapets.   Unknown

270A   15.74   CATCOTT CROSSING CANAL BRIDGE
2-span public outlying bridge carrying road to Catcott over canal. Ferro-concrete beams and decking on a concrete pier and abutments north side. Masonry abutments south side. Handrail parapets.   Still standing

270B   400424   16.48   PUBLIC ROAD OVER CANAL
1-span public outlying bridge carrying road over canal. No information on original construction and materials. Replaced by a modern bridge of reinforced concrete on brick faced abutments. Steel handrail parapets.   Still standing, modernised

271   399424   16.50¹/₂   CATCOTT WALL RHINE BRIDGE
1-span private under bridge crossing stream. Originally timber girders and decking on wooden piers with masonry abutments. Rebuilt brick arch on masonry abutments.   Still standing

271A   393427   17.09   EDINGTON BRIDGE
1-span public outlying bridge carrying road to Edington over canal. Originally No.4 rolled steel girders and old rail decking on masonry abutments. Recently modernised with concrete decking on RSBs. Steel handrail parapets.   Still standing modernised

271B   386427   CHILTON DROVE BRIDGE
1-span public outlying bridge carrying road to Chilton Polden over canal. Originally BH steel rails on timber girders with timber decking on masonry abutments. WI handrail parapets. Recently modernised with concrete decking on RSBs. Steel handrail parapets.   Still standing modernised

271C   376429   WEST DROVE BRIDGE
1-span public outlying bridge carrying road to Chilton Polden over canal. Originally timber girders and timber decking on masonry abutments. WI handrail parapets. Rebuilt with BH rails and timber decking with steel handrail parapets.   Still standing modernised

Bridge No.   Map Ref.   Mile Post   Official Bridge Name
Type and Size and Construction. Present Condition

271D   367431   GOLD CORNER BRIDGE
1-span private outlying bridge carrying occupation road over canal. BH steel rails on timber girders with timber decking on masonry abutments and parapets.   Still standing

271E   EASTERN MOOR BRIDGE
1-span public outlying bridge carrying road to Huntspill over canal. Originally timber girders and timber decking on masonry abutments with handrail parapets.   Still standing modernised

271F   LITTLE MOOR BRIDGE
1-span private outlying bridge carrying occupation road over canal. originally BH steel rails and timber girders with timber decking on masonry abutments.   Still standing modernised

272   385432   17.50^{1}/$_2$ CHILTON ROAD BRIDGE
1-span public under bridge carrying road to Chilton Polden. BH steel rail decking on masonry abutments with WI handrail parapets.   Demolished 1968

273   18.20   MIDDLE FURLONG RHINE BRIDGE
1-span private under bridge crossing rhine. Originally timber girders with longitudinal timbers for permanent way and timber decking on timber piles. Handrail parapets.   Unknown

274   18.31   CHILTON DROVE BRIDGE
1-span public under bridge crossing road to Chilton Polden. Rolled steel main and cross girders with longitudinal timbers on top for permanent way on masonry abutments. WI handrail parapets.   Demolished

275   18.46^{1}/$_2$ BLACK DITCH BRIDGE
3-span private under bridge crossing rhine. Timber girders and timber decking on timber piers. Longitudinal timbers for permanent way. Handrail parapets.   Still standing

276   19.47   BRUE CORNER BRIDGE or CRIPS CORNER BRIDGE
4-span private under bridge crossing River Brue. WI lattice main and cross girders with ferro-concrete decking on CI and steel piles. WI handrail parapets.   Unknown

277   20.18   ISGAR'S CATTLE CREEP
1-span private under bridge crossing occupation road. Brick abutments, walls, arch and parapets.   Unknown

278   21.68   5ft CULVERT
1-span private under bridge crossing rhine. Brick arch and side walls.   Still standing

279   21.70   HUNT'S CATTLE CREEP
1-span private under bridge crossing occupation road. Brick arch and side walls backed with concrete on masonry abutments. WI handrail parapets.   Unknown

280   323469   22.21   5ft CULVERT
1-span private under bridge. Brick arch with masonry side walls.   Still standing

280A   323469   22.21   FOOTBRIDGE OVER STREAM
1-span private outlying bridge, footpath to Locomotive Works over stream. Ferro-concrete beams and decking on brick abutments.   Believed demolished

280B   322470   22.29   CULVERT
1-span private under bridge. Masonry abutments. Brick faced and lined.   Unknown

281   322470   22.29   HIGHBRIDGE STATION FOOTBRIDGE
2-span private over bridge carrying foot passengers. WI girders on CI columns. Masonry abutments faced in brick. Timber decking and steps. WI plate parapets.   GWR portion still standing

Bridge No.   Map Ref.   Mile Post   Official Bridge Name
Type and Size and Construction. Present Condition
281A   322470   22.29   BRIDGE OVER GWR MAIN LINE
1-span public over bridge carrying Highbridge to Bason Bridge road. Originally WI girders on CI columns with corrugated floor plates and WI plate parapets. Masonry abutments. Rebuilt on masonry abutments with concrete decking on RSBs. Steel handrail parapets.   Still standing

Highbridge to Burnham-on-Sea

282   22.44   3ft 6in CULVERT
1-span private under bridge. Brick arch on masonry side walls.   Demolished

283   22.46¹/₂   CHURCH STREET FOOTBRIDGE
1-span public over bridge carrying foot passengers. DH iron rail girders on trestles with timber decking.   Demolished

283A   22.69   BRUE BRIDGE or LOCK BRIDGE
1-span public outlying bridge carrying public road over lock. Rebuilt as 3-span bridge. Originally, masonry abutments, arch and invert. Rebuilt with concrete decking on RSBs. Two masonry flood opening on either side. Steel handrail parapets.   Still standing modernised

283B   23.09   NEW CYCLE BRIDGE or LOCK BRIDGE
1-span private outlying bridge carrying private siding and public footpath over lock. Rebuilt with two spans for water authority pumps and footpath. Masonry abutments, arch and invert with timber decking. This bridge also took a siding over the lock when originally constructed. Rebuilt with masonry arches, abutments and parapets, lock gates and pumps.
                                                                                    Still standing

284   23.18   HAYES CATTLE CREEP
1-span under bridge. No information on construction or materials.   Demolished 1917

285   23.18¹/₂   4ft CULVERT
1-span private under bridge. Brick arch on masonry walls.   Still standing

Glastonbury Mile Post ¹/₄ to Wells Priory

286   509412   1.77¹/₂   HARTLAKE RHINE BRIDGE
1-span private under bridge crossing stream. Timber girders and decking on masonry abutments with WI handrail parapets.
                                                                                    Still standing
287   509412   1.78   HARTLAKE RIVER BRIDGE
1-span private under bridge crossing rhine. Trussed timber girders and decking on masonry abutments. WI handrail parapets.
                                                                                    Still standing

Bridge No. 283A, Brue Bridge, between Highbridge and Burnham. One of many outlying bridges on the branch line. This bridge has been rebuilt on the original abutments. Note flood openings either side.

Andy Read

Bridge No. 283B New Cycle or Lock Bridge. An interestingly rebuilt bridge of masonry and brick arches, abutments and parapets with lock gates and pumps. Also used for a footpath.

Andy Read

Bridge No.   Map Ref.   Mile Post   Official Bridge Name
Type and Size and Construction. Present Condition

288   523434   3.50   COXLEY RIVER BRIDGE
1-span private under bridge crossing stream. Masonry abutments, walls and arch with WI handrail parapets. Still standing

289   527438   3.79¹/₂   COXLEY BRIDGE
1-span public over bridge carrying road to Coxley. Masonry abutments, walls and arch with brick parapets. Still standing

289A   527438   3.79¹/₂   COXLEY BRIDGE (Culvert)
1-span public outlying bridge over stream carrying public road to Coxley. Masonry barrel, arch and invert. Still standing

290   531441   4.26   4ft 2in CULVERT
1-span private under bridge. Masonry arch, walls and invert.   Still standing

291   541452   5.21¹/₂   4ft 2in CULVERT
1-span private under bridge. Masonry arch, walls and invert.   Still standing

292   542452   5.26¹/₂   St ANDREWS MILL STREAM
1-span private under bridge crossing mill stream. Masonry arch on masonry abutments. WI handrail parapets.
                                                                                                       Still standing
293   543453   0.04*   MILL STREAM BRIDGE
1-span private under bridge crossing mill stream carrying S&D Railway to GW Railway, Tucker Street station. Masonry
arch on masonry abutments and brick faced.   Still standing
* Mileage is 0.04 chains on the branch from the S&D to the GWR.

Edington Junction to Bridgwater North

294   383427   0.34   GLASTONBURY CANAL BRIDGE
1-span private under bridge crossing canal. WI main and cross girders with longitudinal timbers for permanent way and
timber decking on brick abutments. WI handrail parapets.   Demolished

295   0.57¹/₂   FLOOD OPENING BRIDGE
1-span private under bridge to dissipate flood water. WI girders and timber decking on masonry abutments with WI
handrail parapets.   Demolished

296   1.25   RHINE BRIDGE
1-span private under bridge crossing rhine. WI girders and timber decking on masonry abutments with WI handrail parapets.   Demolished

Bridge No. 289A, Coxley Bridge. This outlying structure is in fact a culvert rather than a bridge, carrying a road over a diverted stream.

Andy Read

Bridge No. 292, St Andrews Mill Stream, located just outside of Wells and now used to carry a farm track rather than railway track.

Andy Read

Bridge No.   Map Ref.   Mile Post   Official Bridge Name
Type and Size and Construction. Present Condition

296A   379422   1.29   RHINE BRIDGE
1-span private under bridge. No information on construction and materials.   Abutments only survive

296B   376416   1.39   RHINE BRIDGE
1-span private under bridge. No information on construction and Materials.   Abutments only survive

297   376412   1.40   NYDON RHINE BRIDGE or NIDDON BRIDGE
1-span private under bridge crossing rhine. WI girders and timber decking on masonry abutments with WI handrail parapets.   Still standing

298   375409   1.60$^{1}/_{2}$ CATTLE CREEP
1-span private under bridge crossing occupation road. WI girders and timber decking on masonry abutments with WI handrail parapets.   Abutments only survive

299   372407   1.75   DOLE LANE BRIDGE
1-span public under bridge crossing road to fields. Masonry abutments with brick arch and parapets.   Still standing

300   370406   2.09$^{1}/_{2}$ LANDSHIRE BRIDGE
1-span public over bridge carrying road to Chilton Polden. Masonry abutments with brick arch and parapets.   Still standing

301   360408   2.58$^{1}/_{2}$ FLY ARCH BRIDGE
1-span public over bridge carrying road to Cossington. Masonry abutments faced with blue brick. Red brick arch and masonry parapets.   Still standing

302   358408   2.69   5ft CULVERT
1-span private under bridge. Brick arch and invert on masonry abutments.   Still standing

303   356406   3.02   OCCUPATION BRIDGE
1-span private over bridge carrying occupation road and public footpath to Cossington. Masonry abutments and walls with brick arch and parapets.   Still standing

304   354405   3.15   WOOLAVINGTON ROAD BRIDGE
1-span public over bridge carrying road to Highbridge. Masonry abutments and walls with red brick arch. Masonry parapets.   Still standing

305   349400   3.48   GLASTONBURY ROAD BRIDGE
1-span public over bridge carrying Glastonbury to Bridgwater road. Masonry abutments and walls with brick arch.   Still standing

305A   349400   3.48   CULVERT
1-span private under bridge. No information on construction or materials.   Abutments only survive

306   341397   4.14   BAWDRIP BRIDGE
1-span public under bridge, crossing Bawdrip to Bridgwater road. Masonry abutments and walls with red brick arch. Masonry abutments.   Still standing

307   335395   4.41   SEDGMOOR DRAIN BRIDGE
1-span private under bridge crossing Sedgmoor Drain. WI girders and timber decking on masonry abutments faced in brick with WI handrail parapets.   Demolished 1959

308   327393   5.03   BATH ROAD BRIDGE
1-span public over bridge carrying road to Bridgwater. WI girders with WI ceiling plates and timber decking on masonry abutments, faced in brick. WI plate parapets.   Demolished

309   326393   5.11   3ft 9in CULVERT
1-span private under bridge. Masonry walls and abutments with blue brick arch and invert.   Still standing

Bridge No. 306, Bawdrip Bridge, near the site of Bawdrip halt. Note the use of red bricks for the arch whilst the remainder is of masonry.

Andy Read

Bridge No.   Map Ref.   Mile Post   Official Bridge Name
Type and Size and Construction. Present Condition
310   322387   6.16$^{1}/_{2}$ CATTLE CREEP
1-span private under bridge crossing occupation road. WI girders and timber decking on brick abutments with WI handrail parapets.   Unknown

311   309385   6.23   GREAT WESTERN BRIDGE
1-span private under bridge crossing Great Western Railway. WI main and cross girders with timber decking on brick abutments. WI handrail parapets.   Demolished

312   306383   6.42   BRISTOL ROAD BRIDGE
1-span public under bridge crossing road to Bridgwater. WI lattice girders with WI cross girders and timber decking on brick abutments.   Demolished 1959

BCC = Bath City Council
BH = Bull head
CI = Cast iron
DCC = Dorset County Council
MDC = Mendip District Council
RSBs = Rolled steel beams
SCC = Somerset County Council
WI = Wrought iron

Appendix 4

S&DJR Viaducts

A

Bridge No. 1 TWERTON VIADUCT
MP 0.13 Map Reference ST736648
Constructed just south of Bath Junction as the line went through a 180 degree curve to leave Bath in a southerly direction, Twerton Viaduct or the 'Red viaduct' as many local people called it, was an interesting structure. Built in 1873 of limestone, red and blue brick, wrought iron and timber. At 79 yards in length and standing some 28 feet above the Lower Bristol Road and Bellott's Road, it was an impressive if rather unattractive structure. Being constructed on a curve it had an uneven number of spans, only span No. 8 was square. On the up side it had eleven spans whilst the down side had ten. Three-spans were constructed of wrought iron girders on steel columns with timber decking across the two roads. The remaining spans were of limestone piers and abutments faced in red or blue brick with brick arches. The spans varied in size from 23 to 63 feet. The Lower Bristol Road, originally Twerton Road, formed a dangerous 'S' bend to pass under the viaduct on what had become a very busy road. As soon as the S&DJR closed Bath City Council drew up plans to cure this hazard and the viaduct's fate was sealed. Only that much of the viaduct to allow the necessary road improvements was demolished on 4th May 1969, the remaining spans and part of the embankments on both sides were gradually removed over several years. No trace remains today.

Bridge No. 3 GWR VIADUCT
MP 0.31. Map Reference ST733645
By far the smallest viaduct to remain on the S&DJR, in fact several bridges are larger than this viaduct. Constructed in 1873 of limestone with brick built parapets, this structure has had a very uneventful existence. Access across it is now impeded by a wire mesh fence topped with barbed wire which is most important when you consider it crosses the main London–Bristol railway line. As a result of this the parapets have not been vandalised and the general condition is good. This structure is quite elegant when viewed from the up side of the main line looking towards Bath. The two piers of this three-arch viaduct are buttressed on the S&DJR up side as if to compensate for the slight curve in its structure. BR still own and maintain it and as a result it is in good condition with no apparent reason for its demise.

Bridge No. 16 TUCKING MILL VIADUCT
MP 3.21–3.26. Map Reference ST763616
Originally constructed in 1872/73 of local limestone with eight arches totalling 96 yards in length and a height of 63 feet, to carry a single track. Set in the beautiful Horsecombe Vale. Widening was carried out in 1891/2 when the original limestone arches were encapsulated in Staffordshire Blue Brick. Double track was never instated on the viaduct due to a lack of money to widen the track from Midford Viaduct to Horsecombe Vale, together with a new Midford station. After closure of the line in March 1966 track was lifted from this viaduct in late December 1967. Since then vandals have dislodged many of the parapet coping stones and even large parts of the parapet wall itself have been pushed over, at great risk to people walking underneath. BR made a poor job of patching the damaged parapets by using concrete blocks. In order to prevent further vandalism, access across the viaduct was stopped by the construction of 6ft high walls at either end on the trackbed. These walls are capped with razor wire. The condition of this viaduct has deteriorated over the years as trees and shrubs have been

allowed to grow unchecked. Casual structure damage has occurred due to root growth and the resulting water seepage into the arches. The overall condition is said to be poor. In May 1992 BR sold this viaduct to a Mr Weeks.

Bridge No. 18 MIDFORD VIADUCT
MP 3.72–3.80. Map Reference ST763606
Constructed at the same time as Tucking Mill and of identical materials it was also widened at the same time to take double track. This viaduct has eight arches and a total length of 168 yards on a centre curve with a change of gradient mid-way across.. Interestingly the doubling of this structure reduced each span by nine inches, additional strengthening was provided by buttressing some of the piers. The viaduct spans the Frome–Bristol road, the Cam Brook, the abandoned Somersetshire Coal Canal and the short lived GWR branch from Limpley Stoke to Camerton – the 'Titfield Thunderbolt' line. Heavy maintenance was last carried out in 1958 when the parapet walls and railings were completely replaced, along with a great deal of pointing and general repairs to the complete structure. The past 36 winters and 28 years of neglect have taken their toll since then, trees and shrubs have again caused trouble. This viaduct is blocked off on both sides by a chain linked fence set on concrete posts. The overall condition is said to be fair. Planning consent was given in August 1989 for the use of the viaduct as an extension to the Hope & Anchor public house car park, but nothing came of this. Had the work been undertaken the replacement of the ballast with tarmac would have sealed the viaduct's structure from the elements and improved and preserved its overall condition. This viaduct has also been sold to Mr Weeks.

Viaduct No. 22. WELLOW VIADUCT
MP 5.72. Map Reference ST744583
Built at the same time as the previous two viaducts. Wellow's four-arch viaduct is perhaps in the best condition of any of the structures so far covered. When widened in 1892 more use was made of limestone and the quality of workmanship would appear far higher, with the result that this attractive viaduct is in a sound condition. This viaduct crosses the public road into Wellow and a farm track. Ivy now covers much of the structure making it a picture of delight, however causing some damage to the pointing. Fortunately there is little tree or shrub growth on the trackbed due to its use as a farm track, and the arches and piers are in good condition as a result. The main danger to this viaduct's future is

that of road improvements which could warrant its removal as it causes the road to narrow and form a sharp blind bend into the village. However there are no plans at the present to straighten this minor road. Wellow Viaduct is still owned by BR.

Bridge No. 31. HOME FARM VIADUCT
MP 8.37–8.39. Map Reference ST714558
This low six-arch viaduct was originally constructed for single track of brick on masonry abutments and piers. Between 1891 and 1892 the line between Midford and Radstock was widened to take double track and the new portion of this viaduct was constructed from similar materials. The original portion was mostly encapsulated in Staffordshire Blue Brick during this work, which reduced the diameter of its arches. Home Viaduct was still totally intact until 1990. In September 1990 the arch over the narrow road near Paglinch Farm was demolished and both the parapet walls were removed. It must be said that a good job was made of this and the angled off arches were repointed and the original coping stones were re-used along the top of the decapitated walls. Even a nesting owl was given a pointed entrance into one of the arches. All the remaining arches are used by local farmers for storage. This structure is still owned by BR.

Bridge No. 44. NORTH SOMERSET VIADUCT
MP 10.56–10.61. Map Reference ST681548
A Staffordshire Blue Brick and masonry structure of five arches which cannot be described as the most attractive viaduct still standing on the S&DJR, but it is however one of the most interesting. Crossing at a skew angle the Bristol & North Somerset line and the route of the Somersetshire Coal Canal tramway. This viaduct was doubled in width in 1886 but not to a very high standard as repairs were required as early as 1888. Repairs became quite regular and the ever expanding coal mines based around Radstock did not help matters. A low viaduct which appears almost to be two separate structures from the S&D down side as the arches over the B&NS line are of blue brick while the other three arches are of limestone. This viaduct is now in a linear park and walkway along the S&DJR trackbed. Unfortunately it had suffered considerably from vandals resulting in the complete removal of the down side parapet wall on the softer limestone section. Access over the viaduct had been prevented by the construction of breeze block walls on both sides. It had been feared that this viaduct would be demolished due to its worsening condition

but in late 1992 Radstock Town Council, owner of the viaduct, announced that they were to restore the structure. The cost of this work is unknown but the end result is well worth seeing. The trackbed across the viaduct is once again part of the trackbed walk between Radstock and Midsomer Norton.

Bridge No. 61. NETTLEBRIDGE VIADUCT
MP 15.41–15.46. Map Reference ST621507
Nettlebridge has been an 'elusive' viaduct. It was only confirmed in late 1990 that it was still even standing, being hidden away within the secure confines of the Emborough Quarry site. Reports at the time of the closure of the S&DJR indicated a 15 mph speed limit over this viaduct due to its poor condition, but this has proved to be incorrect. Visitors are not welcome unless by prior arrangements with the owner. This lofty structure was originally constructed of limestone for single track. In 1893 the Radstock to Binegar section of the S&DJR was doubled and with it Nettlebridge Viaduct. The new down side portion was constructed of limestone faced in Staffordshire Blue Brick and the workmanship was of far higher standard than that of the previously mentioned viaduct. This in turn is reflected in its excellent overall condition, which is now being insured by the current owner's maintenance of the structure. Thanks to Phillip Blatchford it is hoped that the viaduct still has a long life ahead of it. It has not suffered at the hands of vandals or the growth of trees and shrubs on the trackbed, as a result the membrane protecting the top of the arches and piers has not been damaged by roots. The parapet walls are in good condition and received major repairs in the 1930s, possibly as part of the bridge strengthening required before the introduction of the new LMS 4-6-0 locomotives in 1938/39. At this time the original up side parapet was renewed and is now topped with railings made up of concrete posts and metal cross members. The down side retains its original parapet wall and coping stones in good condition.

Bridge No. 75. HAM WOOD VIADUCT
MP 19.27–19.30. ST610484
This attractive five-arch viaduct is set, not surprisingly by its name, in a deep wooded valley which was once a busy quarry. This viaduct was doubled in 1892 and as such is encased in Staffordshire Blue Brick. Due to the nature of its location it is difficult to really see what its condition now is. Climbing up the embankment to the north of the structure shows the top of the arches to be in need of re-pointing. On the trackbed large shrubs have grown on the

down side but it's doubtful if their roots have yet damaged the membrane. Vandals have again, but to lesser extent, damaged the parapet walls, and these have been repaired by BR with concrete blocks. BR have recently sold Ham Wood Viaduct, Winsor Hill Tunnels and a quarter of a mile of the trackbed to Mr Weeks for a wild life conservation park.

Bridge No. 81. BATH ROAD VIADUCT
MP 20.25–20.31. ST621443
A controversial viaduct. Originally constructed for single track in 1873 of limestone and widened in 1892 with a total length 118 yards. The new up side only lasted 54 years as it collapsed on 1st February 1946. A new brick built viaduct was constructed over the next six months being opened on 1st August. A stone plaque on the new viaduct reads 'Somerset & Dorset Joint Railway, Bath Road Viaduct – reconstructed February to July 1946. V. A. M. Robertson. M.inst.C.E. Engineer – William Cowlin & Sons Ltd. Contractors. Bristol.' Sadly this 'new' half of the viaduct was flawed, as no waterproof membrane was included which has allowed water to enter the structure and damage the arches and piers. The normal parapet vandalism has occurred and at this location is very dangerous with homes and a busy road below the structure. Once again walls have been constructed on the trackbed to stop this activity. The local town council wishes the viaduct to remain as part of the town's heritage and to form part of a long distance footpath from the Ridgeway to Bristol. However with no buyer with sufficient funds coming forward the future of Bath Road Viaduct remains uncertain. In January 1993 it was announced that £350,000 would be required to repair the viaduct to a safe condition and that BR would contribute £100,000 of this: the same amount as demolition would cost. Much as the town, local and county councils want to see this viaduct remain they cannot afford the money to undertake the repair work and we must presume the worst.

Bridge No. 84. CHARLTON ROAD VIADUCT
MP 20.73–21.09. Map Reference ST627436
This superb viaduct is without doubt the S&DJR's architectural masterpiece. Originally of local oolitic limestone and then doubled in 1892 when Staffordshire Blue Brick was used. Built on a centre curve with a falling gradient of 1 in 55 and 1 in 130 changing to a rising gradient of 1 in 66 at the mid-way point, making this viaduct an amazing achievement for its time. The 27 arches are unusual in being of segmental and not semi-circular construction. This design

results in large lateral thrusts and required the 9th and 18th piers to be thicker. Every third pier is buttressed on the outside of the curve to resist the huge lateral forces of heavy and often fast trains. Fortunately this viaduct has been owned and maintained by Showerings as a spectacular backdrop to the work's gardens, being purchased from BR in 1971 for just £5, plus legal costs. Showerings spent some £43,000 on a tarmac surface to keep the rain and frost out of the structure and general repairs to the oolitic parapets and much pointing. Permission to view and walk over this viaduct could be obtained by writing to Showerings at Shepton Mallet, but the company was recently bought by Gaymer's. However, the company changed hands again in late 1994 but it is hoped that the new owners will ensure the future of this important landmark.

Bridge No. 95. PRESTLEIGH VIADUCT
MP 22.75–23.00. Map Reference ST635406
Prestleigh Viaduct was constructed on a curve and a gradient of 1 in 50. The original portion was constructed of rather poor quality limestone which was partially encased in brick during the widening of the viaduct. Prestleigh Viaduct's eleven arches were widened in 1888 using various types of brick and stone, the whole job appearing to have been done as cheaply as possible. Poor workmanship and materials were compounded over the years by the structure's exposed location and little maintenance after BR was formed and none since March 1968 when the track was lifted. Standing proudly in an open valley forming an evocative part of the local landscape, but sadly this idyllic picture could not last for ever. All these factors resulted in the viaduct's overall deterioration to the point where in 1990 it was described as 'will become dangerous very soon'. The following year quantities of brick from the outer edge of the newer portion were to be found at the base of several piers. By the middle of 1992 the viaduct was officially described as dangerous and beyond economic repair. BR put out a contract for demolition during the last quarter of 1992. The contract was undertaken on Saturday 16th January 1993, when the structure was blown up, after which only two piers remained standing. A visit to the location on 8th February showed no sign that a viaduct had once occupied the site, and only a small embankment on each side now remain.

Bridge No. 105. PECKING MILL VIADUCT
MP 25.12–25.15. ST639375
Just before Evercreech Junction on the main A371 road stand the remains of Pecking Mill Viaduct. A

five-span structure of Staffordshire Blue Brick and limestone and one-span of cast iron decking over the road which was removed soon after the track was lifted in 1968. When this viaduct was widened in 1888 no attempt was made to keep the arches of the same radius and this has resulted in a curious mix-match 'double arch' effect. The general condition of Pecking Mill now is very good and shows none of the problems that effect the other viaducts, such as vandal damage or plant growth but has been threatened with demolition should road widening become necessary. BR still own this structure.

Bridge No. 119. COLE VIADUCT
MP 28.42–28.44. ST669338
Cole Viaduct was a simple structure which harmonised well with the local landscape as it crossed the River Brue and a road to Bruton. Just 62 yards in length and some 40 feet in height this five-span structure was doubled in width in 1886. Originally on limestone piers and abutments with brick arches and parapets, the new portion followed this construction and the complete viaduct was then partly faced with blue brick. All repairs appear to have used red brick. It must be presumed that the viaduct became unsafe as no other reason for its demolition in September 1984 can be found. The contract for demolition, along with two other bridges nearby, went to Luke Devenish Ltd of Cheddar.

Bridge No. 122. PITCOMBE VIADUCT
MP 28.79–29.01. Map Reference ST672331
This attractive three-arch structure, originally constructed of limestone but when widened in 1887, various bricks were used. Pitcombe Viaduct dominates the tiny hamlet of Pitcombe with some properties only yards away. The viaduct, shorn of its parapet walls some years ago remains in very good condition and has very little plant life on either the trackbed or ivy on the arches. This may be a small structure but it has several unusual features. A wide metal band covers the joint between the two halves of the structure, the purpose of which is unknown but it would not appear strong enough to be an additional method of securing the two portions together. A stream appears from the centre arch and is the cooling medium for a brick and stone cold store for the surrounding homesteads. These curious structures were at one time common in 'Wessex' before the spread of electricity and the advent of the refrigerator. The viaduct is still owned by BR.

Glastonbury station on 14th May 1967, just after demolition of the footbridge. The rest of the station survived until 1984. Only a few sleepers remain to be retrieved by lorry.

Chris Handley

Midford station just four months after track lifting and demolition of the station buildings. The signalbox survived a few more months.

Chris Handley

Bibliography

The Somerset & Dorset, Then & Now by Mac Hawkins 1986 (Patrick Stephens Ltd).
The Somerset & Dorset, An English Cross Country Railway by Ivo Peters 1974 (OPC).
The Somerset & Dorset in the Fifties Vol. 1 by Ivo Peters 1980 (OPC).
The Somerset & Dorset in the Fifties Vol. 2 by Ivo Peters 1981 (OPC).
The Somerset & Dorset in the Sixties Vol. 3 by Ivo Peters 1982 (OPC).
The Somerset & Dorset in the Sixties Vol. 4 by Ivo Peters 1983 (OPC).
An Historical Survey of the Somerset & Dorset Railway by C. W. Judge & C. R. Potts 1979 (OPC).
Steam on the Somerset & Dorset by G. A. Richardson 1975 (Bradford Barton).
The Railways of Midford by Mike Arlett 1986 (Millstream).
The Colour of Steam Vol. 2, The Somerset & Dorset by R. C. Riley 1984 (Atlantic).
Picture History of the Somerset & Dorset by Robin Atthill 1970 (David & Charles).
Guide to the Somerset & Dorset Line by Brian Macdermott 1982 (Patrick Stephens).
Bournemouth to Evercreech Junction by Vic Mitchell 1987 (Middleton Press).
Bath to Evercreech Junction by Vic Mitchell 1988 (Middleton Press).
Burnham to Evercreech Junction by Vic Mitchell 1989 (Middleton Press).
The Somerset & Dorset Railway by Robin Atthill 1967 (David & Charles).
The Somerset & Dorset from the Footplate by Peter Smith 1987 (OPC).
Highbridge in its Heyday by Colin Maggs 1973 (Oakwood Press).
The Somerset & Dorset Joint Railway by D. S. Barrie & C. A. Clinker 1978 (Oakwood).
Steam Around Bath by Ivo Peters & Mike Arlett 1987 (Millstream).
The Somerset & Dorset in Colour by Mike Arlett & David Lockett 1990 (OPC).
The Last Years of the Somerset & Dorset by Colin Maggs 1991 (Ian Allan).
Radstock Coal & Steam Vols 1 & 2 by Chris Handley 1991 & 1992 (Millstream).
The Last Years of Steam in Bristol & Somerset by Colin Maggs 1992 (Alan Sutton).
Working S&D Steam by Derek Phillips 1990 (Fox & Co).
The Mangotsfield to Bath Branch by Colin Maggs 1992 (Oakwood).
Through Countryside and Coalfield by Mike Vincent 1990 (OPC).
Life on the Railway by John Owen 1989 (Millstream).
Somerset & Avon Railways by Kevin Robertson 1992 (Alan Sutton).
The Bridgwater Branch by J. D. Harrison 1990 (Oakwood).
Track Diagrams of the GWR & BR Section 18 The Somerset & Dorset by R. A. Cooke.
The Somersetshire Coal Canal & Railway by Kenneth Clew 1986 (Brans Head).
Various editions of the The Somerset & Dorset Railway Trust Bulletin and various Railway Magazine articles.

Index

Admiralty siding 137, 144
Ashcott Halt 145

Bailey Gate Creamery 87,88,116
Bailey Gate crossing 87, 89, 116, 136, 146
Bailey Gate station 86, 87, 88, 89, 115, 116, 135, 136, 137, 145, 146
Bason Bridge Creamery 91, 92, 93, 145
Bason Bridge station 91, 92, 101, 104, 149
Bath Devonshire bank 81, 82, 118, 120
Bath Gas Works 97, 104, 149
Bath (Green Park) depot 13, 45, 94, 95, 97, 117, 118
Bath (Green Park) station 17, 45, 46, 47, 48, 49, 50, 51, 94, 96, 117, 118, 141, 146
Bath Junction 45, 46, 47, 104, 142
Bath Junction to Twerton 20, 21, 25
Bath Midland Road Yard 20, 46, 47, 94, 97, 149
Bawdrip Halt 101, 143
Binegar station 22, 53, 66, 68, 69, 72, 106, 108, 125, 145
Blandford station 4, 9, 10, 53, 66, 68, 69, 72, 86, 106, 115, 116, 134, 135, 136
Blandford Army Camp 142
Blandford to Radstock North 50, 55–79, 147
Bournemouth West station 83, 84, 85, 116, 138, 146, 147
Branksome depot 84, 145, 146
Branksome station 83, 84, 89, 116
Braysdown Colliery 144
Bridgwater Wharf and Port 92, 143
Bridgwater branch 11, 12, 92, 93, 101, 143, 144
Bridgwater station 92, 93, 143, 145
Broadstone Junction to Blandford 20, 38–44, 50, 85–89, 99, 149
Bruton 11
Burnham-on-Sea station 12, 97, 100, 101, 142, 145

Cannards Grave 70, 108, 128
Carter's Clay Pit Siding 12, 86, 98, 116, 137, 142, 144, 145
Charlton Marshall Halt 87, 135, 142, 144, 145
Charlton Road Viaduct 21, 71, 100, 108, 127, 128, 161, 187
Chilcompton New Rock Colliery 20
Chilcompton station 56, 57, 66, 72, 73, 77, 106, 108, 124, 125, 145
Chilcompton Tunnel 54, 78, 108, 123, 124, 149
Cole station 61, 64, 109, 112, 130, 146

Cole Viaduct 64, 111, 188
Combe Down Tunnel 80, 81, 82, 104, 119, 148, 154
Corfe Mullen Halt 137, 142, 144
Corfe Mullen Junction 12, 18, 85, 86, 87, 88, 98, 116, 137, 138, 139
Cossington station 92, 101, 102, 143, 144, 145
Creekmoor Halt 116, 142, 146

Devonshire Tunnel 80, 81, 82, 104, 118

Edington Burtle Junction 92, 93, 144
Edington Burtle station 91, 92, 101, 102, 145
Emborough Stone Quarries 66, 108, 125, 146, 149
Evercreech Junction 2, 56, 64, 66, 70, 90, 104, 112, 129, 130, 149
Evercreech Junction to Bason Bridge 51, 89–91, 99, 147, 148
Evercreech Junction station 55, 57–61, 63, 64, 66, 69, 70, 109, 112, 129, 146
Evercreech New station 65, 66, 70, 112, 128, 142, 145

Glastonbury & Street station 11, 14, 20, 90, 92, 101–103, 146, 190
Great Western/Western Region 16, 17, 20

Henstridge station 15, 37, 57, 111, 112, 132, 133, 146
Highbridge to Bason Bridge 20, 21, 34–38, 51, 91, 92, 150
Highbridge depot 37, 50, 93, 99, 147
Highbridge station 12, 13, 50, 92–94, 100, 147, 149
Highbridge Wharf 11, 100
Highbridge Works 93, 94, 100, 142, 149
Holes Bay Junction 51, 83, 116, 143
Horsington 58, 112, 148

Kilmersdon Colliery 27, 30

London, & South Western Railway/SR 11, 16, 52
Lyncombe Vale 81, 119

Mangotsfield to Bath 11, 20, 45–47, 51, 97, 99, 149, 150
Masbury Halt 66, 74, 106, 126, 127, 143, 145, 148
Masbury Summit 23, 66, 67, 71, 74, 108, 126
Mendipadam Works 108, 144
Midford station and yards 19, 51, 82, 104, 119, 120, 144, 145, 148, 190

Midford Viaduct 80, 119, 154, 186
Midland Railway 11, 16, 17
Midsomer Norton station 51, 52, 57, 64, 66, 76, 78, 106, 108, 123, 124, 145, 149
Moorewood 18, 20, 63, 66, 72, 74, 75, 77, 100, 125, 145, 149

Nettlebridge Viaduct 12, 74, 159, 187
North Somerset line 75, 79, 108, 124
Norton Hill Colliery 20, 57, 65, 78, 108, 124, 146

Polsham Halt 102, 143
Prestleigh Viaduct 65, 70, 108, 128, 162, 188
Pylle station 18, 90, 91, 103, 104, 142, 144, 145

Radstock to Writhlington 21–28, 29–34, 51, 52, 79
Radstock depot 31, 32, 75, 79
Radstock spur 26, 30, 56
Radstock station 15, 24, 29, 31, 35, 54, 64, 108, 122, 143, 145

Shapwick station 9, 91, 101, 145
Shepton Mallet station 55, 66–70, 108, 127, 128, 145, 150, 192
Shepton Montague 130
Shillingstone station 51, 53, 55, 114, 116, 133, 135, 145
Shoscombe & Single Hill Halt 79, 105, 107, 108, 122, 142
South Midland Union Railway 11
Spetisbury station/Halt 43, 84, 85, 87, 89, 116, 135, 136, 143, 144
Stalbridge station 14, 58, 112, 113, 146
Stourpaine & Durweston Halt 55, 114, 116, 134, 142, 144
Sturminster Newton station 55, 57, 113, 116, 133, 134, 146

Templecombe depot 110, 112, 145
Templecombe Junctions 23, 58, 112, 131, 142
Templecombe Lower Halt 24, 58, 97, 111, 112, 131, 132, 146
Templecombe Upper station 10, 12, 52, 56, 57, 97
Templecombe Yards 52, 97, 131, 143, 146
Tucking Mill Viaduct 104, 119, 154, 185, 186
Twerton Bakery Siding 20, 82, 185

Wellow station 51, 79, 80, 81, 105, 120, 121, 185
Wellow Valley 79, 185
Wells Priory branch 11, 12, 92, 101, 102, 143
Wells Priory station 92, 144, 145
West Pennard station 92, 103, 104, 144, 145
Wimborne Junction 12, 98, 142
Wimborne station 11, 20, 21, 51, 58, 83–85, 98, 142, 145, 146
Wincanton station 62, 63, 110, 130, 131, 142, 145, 146
Winsor Hill Tunnel 19, 66, 69, 70 71, 108, 127, 148, 160
Winsor Hill Quarry Sidings 66, 70–74, 108, 127, 143, 144
Writhlington Colliery 20, 21, 28, 108, 122, 147, 150
Writhlington to Bath 50, 79–82, 99
Wyke Champflower 64, 148

A strange sight just behind the goods shed at Shepton Mallet, in March 1968. This old coach, possibly of LNWR or MR parentage, was being used as a store room. To keep vermin and damp at bay, it was placed up on pillars in the form of large diameter pipes.

Michael Gates